Professional Examinations

CW01424483

Management Level

Paper F2

Financial Management

EXAM PRACTICE KIT

CIMA

PUBLISHING

WORKING TOGETHER FOR YOU

ELSEVIER

KAPLAN)

PUBLISHING

CIMA Publishing is an imprint of Elsevier
The Boulevard, Langford Lane, Kidlington, Oxford, OX5 1GB, UK
225 Wyman Street, Waltham, MA 02451, USA
Kaplan Publishing UK, Unit 2 The Business Centre, Molly Millars Lane, Wokingham, Berkshire RG41 2QZ

Acknowledgements

We are grateful to the Chartered Institute of Management Accountants for permission to reproduce past examination questions. The answers to CIMA Exams have been prepared by Kaplan Publishing, except in the case of the CIMA November 2011 answers where the official CIMA answers have been reproduced.

British Library Cataloguing in Publication Data

A catalogue record for this book is available from the British Library

ISBN: 978 0 85732 498 6

Printed and bound in Great Britain

11 12 11 10 9 8 7 6 5 4 3 2 1

CONTENTS

Section

Key features in this edition

In addition to providing a wide ranging bank of real past exam questions (including those from the equivalent paper of the old syllabus, i.e. Paper 8 Financial Analysis), we have also included in this edition:

- Paper specific information and advice on exam technique.

- Guidance to make your revision for this particular subject as effective as possible.

- Enhanced tutorial answers packed with specific key answer tips, technical tutorial notes and exam technique tips from our experienced tutors.

You will find a wealth of other resources to help you with your studies on the following sites:

www.EN-gage.co.uk

www.cimaglobal.com

INDEX TO QUESTIONS AND ANSWERS

INTRODUCTION

The style and contents of the current Paper F2 exam questions is different to old syllabus Paper 8 questions. However, many of the old syllabus exam questions are still relevant to the new exam paper and so are included within this exam practice kit.

The more recent CIMA exam questions (from 2005) are labelled as such in the index.

KEY TO THE INDEX

PAPER ENHANCEMENTS

We have added the following enhancements to the answers in this exam practice kit:

Key answer tips

Many answers include key answer tips to help your understanding of each question.

Tutorial note

Many answers include more tutorial notes to explain some of the technical points in more detail.

Top tutor tips

For selected questions, we "walk through the answer" giving guidance on how to approach the questions with helpful 'tips from a top tutor', together with technical tutor notes.

These answers are indicated with the "footsteps" icon in the index.

SECTION A-TYPE QUESTIONS

SECTION B-TYPE QUESTIONS

SPECIMEN PAPER QUESTIONS

ANALYSIS OF PAST EXAM PAPER

The table below summarises the key topics that have been tested in the new syllabus examinations to date.

	Specimen	May 10	Nov 10	Mar 11	May 11	Sep 11
Group Financial Statements						
1 Preparing a complete set of consolidated financial statements:						
• consolidated statement of comprehensive income;	Q1	Q6	Q3	Q1	Q6	
• consolidated statement of financial position;	Q4	Q4	Q6	Q6	Q6	Q1
• consolidated statement of cash flows;	Q6					Q6
• consolidated SOCIE;					Q2	
2 Discuss the principles of consolidation;		Q1		Q6		Q1
3 Acquisitions/disposals part way through an accounting period, including piecemeal acquisitions;		Q6	Q6		Q2	
4 Joint ventures;	Q4					
5 Accounting for capital schemes and foreign exchange rates.					Q6	
Issues in Recognition and Measurement						
1 The problems of profit measurement;	Q5					Q4
2 Changing price levels;	Q4	Q2				Q4
3 The principle of substance over form;	Q3					Q2
4 Financial instruments;				Q4	Q4	

PAPER F2 : FINANCIAL MANAGEMENT

	Specimen	May 10	Nov 10	Mar 11	May 11	Sep 11
5 Amortised cost, fair value and hedge accounting;			Q4, Q6			Q2
6 Pension schemes and share-based payments.	Q3	Q2	Q1	Q3	Q1	Q2
Analysis and Interpretation of Financial Accounts						
1 Interpreting accounting ratios;	Q7	Q7	Q5, Q7	Q7	Q7	Q5, Q7
2 Earnings per Share;		Q3				Q7
3 The limitations of ratio and financial statements analysis;	Q7	Q7	Q5	Q7		Q5
4 Performance and position analysis;		Q7	Q7	Q5, Q7	Q7	Q7
5 Segmental analysis.					Q3	
Developments in External Reporting						
1 Extending the scope and quality of external reports;	Q2				Q5	Q3
2 The interaction of a business with society and the environment;						Q3
3 "Human resource accounting,"			Q2	Q2		
4 IFRS and US GAAP.		Q5				

EXAM TECHNIQUE

- Use the allocated **20 minutes reading and planning time** at the beginning of the exam:
  - read the questions and examination requirements carefully, and
  - begin planning your answers.

  See the Paper Specific Information for advice on how to use this time for this paper.

- **Divide the time** you spend on questions in proportion to the marks on offer:
  - there are 1.8 minutes available per mark in the examination
  - within that, try to allow time at the end of each question to review your answer and address any obvious issues

  Whatever happens, always keep your eye on the clock and **do not over run on any part of any question!**

- Spend the last **five minutes** of the examination:
  - reading through your answers, and
  - **making any additions or corrections**.

- If you **get completely stuck** with a question:
  - leave space in your answer book, and
  - **return to it later.**

- Stick to the question and **tailor your answer** to what you are asked.
  - pay particular attention to the verbs in the question.

- If you do not understand what a question is asking, **state your assumptions**.

  Even if you do not answer in precisely the way the examiner hoped, you should be given some credit, if your assumptions are reasonable.

- You should do everything you can to make things easy for the marker.

  The marker will find it easier to identify the points you have made if your **answers are legible**.

- **Written questions**:

  Your answer should have:
  - a clear structure
  - a brief introduction, a main section and a conclusion

  Be concise:

  It is better to write a little about a lot of different points than a great deal about one or two points.

- **Computations**:

  It is essential to include all your workings in your answers.

  Many computational questions require the use of a standard format:

  e.g. income tax computations, corporation tax computations and capital gains.

  Be sure you know these formats thoroughly before the exam and use the layouts that you see in the answers given in this book and in model answers.

- **Reports, memos and other documents**:

  Some questions ask you to present your answer in the form of a report, a memo, a letter or other document.

  Make sure that you use the correct format – there could be easy marks to gain here.

PAPER SPECIFIC INFORMATION

THE EXAM

FORMAT OF THE EXAM

		Number of marks
Section A:	Five compulsory medium answer questions, each worth ten marks. A short scenario may be given, to which some or all questions relate.	50
Section B:	One or two compulsory questions. Short scenarios may be given, to which questions relate.	50
		100

Total time allowed: 3 hours plus 20 minutes reading and planning time.

Note that questions will be drawn from all areas of the syllabus.

PASS MARK

The pass mark for all CIMA Qualification examination papers is 50%.

READING AND PLANNING TIME

Remember that all three hour paper based examinations have an additional 20 minutes reading and planning time.

CIMA GUIDANCE

CIMA guidance on the use of this time is as follows:

You are not allowed to open or write in your answer book during the 20 minutes, but there's plenty you can do to plan your approach to the paper.

Although it is tempting to plan answers to the Section A questions, your time may be better spent studying Sections B so that clues and context used in scenarios which support these questions can be really appreciated and used to develop answers.

The examiner strongly recommends that you use your reading time to read the scenario based questions thoroughly, including an analysis of the nuances of the sub questions associated with them.

FURTHER GUIDANCE

As all questions are compulsory, there are no decisions to be made about choice of questions, other than in which order you would like to tackle them.

Therefore, in relation to F2, we recommend that you take the following approach with your reading and planning time:

- **Skim through the whole paper**, assessing the level of difficulty of each question.

- **Write down** on the question paper next to the mark allocation **the amount of time you should spend on each part.** Do this for each part of every question.

- **Decide the order** in which you think you will attempt each question:

    This is a personal choice and you have time on the revision phase to try out different approaches, for example, if you sit mock exams.

    A common approach is to tackle the question you think is the easiest and you are most comfortable with first.

    Others may prefer to tackle the longest questions first, or conversely leave them to the last.

    Psychologists believe that you usually perform at your best on the second and third question you attempt, once you have settled into the exam, so not tackling the bigger Section B questions first may be advisable.

    It is usual however that students tackle their least favourite topic and/or the most difficult question in their opinion last.

    Whatever your approach, you must make sure that you leave enough time to attempt all questions fully and be very strict with yourself in timing each question.

- **For each question** in turn, read the requirements and then the detail of the question carefully.

    Always read the requirement first as this enables you to **focus on the detail of the question with the specific task in mind**.

    For Section B questions:

    Take notice of the format required (e.g. notes, memo, letter) and identify the recipient of the answer. You need to do this to judge the level of financial sophistication required in your answer and whether the use of a formal reply or informal bullet points would be satisfactory.

    Plan your beginning, middle and end and the key areas to be addressed and your use of titles and sub-titles to enhance your answer.

    Consider what calculations are required. Don't worry if you are unsure of some adjustments, focus on the areas that you can attempt. These are where you will score marks in your answer.

For all questions:

Spot the easy marks to be gained in a question. Make sure that you do these parts first when you tackle the question.

Don't go overboard in terms of planning time on any one question – you need a good measure of the whole paper and a plan for all of the questions at the end of the 20 minutes.

By covering all questions you can often help yourself as you may find that facts in one question may remind you of things you should put into your answer relating to a different question.

- With your plan of attack in mind, **start answering your chosen question** with your plan to hand, as soon as you are allowed to start.

DETAILED SYLLABUS

The detailed syllabus and study guide written by CIMA can be found at:

www.cimaglobal.com

MATHMATICAL TABLES AND FORMULAE

Present value table

Present value of $1 i.e. that is $(1 - r)^{-n}$ where r = interest rate; n = number of periods until payment or receipt.

Periods	Interest rates (r)									
(n)	1%	2%	3%	4%	5%	6%	7%	8%	9%	10%
1	0.990	0.980	0.971	0.962	0.952	0.943	0.935	0.926	0.917	0.909
2	0.980	0.961	0.943	0.925	0.907	0.890	0.873	0.857	0.842	0.826
3	0.971	0.942	0.915	0.889	0.864	0.840	0.816	0.794	0.772	0.751
4	0.961	0.924	0.888	0.855	0.823	0.792	0.763	0.735	0.708	0.683
5	0.951	0.906	0.863	0.822	0.784	0.747	0.713	0.681	0.650	0.621
6	0.942	0.888	0.837	0.790	0.746	0.705	0.666	0.630	0.596	0.564
7	0.933	0.871	0.813	0.760	0.711	0.665	0.623	0.583	0.547	0.513
8	0.923	0.853	0.789	0.731	0.677	0.627	0.582	0.540	0.502	0.467
9	0.914	0.837	0.766	0.703	0.645	0.592	0.544	0.500	0.460	0.424
10	0.905	0.820	0.744	0.676	0.614	0.558	0.508	0.463	0.422	0.386
11	0.896	0.804	0.722	0.650	0.585	0.527	0.475	0.429	0.388	0.350
12	0.887	0.788	0.701	0.625	0.557	0.497	0.444	0.397	0.356	0.319
13	0.879	0.773	0.681	0.601	0.530	0.469	0.415	0.368	0.326	0.290
14	0.870	0.758	0.661	0.577	0.505	0.442	0.388	0.340	0.299	0.263
15	0.861	0.743	0.642	0.555	0.481	0.417	0.362	0.315	0.275	0.239
16	0.853	0.728	0.623	0.534	0.458	0.394	0.339	0.292	0.252	0.218
17	0.844	0.714	0.605	0.513	0.436	0.371	0.317	0.270	0.231	0.198
18	0.836	0.700	0.587	0.494	0.416	0.350	0.296	0.250	0.212	0.180
19	0.828	0.686	0.570	0.475	0.396	0.331	0.277	0.232	0.194	0.164
20	0.820	0.673	0.554	0.456	0.377	0.312	0.258	0.215	0.178	0.149

Periods	Interest rates (r)									
(n)	11%	12%	13%	14%	15%	16%	17%	18%	19%	20%
1	0.901	0.893	0.885	0.877	0.870	0.862	0.855	0.847	0.840	0.833
2	0.812	0.797	0.783	0.769	0.756	0.743	0.731	0.718	0.706	0.694
3	0.731	0.712	0.693	0.675	0.658	0.641	0.624	0.609	0.593	0.579
4	0.659	0.636	0.613	0.592	0.572	0.552	0.534	0.516	0.499	0.482
5	0.593	0.567	0.543	0.519	0.497	0.476	0.456	0.437	0.419	0.402
6	0.535	0.507	0.480	0.456	0.432	0.410	0.390	0.370	0.352	0.335
7	0.482	0.452	0.425	0.400	0.376	0.354	0.333	0.314	0.296	0.279
8	0.434	0.404	0.376	0.351	0.327	0.305	0.285	0.266	0.249	0.233
9	0.391	0.361	0.333	0.308	0.284	0.263	0.243	0.225	0.209	0.194
10	0.352	0.322	0.295	0.270	0.247	0.227	0.208	0.191	0.176	0.162
11	0.317	0.287	0.261	0.237	0.215	0.195	0.178	0.162	0.148	0.135
12	0.286	0.257	0.231	0.208	0.187	0.168	0.152	0.137	0.124	0.112
13	0.258	0.229	0.204	0.182	0.163	0.145	0.130	0.116	0.104	0.093
14	0.232	0.205	0.181	0.160	0.141	0.125	0.111	0.099	0.088	0.078
15	0.209	0.183	0.160	0.140	0.123	0.108	0.095	0.084	0.079	0.065
16	0.188	0.163	0.141	0.123	0.107	0.093	0.081	0.071	0.062	0.054
17	0.170	0.146	0.125	0.108	0.093	0.080	0.069	0.060	0.052	0.045
18	0.153	0.130	0.111	0.095	0.081	0.069	0.059	0.051	0.044	0.038
19	0.138	0.116	0.098	0.083	0.070	0.060	0.051	0.043	0.037	0.031
20	0.124	0.104	0.087	0.073	0.061	0.051	0.043	0.037	0.031	0.026

Cumulative present value of $1

This table shows the Present Value of $1 per annum, Receivable or Payable at the end of each year for n years $\dfrac{1-(1+r)^{-n}}{r}$

Periods (n)	Interest rates (r)									
	1%	2%	3%	4%	5%	6%	7%	8%	9%	10%
1	0.990	0.980	0.971	0.962	0.952	0.943	0.935	0.926	0.917	0.909
2	1.970	1.942	1.913	1.886	1.859	1.833	1.808	1.783	1.759	1.736
3	2.941	2.884	2.829	2.775	2.723	2.673	2.624	2.577	2.531	2.487
4	3.902	3.808	3.717	3.630	3.546	3.465	3.387	3.312	3.240	3.170
5	4.853	4.713	4.580	4.452	4.329	4.212	4.100	3.993	3.890	3.791
6	5.795	5.601	5.417	5.242	5.076	4.917	4.767	4.623	4.486	4.355
7	6.728	6.472	6.230	6.002	5.786	5.582	5.389	5.206	5.033	4.868
8	7.652	7.325	7.020	6.733	6.463	6.210	5.971	5.747	5.535	5.335
9	8.566	8.162	7.786	7.435	7.108	6.802	6.515	6.247	5.995	5.759
10	9.471	8.983	8.530	8.111	7.722	7.360	7.024	6.710	6.418	6.145
11	10.368	9.787	9.253	8.760	8.306	7.887	7.499	7.139	6.805	6.495
12	11.255	10.575	9.954	9.385	8.863	8.384	7.943	7.536	7.161	6.814
13	12.134	11.348	10.635	9.986	9.394	8.853	8.358	7.904	7.487	7.103
14	13.004	12.106	11.296	10.563	9.899	9.295	8.745	8.244	7.786	7.367
15	13.865	12.849	11.938	11.118	10.380	9.712	9.108	8.559	8.061	7.606
16	14.718	13.578	12.561	11.652	10.838	10.106	9.447	8.851	8.313	7.824
17	15.562	14.292	13.166	12.166	11.274	10.477	9.763	9.122	8.544	8.022
18	16.398	14.992	13.754	12.659	11.690	10.828	10.059	9.372	8.756	8.201
19	17.226	15.679	14.324	13.134	12.085	11.158	10.336	9.604	8.950	8.365
20	18.046	16.351	14.878	13.590	12.462	11.470	10.594	9.818	9.129	8.514

Periods (n)	Interest rates (r)									
	11%	12%	13%	14%	15%	16%	17%	18%	19%	20%
1	0.901	0.893	0.885	0.877	0.870	0.862	0.855	0.847	0.840	0.833
2	1.713	1.690	1.668	1.647	1.626	1.605	1.585	1.566	1.547	1.528
3	2.444	2.402	2.361	2.322	2.283	2.246	2.210	2.174	2.140	2.106
4	3.102	3.037	2.974	2.914	2.855	2.798	2.743	2.690	2.639	2.589
5	3.696	3.605	3.517	3.433	3.352	3.274	3.199	3.127	3.058	2.991
6	4.231	4.111	3.998	3.889	3.784	3.685	3.589	3.498	3.410	3.326
7	4.712	4.564	4.423	4.288	4.160	4.039	3.922	3.812	3.706	3.605
8	5.146	4.968	4.799	4.639	4.487	4.344	4.207	4.078	3.954	3.837
9	5.537	5.328	5.132	4.946	4.772	4.607	4.451	4.303	4.163	4.031
10	5.889	5.650	5.426	5.216	5.019	4.833	4.659	4.494	4.339	4.192
11	6.207	5.938	5.687	5.453	5.234	5.029	4.836	4.656	4.486	4.327
12	6.492	6.194	5.918	5.660	5.421	5.197	4.988	7.793	4.611	4.439
13	6.750	6.424	6.122	5.842	5.583	5.342	5.118	4.910	4.715	4.533
14	6.982	6.628	6.302	6.002	5.724	5.468	5.229	5.008	4.802	4.611
15	7.191	6.811	6.462	6.142	5.847	5.575	5.324	5.092	4.876	4.675
16	7.379	6.974	6.604	6.265	5.954	5.668	5.405	5.162	4.938	4.730
17	7.549	7.120	6.729	6.373	6.047	5.749	5.475	5.222	4.990	4.775
18	7.702	7.250	6.840	6.467	6.128	5.818	5.534	5.273	5.033	4.812
19	7.839	7.366	6.938	6.550	6.198	5.877	5.584	5.316	5.070	4.843
20	7.963	7.469	7.025	6.623	6.259	5.929	5.628	5.353	5.101	4.870

Formulae

Annuity

Present value of an annuity of $1 per annum receivable or payable for n years, commencing in one year, discounted at r% per annum:

$$PV = \frac{1}{r}\left[1 - \frac{1}{[1+r]^n}\right]$$

Perpetuity

Present value of $1 per annum, payable or receivable in perpetuity, commencing in one year, discounted at r% per annum:

$$PV = \frac{1}{r}$$

Growing perpetuity

Present value of $1 per annum, receivable or payable, commencing in one year, growing in perpetuity at a constant rate of g% per annum, discounted at r% per annum:

$$PV = \frac{1}{r - g}$$

APPROACH TO REVISION

QUESTION PRACTICE IS THE KEY TO SUCCESS

Success in management level examinations relies upon you acquiring a firm grasp of the required knowledge at the tuition phase. In order to be able to do the questions, knowledge is essential.

However, the difference between success and failure often hinges on your exam technique on the day and making the most of the revision phase of your studies.

The **study text** is the starting point, designed to provide the underpinning knowledge to tackle all questions. However, in the revision phase, pouring over text books is not the answer.

The **online fixed tests** help you consolidate your knowledge and understanding and are a useful tool to check whether you can remember key topic areas.

Revision cards are designed to help you quickly revise a topic area, however you then need to practice questions. There is a need to progress to full exam standard questions as soon as possible, and to tie your exam technique and technical knowledge together.

The importance of question practice cannot be over-emphasised.

The recommended approach below is designed by expert tutors in the field, in conjunction with their knowledge of the examiner and their knowledge of past exams.

The approach taken is to revise by syllabus area. However, with the management level papers, a multi syllabus area approach is often required to answer the scenario based questions.

You need to practice as many questions as possible in the time you have left.

OUR AIM

Our aim is to get you to the stage where you can attempt exam standard questions confidently, to time, in a closed book environment, with no supplementary help (i.e. to simulate the real examination experience).

Practising your exam technique on real past examination questions, in timed conditions, is also vitally important for you to assess your progress and identify areas of weakness that may need more attention in the final run up to the examination.

In order to achieve this we recognise that initially you may feel the need to practice some questions with open book help and exceed the required time.

The approach below shows you which questions you should use to build up to coping with exam standard question practice, and references to the sources of information available should you need to revisit a topic area in more detail.

Remember that in the real examination, all you have to do is:

- attempt all questions required by the exam

- only spend the allotted time on each question, and

- get them at least 50% right!

Try and practice this approach on every question you attempt from now to the real exam.

EXAMINER COMMENTS

Form looking at the post-exam guidance, the common mistakes are as follows:

- misallocation of time

- running out of time

- showing signs of spending too much time on an earlier questions and clearly rushing the answer to a subsequent question

- not applying knowledge to the scenario given

- not writing enough and

- not answering the question and/ or including a lot of irrelevant detail.

Good exam technique is vital.

THE F2 REVISION PLAN

Stage 1: Assess areas of strengths and weaknesses

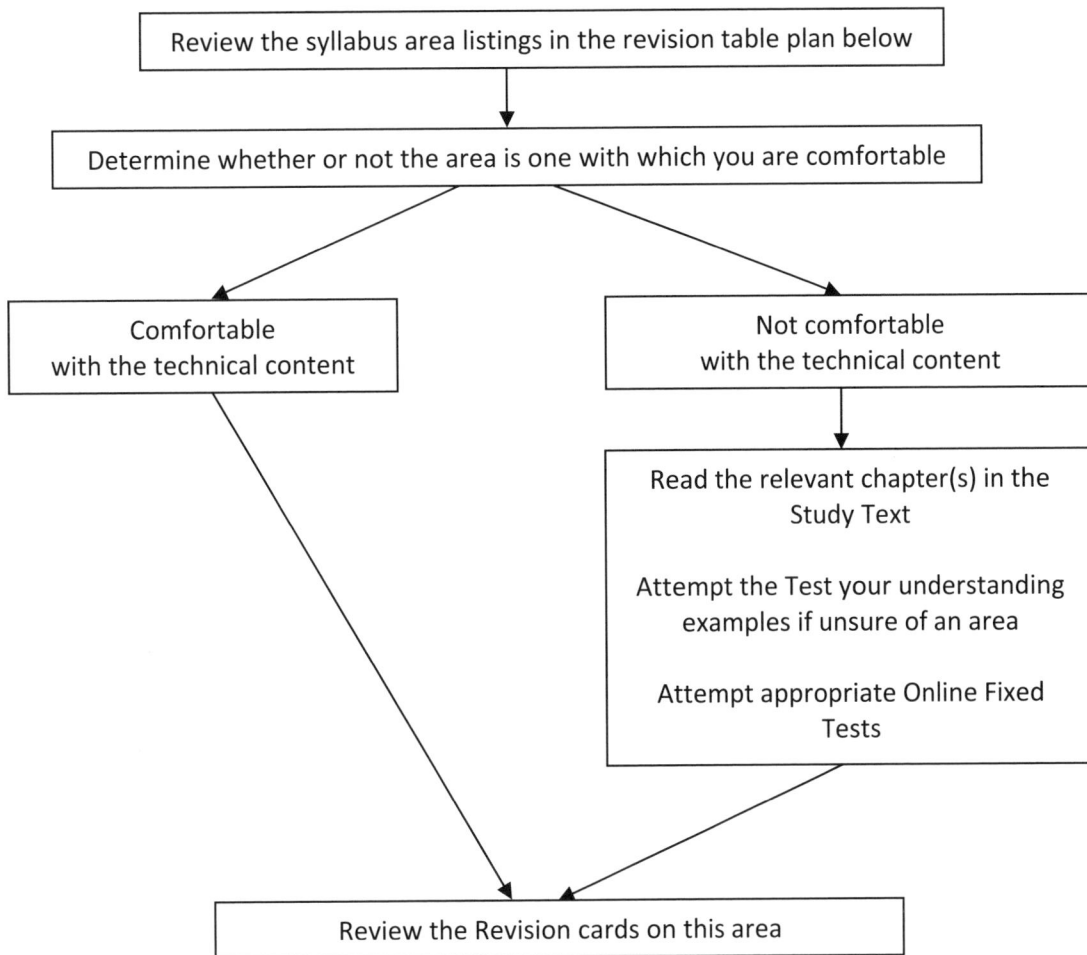

```
┌─────────────────────────────────────────────────────────────┐
│   Review the syllabus area listings in the revision table     │
│   plan below                                                   │
└─────────────────────────────────────────────────────────────┘
                              ↓
┌─────────────────────────────────────────────────────────────┐
│  Determine whether or not the area is one with which you       │
│  are comfortable                                               │
└─────────────────────────────────────────────────────────────┘
         ↙                                        ↘
┌──────────────────────┐              ┌──────────────────────┐
│  Comfortable          │              │  Not comfortable      │
│  with the technical   │              │  with the technical   │
│  content              │              │  content              │
└──────────────────────┘              └──────────────────────┘
                                                  ↓
                              ┌──────────────────────────────────┐
                              │  Read the relevant chapter(s) in   │
                              │  the Study Text                    │
                              │                                    │
                              │  Attempt the Test your             │
                              │  understanding examples if unsure  │
                              │  of an area                        │
                              │                                    │
                              │  Attempt appropriate Online Fixed  │
                              │  Tests                             │
                              └──────────────────────────────────┘
         ↘                                        ↙
┌─────────────────────────────────────────────────────────────┐
│        Review the Revision cards on this area                 │
└─────────────────────────────────────────────────────────────┘
```

Stage 2: Practice questions

Follow the order of revision of syllabus areas as recommended in the revision table plan below and attempt the questions in the order suggested.

Try to avoid referring to text books and notes and especially the model answer until you have completed your attempt.

Try to answer the question in the allotted time.

Review your attempt with the model answer and assess how much of the answer you achieved in the allocated exam time.

Fill in the self-assessment box and decide on your best course of action.

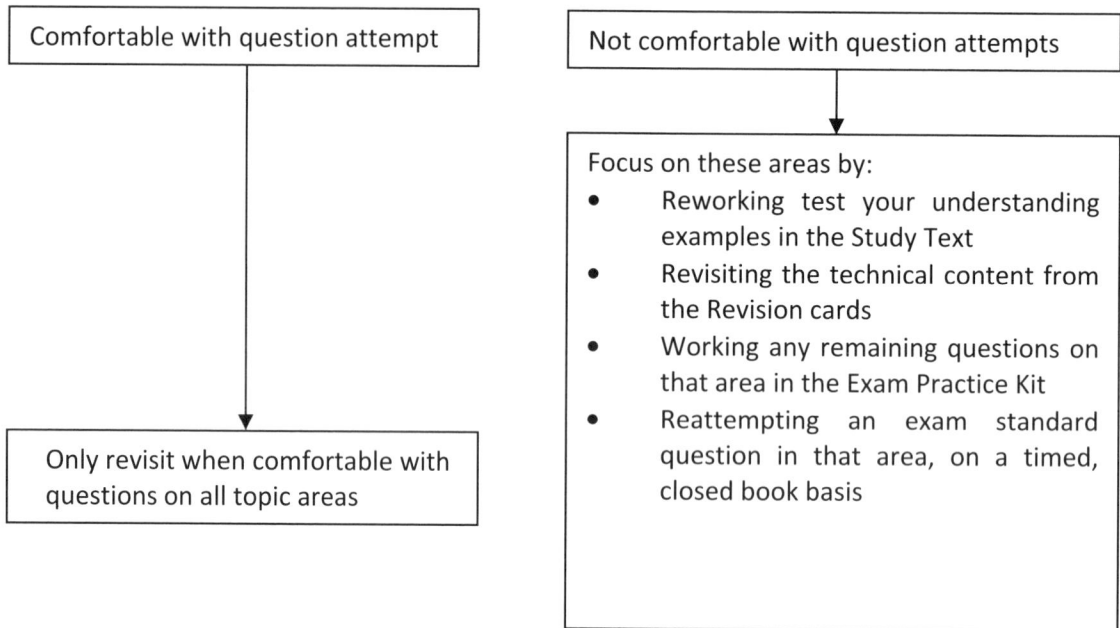

Comfortable with question attempt	Not comfortable with question attempts

Focus on these areas by:

- Reworking test your understanding examples in the Study Text
- Revisiting the technical content from the Revision cards
- Working any remaining questions on that area in the Exam Practice Kit
- Reattempting an exam standard question in that area, on a timed, closed book basis

Only revisit when comfortable with questions on all topic areas

Note that:

The "footsteps questions" give guidance on exam techniques and how you should have approached the question.

Stage 3: Final pre-exam revision

We recommend that you **attempt at least one three hour mock examination** containing a set of previously unseen exam standard questions.

It is important that you get a feel for the breadth of coverage of a real exam without advanced knowledge of the topic areas covered – just as you will expect to see on the real exam day.

Ideally a mock examination offered by your tuition provider should be sat in timed, closed book, real exam conditions.

THE DETAILED REVISION PLAN

Syllabus area	Study Text Chapter	Questions to attempt	Tutor guidance	Date attempted	Self assessment
Group Financial Statements	4–10		You can expect to be tested on consolidations as one long section B question and also in a 10 mark question. Practise is the key to success.		
Calculation of goodwill and non-controlling interest; Associates and joint ventures	4–6	Q1 ST Q6 MX Q7 AB, CD & EF Q47 AT Q51 AJ	There will be marks for the more basic elements of consolidation and so your aim is to do these well. Make sure that you are practised at the 5 workings for the statement of financial position. Make sure that you learn both approaches (fair value and proportion of net assets) for valuing the non-controlling interest and goodwill. Make sure you learn how to account for an associate and a joint venture.		
Acquisitions and disposals of subsidiaries	7	Q3 SGB Q5 AB, GH, JK & LM Q49 AX	The rules on acquisitions and disposals are regularly examined in F2. The key thing to look for in a change to group structure is any change to control. Learn the calculation for group profit on disposal.		

Attempted
1, 2, 3, 4,

Complex group structures	8	Q48 Purple	Make sure you can identify whether you have control over a sub-subsidiary and that you can calculate the effective ownership the parent company has. Getting the group structure correct should set you up for all of the key consolidation workings. If you can remember the indirect holding adjustment to goodwill and the NCI then that is good but there may be easier marks to pick up in the consolidation.
Statement of cash flows	10	Q52 EAG	The basic workings are the same as for individual cash flows and so this is an area where you can expect to score high marks, so long as you have practised. Remember to adjust your workings for the affect of any acquisition or disposal of a subsidiary.
Foreign exchange	9	Q2 Home and foreign Q53 DX & EY	Learn the exchange rates that should be used to translate individual transactions (monetary / non monetary) and an overseas subsidiary. Most of the consolidation workings remain the same but spend time learning the calculation of the foreign exchange gain or loss that goes into reserves (other comprehensive income) as this is worth a significant number of marks when foreign subsidiaries are examined in a 25 mark question.

Issues in Recognition and measurement	12–16	You should review the syllabus content and make sure that you can have an attempt at each of the accounting issues. You can expect a couple of 10 mark section A questions on these topics. The section A questions are often where candidates struggle in the exam so it is well worth trying to get ahead on these.
Financial instruments	13	Q15 AZG Q17 DG Q24 QWE There are some tricky areas in this part of the syllabus such as accounting for derivatives and hedging. However the more commonly tested areas are the accounting for liabilities, charging the effective interest rate, and the four categories of financial asset. Make sure you learn these. In recent years we have often seen financial instruments being tested within a 25 mark consolidation.
Pensions and share based payments	14–15	Q11 CBA Q12 FDE Q19 LBP Spec Q3 RP Make sure you know how to calculate the actuarial difference on a defined benefit pension plan. Share based payments is new to the F2 syllabus and has so far been examined in every sitting. Learn the difference between a cash settled share based payment (liability) and equity settled (reserve).

Substance over form	16	Q13 LMN Q14 GHK Spec Q4 JKA	The principal of substance over form is key to financial reporting and therefore regularly tested. As well as the 10 mark section A questions we have also seen this area tested in the context of a 25 mark interpretation where adjustments need to be made.
Analysis and interpretation of financial accounts	2	Q60 TYD Q62 TEX Q65 DAS Q69 FJK Spec Q7 XYZ	It is likely that one of your section B questions, for around 25 marks will be to prepare a report on a companies performance and position. The key to this is to read the scenario carefully and use the specific information given by the examiner. Some of these questions will require adjustments to be made to the accounts, for example to report the substance of a transaction. A range of question styles has been selected for you to attempt.
Earnings per share	3	Q27 JKL Q29 BAQ Q30 AGZ	Earnings per share is regularly tested as a 10 mark question.

| Developments in external reporting | 11 | Q38 Env discs Q39 Intellectual assets Q40 IASB & FASB Q77 BCA | An easy 10% of the syllabus to score well on. You need to know about how narrative reporting (sustainability and operating and financial reviews) complements the financial statements and about the current issues in international harmonisations, in particular US GAAP convergence. Prepare for this by reviewing Ch 11 and also using your Revision cards as you should be able to learn the key facts.

We would mostly expect a 10 mark section A question on one of the topics although it could be tested as a part b of one of the 25 mark questions, this has not been seen in recent exams however. | |
| --- | --- | --- | --- | --- |

Note that not all of the exam practice kit questions are referred to in the programme above. We have recommended a range of questions to build up from the longer questions in your study text to the exam scenarios that often combine different topics.

These questions, especially the long consolidations, will be tricky so try not to lose confidence when you attempt them. Try to reward yourself for the parts of questions that you are getting right as these will all score marks in the exam. One of the principal aims of a revision course is for your tutor to guide you as to how to begin these questions so you can show the examiner all of the things that you can do within a question.

The remaining questions are available in the exam practice kit for extra practice for those who require more questions on some areas. If you are booked on to a revision course then we will use the exam practice kit questions in class to cover off the key syllabus areas.

Section 1

SECTION A-TYPE QUESTIONS

GROUP FINANCIAL STATEMENTS

1 ST (MAY 06 EXAM)

The income statements of ST and two entities in which it holds investments are shown below for the year ended 31 January 20X6:

	ST $000	UV $000	WX $000
Revenue	1,800	1,400	600
Cost of sales	(1,200)	(850)	(450)
Gross profit	600	550	150
Operating expenses	(450)	(375)	(74)
Profit from operations	150	175	76
Finance cost	(16)	(12)	–
Interest income	6	–	–
Profit before tax	140	163	76
Income tax expense	(45)	(53)	(26)
Profit for the period	95	110	50

Notes:

Note 1 – Investments by ST

Several years ago ST acquired 70% of the issued ordinary share capital of UV. On 1 February 20X5, ST acquired 50% of the issued share capital of WX, an entity set up under a contractual arrangement as a joint venture between ST and one of its suppliers. The directors of ST have decided to adopt a policy of proportionate consolidation wherever appropriate and permitted by International Financial Reporting Standards.

Note 2 – UV's borrowings

During the financial year ended 31 January 20X6, UV paid the full amount of interest due on its 6% debenture loan of $200,000. ST invested $100,000 in the debenture when it was issued three years ago.

Note 3 – Intra-group trading

During the year, WX sold goods to ST for $20,000. Half of the goods remained in ST's inventories at 31 January 20X6. WX's gross profit margin on the sale was 20%.

Required:

Prepare the consolidated income statement of the ST group for the year ended 31 January 20X6. (Total: 10 marks)

2 HOME AND FOREIGN (NOV 06 EXAM)

The income statements for Home and its wholly owned subsidiary Foreign for the year ended 31 July 20X6 are shown below:

	Home	Foreign
	$000	Crowns 000
Revenue	3,000	650
Cost of sales	(2,400)	(550)
Gross profit	600	100
Distribution costs	(32)	(41)
Administrative expenses	(168)	(87)
Finance costs	(15)	(10)
Profit (Loss) before tax	385	(38)
Income tax	(102)	10
Profit (Loss) for the period	283	(28)

Notes:

1 The presentation currency of the group is the dollar ($) and Foreign's functional currency is the Crown.

2 Home acquired 100% of the ordinary share capital of Foreign on 1 August 20X4 for 204,000 Crowns. Foreign's share capital at that date comprised 1,000 ordinary shares of 1 Crown each, and its reserves were 180,000 Crowns. In view of its subsidiary's losses, Home's directors conducted an impairment review of the goodwill at 31 July 20X6. They concluded that the goodwill had lost 20% of its value during the year (before taking exchange differences into account). The impairment should be reflected in the consolidated financial statements for the year ended 31 July 20X6. It is group policy to value the non-controlling interest at acquisition at the proportionate share of the fair value of the net assets.

3 On 1 June 20X6, Home purchased an item of plant for 32,000 Florins. At the year end, the payable amount had not yet been settled. No exchange gain or loss in respect of this item is reflected in Home's income statement above.

4   Exchange rates are as follows:

On 1 August 20X4:	1.7 Crowns = $1
On 31 July 20X6:	2.2 Crowns = $1
Average rate for year ended 31 July 20X6:	2.4 Crowns = $1
On 1 June 20X6:	1.5 Florins = $1
On 31 July 20X6:	1.6 Florins = $1

5   During the year, Foreign made sales of 50,000 Crowns to Home. None of the items remained in inventory at the year end.

Required:

Prepare the consolidated income statement for the Home group for the year ended 31 July 20X6. (Work to the nearest $100.)   **(Total: 10 marks)**

3   **SGB (MAY 09 EXAM)**

SGB prepares its accounts to 31 December. The entity acquired 1,600,000 of the 2,000,000 $1 ordinary shares of FMA in 20X6 for $2,800,000. The retained earnings at the date of acquisition were $1,000,000. It is group policy to value the non-controlling interest at acquisition at fair value. The fair value of the non-controlling interest at the acquisition date was $680,000.

The goodwill arising on acquisition suffered impairment in 20X7 and was written down by 20%.

SGB sold 1,000,000 of the shares in FMA for $2,500,000 on 1 October 20X8. The fair value of the remaining holding on 1 October 20X8 was $1,200,000.

The profits of both entities accrue evenly throughout the year. The retained earnings of FMA at 31 December 20X7 were $1,150,000. SGB is charged tax at 30% on profits earned in the period. SGB have not recorded the tax arising on their disposal of the shares.

The income statements for both entities for the year ended 31 December 20X8 are presented below:

	SGB	FMA
	$000	$000
Revenue	8,200	3,600
Cost of sales	(4,300)	(1,900)
Gross profit	3,900	1,700
Distribution costs	(1,200)	(800)
Administrative expenses	(800)	(600)
Profit before tax	1,900	300
Income tax expense	(600)	(100)
Profit for the period	1,300	200

Required:

Prepare the consolidated income statement in accordance with IAS 1 Presentation of Financial Statements for the SGB group for the year ended 31 December 20X8.

(Total: 10 marks)

√4   AAY (MAY 08 EXAM)

Summarised statements of changes in equity for the year ended 31 March 20X8 for AAY and its only subsidiary, BBZ, are shown below:

	AAY	BBZ
	$000	$000
Balance at 1 April 20X7	662,300	143,700
Profit for the period	81,700	22,000
Dividends	(18,000)	(6,000)
Balance at 31 March 20X8	726,000	159,700

Notes:

1   AAY acquired 80% of the issued share capital of BBZ on 1 April 20X5, when BBZ's total equity was $107.7 million. The first dividend BBZ has paid since acquisition is the amount of $6 million shown in the summarised statement above. The profit for the period of $81.7 million in AAY's summarised statement of changes in equity above does not include its share of the dividend paid by BBZ.

2   The only consolidation adjustment required is in respect of intra-group trading. BBZ regularly supplies goods to AAY. The amount included in the inventory of AAY in respect of goods purchased from BBZ at the beginning and end of the accounting period was as follows:

1 April 20X7 $2 million

31 March 20X8 $3 million

BBZ earns a profit on intra-group sales of 25% on cost.

3   It is group policy to value the non-controlling interest at acquisition at the proportionate share of the fair value of the net assets.

Required:

Prepare a summarised consolidated statement of changes in equity for the AAY Group for the year ended 31 March 20X8.

(Total: 10 marks)

√5   AB, GH, JK & LM (MAY 10 EXAM)

DF is preparing its consolidated financial statements for the year ended 31 December 20X9. DF has a number of investments in other entities. Details of some of these investments are provided below:

Investment in AB

DF acquired 90% of the issued ordinary share capital of AB on 1 July 20X9 for $6 million, when the book value of the net assets was $5.8 million. The fair value of these net assets was estimated at $6.8 million at the date of acquisition. The difference between the fair value and book value of the net assets related to depreciable property with a remaining useful life at the date of acquisition of 40 years.

Investment in GH

DF acquired 40% of the issued ordinary share capital of GH on 1 January 20X8 for $2 million, when the book value of the net assets was $5.5 million. The fair value of these net assets was estimated at $6 million at the date of acquisition.

Investment in JK

At the date of acquisition of AB, AB held 65% of the issued ordinary share capital of JK. The operations of JK do not fit within the strategic plans of DF and so the directors plan to sell this investment. The investment is currently being actively marketed with a view to selling it within the next 4 months.

Investment in LM

DF acquired 15% of the issued ordinary share capital of LM on 1 January 20X4 for $1 million. On 1 October 20X9, DF acquired a further 40% of issued ordinary share capital for $4.5 million. The fair value of the net assets at 1 October 20X9 was $12 million and on 1 January 20X4 was $8 million. The previously held interest had a fair value on 1 October 20X9 of $1.7 million.

The group policy is to value non-controlling interest at the date of acquisition at the proportionate share of the fair value of the net assets.

Required:

(a)   Explain the basis on which each of the investments should be accounted for in the consolidated financial statements of the DF Group for the year ended 31 December 20X9 (calculations are not required). **(8 marks)**

(b)   Briefly explain the impact of the investment in AB, in the consolidated income statement for the year ended 31 December 20X9. **(2 marks)**

(Total: 10 marks)

6   MX (MAY 10 EXAM)

MX acquired 80% of the 1 million issued $1 ordinary share capital of FZ on 1 May 20X9 for $1,750,000 when FZ's retained earnings were $920,000.

The carrying value was considered to be the same as fair value with the exception of the following:

•   The carrying value of FZ's property, plant and equipment at 1 May 20X9 was $680,000. The market value at that date was estimated at $745,000. The remaining useful life of the property, plant and equipment was estimated at 5 years from the date of acquisition.

•   FZ had a contingent liability with a fair value of $100,000. There was no change to the value of this liability at the year-end.

MX estimates that the costs of reorganising the combined entity following acquisition will be $200,000.

MX depreciates all assets on a straight line basis over their estimated useful lives on a monthly basis.

FZ sold goods to MX with a sales value of $300,000 during the 8 months since the acquisition. All of these goods remain in MX's inventories at the year end. FZ makes 20% gross profit margin on all sales.

The retained earnings reported in the financial statements of MX and FZ as at 31 December 20X9 are $3.2 million and $1.1 million respectively. There has been no impairment to goodwill since the date of acquisition.

The group policy is to measure non-controlling interest at fair value at the date of acquisition. The fair value of non-controlling interest at 1 May 20X9 was $320,000.

Required:

Calculate the amounts that will appear in the consolidated statement of financial position of the MX Group as at 31 December 20X9 for:

(i) **Goodwill;**

(ii) **Consolidated retained earnings; and**

(iii) **Non-controlling interest.**

(Total: 10 marks)

7 ✓ AB, CD & EF (NOV 10 EXAM)

The income statements for AB, CD and EF for the year ended 30 June 20X9 are shown below.

	AB	CD	EF
	$000	$000	$000
Revenue	2,000	1,500	800
Cost of Sales	(1,200)	(1,000)	(500)
Gross profit	800	500	300
Distribution costs	(400)	(120)	(80)
Administrative expenses	(240)	(250)	(100)
Other income	40	–	–
Profit before tax	200	130	120
Income tax expense	(50)	(40)	(20)
Profit for the year	150	90	100

Additional information

1 AB acquired 80% of the ordinary share capital of CD on 1 July 20X7 for $4,100,000. At the date of acquisition the fair value of the net assets of CD was $5,000,000. The group policy is to value non-controlling interest at fair value and at the date of acquisition the fair value of the non-controlling interest was $1,100,000. No impairment of goodwill arose in the year ended 30 June 20X8, however an impairment review conducted on 30 June 20X9 showed goodwill had been impaired by 15%. Impairment is charged to administrative expenses.

2 AB acquired 20% of the ordinary share capital of EF on 1 October 20X8. The interest acquired enables AB to exercise significant influence over the operating and financial policies of EF.

3   During the year to 30 June 20X9, AB and CD paid ordinary dividends of $100,000 and $50,000 respectively. Income from investments is shown in "Other income".

4   Included in the fair value uplift on the acquisition of CD were depreciable assets with a remaining useful life at the acquisition date of 12 years. The fair value of these assets was found to be $240,000 higher than book value. The group policy is to depreciate non-current assets on a straight line basis over their estimated economic useful life. Depreciation is charged to administrative expenses.

5   EF sold goods to AB on 1 May 20X9 with a sales value of $80,000. Half of these goods remain in AB's inventories at the year end. EF makes 25% profit margin on all sales.

Required:

Prepare the consolidated income statement for the AB group for the year ended 30 June 20X9.

(Total: 10 marks)

8   KL, LM & NP (MAR 11 EXAM)

The income statements for KL, LM and NP for the year ended 31 December 20X1 are shown below.

	KL	LM	NP
	$000	$000	$000
Revenue	4,000	1,500	1,200
Cost of Sales	(2,300)	(1,000)	(800)
Gross profit	1,700	500	400
Distribution costs	(900)	(120)	(80)
Administrative expenses	(350)	(150)	(100)
Other income	70	–	–
Profit before tax	520	230	220
Income tax expense	(250)	(80)	(100)
Profit for the year	270	150	120

Additional information

1   KL acquired 70% of the ordinary share capital of LM on 1 January 20X0 for $8,200,000. At the date of acquisition the net assets of LM were assessed to have a fair value of $10,000,000. The only fair value adjustment required on acquisition related to depreciable assets (see note 2 below). The group policy is to value non-controlling interest at fair value at the date of acquisition. The fair value of the non-controlling interest at the date of acquisition was $2,200,000.

2   At the date of acquisition, depreciable assets of LM with a remaining useful life at that date of 6 years had a fair value of $240,000 more than their book value. The group policy is to depreciate non-current assets on a straight line basis over their remaining economic useful life. Depreciation is charged to administrative expenses.

3   No impairment of goodwill arose in the year ended 31 December 20X0, however an impairment review conducted on 31 December 20X1 showed goodwill being impaired by 15%. Impairment losses are charged to administrative expenses.

4   KL acquired 40% of the ordinary share capital of NP on 1 October 20X1. KL is now able to exercise significant influence over the operating and financial policies of NP.

5   During the year to 31 December 20X1, KL and LM paid ordinary dividends of $300,000 and $100,000 respectively. Income from investments is included within other income.

6   LM sold goods to KL on 1 November 20X1 with a sales value of $140,000. Half of these goods remain in KL's inventories at the year end. LM makes 20% profit margin on all sales.

Required:

Prepare the consolidated income statement for the KL group for the year ended 31 December 20X0. (Round all workings to the nearest $000)

(Total: 10 marks)

9   RBE (MAY 11 EXAM)

RBE owns 70% of the ordinary share capital of DCA. The total group equity as at 31 December 20X0 was $4,000,000, which included $650,000 attributable to non-controlling interest.

RBE purchased a further 20% of the ordinary share capital of DCA on 1 October 20X1 for $540,000.

During the year to 31 December 20X1, RBE issued 2 million $1 ordinary shares, fully paid, at $1.30 per share.

Dividends were paid by both group entities in April 20X1. The dividends paid by RBE and DCA were $200,000 and $100,000, respectively.

Total comprehensive income for the year ended 31 December 20X1 for RBE was $900,000 and for DCA was $600,000. Income is assumed to accrue evenly throughout the year.

Required:

(a)   **Explain the impact of the additional 20% purchase of DCA's ordinary share capital by RBE on the equity of the RBE group.**   **(3 marks)**

(b)   **Prepare the consolidated statement of changes in equity for the year ended 31 December 20X1 for the RBE group, showing the total equity attributable to the parent and to the non-controlling interest.**   **(7 marks)**

(Total: 10 marks)

10   SD (SEP 11 EXAM)

SD acquired 60% of the 1 million $1 ordinary shares of KL on 1 July 20X0 for $3,250,000 when KL's retained earnings were $2,760,000. The group policy is to measure non-controlling interests at fair value at the date of acquisition. The fair value of non-controlling interests at 1 July 20X0 was $1,960,000. There has been no impairment of goodwill since the date of acquisition.

SD acquired a further 20% of KL's share capital on 1 March 20X1 for $1,000,000.

The retained earnings reported in the financial statements of SD and KL as at 30 June 20X1 are $9,400,000 and $3,400,000 respectively.

KL sold goods for resale to SD with a sales value of $750,000 during the period from 1 March 20X1 to 30 June 20X1. 40% of these goods remain in SD's inventories at the year-end. KL applies a mark-up of 25% on all goods sold.

Profits of both entities can be assumed to accrue evenly throughout the year.

Required:

Calculate the amounts that will appear in the consolidated statement of financial position of the SD Group as at 30 June 20X1 for:

(i)   Goodwill;

(ii)   Consolidated retained earnings; and

(iii)   Non-controlling interest.

(Total: 10 marks)

ISSUES IN RECOGNITION AND MEASUREMENT

11   CBA (NOV 06 EXAM)

CBA is a listed entity that runs a defined benefit pension scheme on behalf of its employees. In the financial year ended 30 September 20X6, the scheme suffered an actuarial loss of $7.2 million. The entity's directors are aware of the relevant Accounting Standard, IAS 19 Employee Benefits, but do not have sufficient knowledge to apply it. They have asked you, the financial controller, to write a short briefing paper, setting out an outline of the options for accounting for the actuarial loss in accordance with the Standard.

Required:

Prepare the briefing paper explaining the options and identifying, as far as possible from the information given, the potential impact on the financial statements of CBA of the three alternative accounting treatments.

(Total: 10 marks)

12   FDE (MAY 09 EXAM)

FDE is finalising its accounts for the year ended 31 March 20X9. FDE operates a defined benefit pension scheme for all its eligible employees. The current service cost of operating the scheme was $7.8 million for the year ended 31 March 20X9. At 31 March 20X8, the fair value of the pension scheme assets was $73 million and the present value of the pension scheme liabilities was $80 million. $8.8 million of unrecognised actuarial losses were brought forward at 1 April 20X8.

FDE made contributions to the scheme in the year of $8.8 million. The expected return on the pension scheme assets is 8.219% and the interest cost for the year is $10.2 million. The pension scheme paid out $4 million in benefits in the year to 31 March 20X9.

FDE adopts IAS 19 Employee Benefits and follows the corridor approach in recognising actuarial gains and losses. As at 31 March 20X9, the fair value of pension scheme assets was $84 million and the present value of pension scheme liabilities was $95 million. The average remaining service lives of employees who participate in the scheme is 10 years.

Required:

(a)   **Calculate the expense, in respect of the pension scheme, that FDE will include in its income statement for the year ended 31 March 20X9.**   **(3 marks)**

(b)   **Calculate the net pension asset or liability that will appear in the statement of financial position of FDE as at 31 March 20X9.**   **(5 marks)**

(c)   **IAS 19 currently permits alternative treatments for actuarial gains or losses. Briefly explain the impact of adopting ONE of these alternative treatments on the financial statements of FDE.**   **(2 marks)**

(Total: 10 marks)

13   LMN (MAY 06 EXAM)

LMN trades in motor vehicles which are manufactured and supplied by their manufacturer, IJK. Trading between the two entities is subject to a contractual agreement, the principal terms of which are as follows:

- LMN is entitled to hold on its premises at any one time up to 80 vehicles supplied by IJK. LMN is free to specify the ranges and models of vehicle supplied to it. IJK retains legal title to the vehicles until such time as they are sold to a third party by LMN.

- While the vehicles remain on its premises, LMN is required to insure them against loss or damage.

- The price at which vehicles are supplied is determined at the time of delivery; it is not subject to any subsequent alteration.

- When LMN sells a vehicle to a third party, it is required to inform IJK within three working days. IJK submits an invoice to LMN at the originally agreed price; the invoice is payable by LMN within 30 days.

- LMN is entitled to use any of the vehicles supplied to it for demonstration purposes and road testing. However, if more than a specified number of kilometres are driven in a vehicle, LMN is required to pay IJK a rental charge.

- LMN has the right to return any vehicle to IJK at any time without incurring a penalty, except for any rental charge incurred in respect of excess kilometres driven.

Required:

Discuss the economic substance of the contractual arrangement between the two entities in respect of the recognition of inventory and of sales. Refer, where appropriate, to IAS 18 Revenue.

(Total: 10 marks)

14 GHK (MAY 09 EXAM)

GHK is preparing its financial statements to 31 January 20X9 in accordance with International Financial Reporting Standards (IFRS). The financial director is querying the treatment of two transactions that occurred during the year.

Property sale

On 1 February 20X8, GHK sold a property to a financial institution for $65 million. The property had originally been purchased 10 years ago for $60 million and was depreciated at 2% per annum straight line, with a full year's depreciation charge being recorded in the year of purchase and none in the year of sale. The financial accountant has derecognised the property and recorded the subsequent gain on disposal in the income statement for the year ended 31 January 20X9.

Under the terms of the sale agreement GHK has a call option to repurchase the property at any time in the next five years. The repurchase price of $65 million set at the start of the agreement will increase by $2.5 million after the first year and $3 million in the following year. The financial institution can require GHK to repurchase the property on 1 February 20Y1 for $74 million, if GHK fails to exercise the option before that date.

Share issue

GHK issued 10 million $1 cumulative non-redeemable 6% preference shares during the year. The proceeds of the issue were debited to cash and credited to equity. Issue costs paid of $50,000 were debited to share premium and the dividend paid shortly before the year end was debited to retained earnings.

Required:

(a) **Explain how the sale of property transaction should be treated in accordance with IFRS. Prepare any correcting journal entries that are required to be made to the financial statements for the year to 31 January 20X9 in respect of this sale of property transaction.** **(6 marks)**

(b) **Explain how the share issue should have been classified in accordance with IAS 32 Financial instruments: presentation, and prepare any correcting journal entries that are required to be made to the financial statements for the year to 31 January 20X9 in respect of this share issue transaction.** **(4 marks)**

(Total: 10 marks)

15   AZG (MAY 08 EXAM)

On 1 February 20X6, the directors of AZG decided to enter into a forward foreign exchange contract to buy 6 million florins at a rate of $1 = 3 florins, on 31 January 20X9. AZG's year end is 31 March.

Relevant exchange rates were as follows:

1 February 20X6 $1	= 3.0 florins
31 March 20X6 $1	= 2.9 florins
31 March 20X7 $1	= 2.8 florins

Required:

(a)   Identify the three characteristics of a derivative financial instrument as defined in IAS 39 Financial Instruments: Recognition and Measurement.   **(3 marks)**

(b)   Describe the requirements of IAS 39 in respect of the recognition and measurement of derivative financial instruments.   **(2 marks)**

(c)   Prepare relevant extracts from AZG's income statement and statement of financial position to reflect the forward foreign exchange contract at 31 March 20X7, with comparatives. (Note: ignore discounting when measuring the derivative).   **(5 marks)**

(Total: 10 marks)

16   BGA (NOV 07 EXAM)

The following information relates to the defined benefits pension scheme of BGA, a listed entity:

The present value of the scheme obligations at 1 November 20X6 was $18,360,000, while the fair value of the scheme assets at that date was $17,770,000. During the financial year ended 31 October 20X7, a total of $997,000 was paid into the scheme in contributions. Current service cost for the year was calculated at $1,655,000, and actual benefits paid were $1,860,300. The applicable interest cost for the year was 6.5% and the expected return on plan assets was 9.4%.

The present value of the scheme obligations at 31 October 20X7 was calculated as $18,655,500 and the fair value of scheme assets at that date was $18,417,180.

BGA adopts the '10% corridor' criterion in IAS 19 Employee Benefits for determining the extent of recognition of actuarial gains and losses. The average remaining service life of the employees was 10 years. Net unrecognised actuarial losses on 1 November 20X6 were $802,000.

Required:

(a)   Calculate the actuarial gain or loss on BGA's pension scheme assets and liabilities for the year ended 31 October 20X7.   **(8 marks)**

(b)   Calculate the extent to which, if at all, actuarial gains or losses should be recognised in BGA's income statement for the year ended 31 October 20X7, using the '10% corridor' criterion.   **(2 marks)**

(Total: 10 marks)

17   DG (NOV 09 EXAM)

(a)   **Financial Instrument**

DG acquired 500,000 shares in HJ, a listed entity, for $3.50 per share on 28 May 20X9. The costs associated with the purchase were $15,000 and were included in the cost of the investment. The directors plan to realise this investment before the end of 20X9. The investment was designated on acquisition as held for trading. There has been no further adjustment made to the investment since the date of purchase. The shares were trading at $3.65 each on 30 June 20X9.

(b)   **Financial Instrument**

DG purchased a bond with a par value of $5 million on 1 July 20X8. The bond carries a 5% coupon, payable annually in arrears and is redeemable on 30 June 20Y3 at $5.8 million. DG fully intends to hold the bond until the redemption date. The bond was purchased at a 10% discount. The effective interest rate on the bond is 10.26%. The interest due for the year was received and credited to investment income in the income statement.

Required:

Explain how financial instruments (a) and (b) should be classified, initially measured and subsequently measured. Prepare any journal entries required to correct the accounting treatment for the year to 30 June 20X9.

(Total: 10 marks)

18   JK (MAY 10 EXAM)

JK is a motor dealership which prepares its financial statements to 30 November. In the year to 30 November 20X9, transactions included the following:

(a)   JK had motor vehicles on its premises that were supplied by a car manufacturer, SB. Trading between JK and SB was subject to a contractual agreement. This agreement stated that JK could hold up to 100 vehicles on its premises although the legal title of the vehicles remained with SB until they were sold by JK to a third party. JK was required to inform SB within 5 working days of any sale, at which time SB would raise an invoice at the price agreed at the original date of delivery. JK had the right to return any vehicle at any time without incurring a penalty. JK was responsible for insuring all the vehicles on its property.

Required:

Briefly discuss the economic substance of JK's contractual agreement with SB and explain which entity should recognise the vehicles in inventory during the period that they were held at JK's premises.   **(5 marks)**

(b) JK granted 1,000 share appreciation rights (SARs) to its 120 employees on 1 December 20X7. To be eligible, employees must remain employed for 3 years from the grant date. The rights must be exercised in December 20Y0. In the year to 30 November 20X8, 12 staff left and a further 15 were expected to leave over the following two years.

In the year to 30 November 20X9 8 staff left and a further 10 were expected to leave in the following year.

The fair value of each SAR was $15 at 30 November 20X8 and $17 at 30 November 20X9

Required:

Prepare the accounting entries to record, for the year to 30 November 20X9, the expense associated with the SARs. **(5 marks)**

(Total: 10 marks)

19 LBP (NOV 10 EXAM)

LBP granted share options to its 600 employees on 1 October 20X7. Each employee will receive 500 share options provided they continue to work for LBP for four years from the grant date. The fair value of each option at the grant date was $1.48.

The actual and expected staff movement over the 4 years to 30 September 20Y1 is given below:

20X8 20 employees left and another 50 were expected to leave over the next three years

20X9 A further 25 employees left and another 40 were expected to leave over the next two years

20Y0 A further 15 employees left and another 20 were expected to leave the following year

20Y1 No actual figures are available to date

The sales director of LBP has stated in the board minutes that he disagrees with the treatment of the share options. No cash has been paid out to employees, therefore he fails to understand why an expense is being charged against profits.

Required:

(a) **Calculate the charge to the income statement for the year ended 30 September 20Y0 for LBP in respect of the share options and prepare the journal entry to record this.** **(6 marks)**

(b) **Explain the principles of recognition and measurement for share-based payments as set out in *IFRS 2 Share-based Payments* so as to address the concerns of the sales director.** **(4 marks)**

(Total: 10 marks)

20   BCL (NOV 10 EXAM)

BCL entered into a forward contract on 31 July 20X0 to purchase B$2 million at a contracted rate of A$1: B$0.64 on 31 October 20X0.   The contract cost was nil.   BCL prepares its financial statements to 31 August 20X0. At 31 August 20X0 an equivalent contract for the purchase of B$2 million could be acquired at a rate of A$1: B$0.70.

Required:

(a)   **Explain how this financial instrument should be classified and prepare the journal entry required for its measurement as at 31 August 20X0.**   **(6 marks)**

(b)   **Assume now that the instrument described above was designated as a hedging instrument in a cash flow hedge, and that the hedge was 100% effective.**

   (i)   **Explain how the gain or loss on the instrument for the year ended 31 August 20X0 should now be recorded and why different treatment is necessary.**

   (ii)   **Prepare an extract of the statement of total comprehensive income for BCL for the year ended 31 August 20X0, assuming the profit for the year of BCL was A$1 million, before accounting for the hedging instrument.**   **(4 marks)**

                              (Total: 10 marks)

21   JKL (MAR 11 EXAM)

(a)   JKL granted share options to its 300 employees on 1 January 20X7.   Each employee will receive 1,000 share options provided they continue to work for JKL for 3 years from the grant date.   The fair value of each option at the grant date was $1.22.

The actual and expected staff movement over the 3 years to 31 December 20X9 is provided below:

20X7   25 employees left and another 40 were expected to leave over the next two years.

20X8   A further 15 employees left and another 20 were expected to leave the following year.

Required:

   (i)   **Calculate the charge to JKL's income statement for the year ended 31 December 20X8 in respect of the share options and prepare the journal entry to record this.**

   (ii)   **Explain how the recognition and measurement of a share-based payment would differ if it was to be settled in cash rather than in equity, in accordance with IFRS 2 *Share-based Payments*.**   **(6 marks)**

(b)   JKL operates a defined benefit pension plan.   The fair value of the plan assets at 31 December 20X8 was $13.1 million.   The present value of the plan liabilities at 31 December 20X8 was £13.9 million. JKL currently adopts the corridor approach for the treatment of actuarial gains and losses.   Unrecognised actuarial losses as at 31 December 20X8 totalled $0.5 million.

Required:

   (i)   **Calculate the net pension asset or liability that would be included in JKL's statement of financial position as at 31 December 20X8.**

   (ii)   **Explain what other options the directors have for the treatment of actuarial gains or losses, in accordance with IAS 19 *Employee Benefits*.**   **(4 marks)**

                              (Total: 10 marks)

22 ✓ MNB (MAR 11 EXAM)

(a)   MNB acquired an investment in a debt instrument on 1 January 20X0 at its par value of $3 million. Transaction costs relating to the acquisition were $200,000. The investment earns a fixed annual return of 6%, which is received in arrears. The principal amount will be repaid to MNB in 4 years' time at a premium of $400,000. The investment has been correctly classified as held to maturity. The investment has an effective interest rate of approximately 7.05%.

Required:

(i)   Explain how this financial instrument will be initially recorded AND subsequently measured in the financial statements of MNB, in accordance with IAS 39 *Financial Instruments: Recognition and Measurement*.

(ii)   Calculate the amounts that would be included in MNB's financial statements for the year to 31 December 20X0 in respect of this financial instrument.

(6 marks)

(b)   MNB acquired 100,000 shares in AB on 25 October 20X0 for $3 per share. The investment resulted in MNB holding 5% of the equity shares of AB. The related transaction costs were $12,000. AB's shares were trading at $3.40 on 31 December 20X0. The investment has been classified as held for trading.

Required:

Prepare the journal entries to record the initial AND subsequent measurement of this financial instrument in the financial statements of MNB for the year to 31 December 20X0.   **(5 marks)**

(Total: 10 marks)

23 ✓ EAU (MAY 11 EXAM)

(a)   EAU operates a defined benefit pension plan for its employees. At 1 January 20X8 the fair value of the pension plan assets was $2,600,000 and the present value of the plan liabilities was $2,900,000.

The actuary estimates that the current and past service costs for the year ended 31 December 20X8 is $450,000 and $90,000 respectively. The past service cost is caused by an increase in pension benefits. The plan liabilities at 1 January and 31 December 20X8 correctly reflect the impact of this increase.

The interest cost on the plan liabilities is estimated at 8% and the expected return on plan assets at 5%.

The pension plan paid $240,000 to retired members in the year to 31 December 20X8. EAU paid $730,000 in contributions to the pension plan and this included $90,000 in respect of past service costs.

At 31 December 20X8 the fair value of the pension plan assets is $3,400,000 and the present value of the plan liabilities is $3,500,000.

In accordance with the amendment to IAS 19 *Employee Benefits*, EAU recognises actuarial gains and losses in other comprehensive income in the period in which they occur.

Required:

Calculate the actuarial gains or losses on pension plan assets and liabilities that will be included in other comprehensive income for the year ended 31 December 20X8. (Round all figures to the nearest $000). *300* **(5 marks)**

(b) EAU granted 1,000 share appreciation rights (SARs) to its employees on 1 January 20X7. To be eligible, employees must remain employed for 3 years from the date of issue and the rights must be exercised in January 20Y0, with settlement due in cash.

In the year to 31 December 20X7, 32 staff left and a further 35 were expected to leave over the following two years.

In the year to 31 December 20X8, 28 staff left and a further 10 were expected to leave in the following year.

No actual figures are available as yet for 20X9.

The fair value of each SAR was $8 at 31 December 20X7 and $12 at 31 December 20X8.

Required:

Prepare the accounting entry to record the expense associated with the SARs, for the year to 31 December 20X8, in accordance with IFRS 2 *Share-based Payments.*
(5 marks)

(Total: 10 marks)

24 ✓ QWE (MAY 11 EXAM)

(a) QWE issued 10 million 5% convertible $1 bonds 20X5 on 1 January 20X0. The proceeds were credited to non-current liabilities and debited to bank. The 5% interest paid has been charged to finance costs in the year to 31 December 20X0.

The market rate of interest for a similar bond with a five year term but no conversion is 7%.

Required:

Explain AND demonstrate how this convertible instrument would be initially measured in accordance with IAS 32 *Financial Instruments: Presentation* AND subsequently measured in accordance with IAS 39 *Financial Instruments: Recognition and Measurement* in the financial statements for the year ended 31 December 20X0. **(7 marks)**

(b) The directors of QWE want to avoid increasing the gearing of the entity. They plan to issue 5 million 6% cumulative redeemable $1 preference shares in 20X1.

Required:

Explain how the preference shares would be classified in accordance with IAS 32 *Financial Instruments: Presentation* AND the impact that this issue will have on the gearing of QWE. **(3 marks)**

(Total: 10 marks)

25 VB (SEP 11 EXAM)

(a) **Financial instruments**

VB acquired 40,000 shares in another entity, JK, in March 20X2 for $2.68 per share. The investment was classified as available for sale on initial recognition. The shares were trading at $2.96 per share on 31 July 20X2. Commission of 5% of the value of the transaction is payable on all purchases and disposals of shares.

Required:

(i) **Prepare the journal entries to record the initial recognition of this financial asset and its subsequent measurement at 31 July 20X2 in accordance with IAS 39** *Financial Instruments: Recognition and Measurement.* **(3 marks)**

The directors of VB are concerned about the value of VB's investment in JK and in an attempt to hedge against the risk of a fall in its value, are considering acquiring a derivative contract. The directors wish to use hedge accounting in accordance with IAS 39.

Required:

(ii) **Discuss how both the available for sale investment and any associated derivative contract would be subsequently accounted for, assuming that the criteria for hedge accounting were met, in accordance with IAS 39. (3 marks)**

(b) **Share options**

VB granted share options to its 500 employees on 1 August 20X0. Each employee will receive 1,000 share options provided they continue to work for VB for the four years following the grant date. The fair value of the options at the grant date was $1.30 each. In the year ended 31 July 20X1, 20 employees left and another 50 were expected to leave in the following three years. In the year ended 31 July 20X2, 18 employees left and a further 30 were expected to leave during the next two years.

Required:

Prepare the journal entry to record the charge to VB's income statement for the year ended 31 July 20X2 in respect of the share options, in accordance with IFRS 2 *Share-based Payments.* **(4 marks)**

(Total: 10 marks)

26 OVS (SEP 11 EXAM)

(a) OVS is a car dealership and prepares its financial statements to 30 June. In the year to 30 June 20X1, it held a number of vehicles at a number of different sites. The vehicles were supplied by GH, a car manufacturer, which is OVS's main supplier. Under the trading terms agreed with GH, OVS is entitled to hold up to a maximum of 1,000 vehicles although legal title remains with GH until the vehicle is sold to a third party. OVS is able to use the cars for demonstration purposes and can relocate the vehicles between sites, provided the mileage on any individual vehicle does not exceed 1,500 miles. Breach of this mileage limit would result in OVS incurring a penalty.

OVS has the right to return vehicles at any time within six months of delivery, with no charge. OVS is responsible for insuring all the vehicles on its premises.

Required:

Discuss the economic substance of OVS's trading agreement with GH in respect of the vehicles, concluding which entity should recognise the vehicles as inventory for the period that they are held by OVS. **(6 marks)**

(b) OVS is considering acquiring an entity called RT which is based overseas. RT operates car dealerships throughout Eastern Europe and the directors view this entity as an excellent strategic fit with the OVS business model. They are reviewing the financial statements of RT (which are prepared on a historic cost accounting basis), but are aware that RT is currently operating in an economic environment that is subject to high inflation.

Required:

Discuss the potential drawbacks of using RT's financial statements as a basis for making business decisions in times of high inflation. **(4 marks)**

(Total: 10 marks)

FINANCIAL STATEMENT ANALYSIS

27 JKL

JKL is a listed entity preparing financial statements to 31 August. At 1 September 20X3, JKL had 6,000,000 50¢ shares in issue. On 1 February 20X4, the entity made a rights issue of 1 for 4 at 125¢ per share; the issue was successful and all rights were taken up. The market price of one share immediately prior to the issue was 145¢ per share. Earnings after tax for the year ended 31 August 20X4 were $2,763,000.

Several years ago, JKL issued a convertible loan of $2,000,000. The loan carries an interest rate of 7% and its terms of conversion (which are at the option of the stockholder) are as follows:

For each $100 of loan stock:

Conversion at 31 August 20X8	105 shares
Conversion at 31 August 20X9	103 shares

JKL is subject to an income tax rate of 32%.

Required:

(a) **Calculate basic earnings per share and diluted earnings per share for the year ended 31 August 20X4.** **(7 marks)**

(b) **The IASB Framework for the Preparation and Presentation of Financial Statements states that the objective of financial statements is to provide information that is:**

'useful to a wide range of users in making economic decisions'.

Explain to a holder of ordinary shares in JKL both the usefulness and limitations of the diluted earnings per share figure. **(3 marks)**

(Total: 10 marks)

28   CB (MAY 05 EXAM)

On 1 February 20X4, CB, a listed entity, had 3,000,000 ordinary shares in issue.

On 1 March 20X4, CB made a rights issue of 1 for 4 at $6.50 per share. The issue was completely taken up by the shareholders.

Extracts from CB's financial statements for the year ended 31 January 20X5 are presented below:

CB: Extracts from income statement for the year ended 31 January 20X5

	$000
Operating profit	1,380
Finance cost	(400)
Profit before tax	980
Income tax expense	(255)
Profit for the period	725

CB: Extracts from summarised statement of changes in equity for the year ended 31 January 20X5

	$000
Balance at 1 February 20X4	7,860
Issue of share capital	4,875
Surplus on revaluation of properties	900
Profit for the period	725
Equity dividends	(300)
Balance at 31 January 20X5	14,060

Just before the rights issue, CB's share price was $7.50, rising to $8.25 immediately afterwards. The share price at close of business on 31 January 20X5 was $6.25.

At the beginning of February 20X5, the average price earnings (P/E) ratio in CB's business sector was 28.4, and the P/E of its principal competitor was 42.5.

Required:

(a)   Calculate the earnings per share for CB for the year ended 31 January 20X5, and its P/E ratio at that date.   **(6 marks)**

(b)   Discuss the significance of P/E ratios to investors and CB's P/E ratio relative to those of its competitor and business sector.   **(4 marks)**

(Total: 10 marks)

29   BAQ (MAY 07 EXAM)

BAQ is a listed entity with a financial year end of 31 March. At 31 March 20X7, it had 8,000,000 ordinary shares in issue.

The directors of BAQ wish to expand the business's operations by acquiring competitor entities. They intend to make no more than one acquisition in any financial year.

The directors are about to meet to discuss two possible acquisitions. Their principal criterion for the decision is the likely effect of the acquisition on group earnings per share.

Details of the possible acquisitions are as follows:

1   Acquisition of CBR

- 100% of the share capital of CBR could be acquired on 1 October 20X7 for a new issue of shares in BAQ;
- CBR has 400,000 ordinary shares in issue;
- Four CBR shares would be exchanged for three new shares in BAQ;
- CBR's profit after tax for the year ended 31 March 20X7 was $625,000 and the entity's directors are projecting a 10% increase in this figure for the year ending 31 March 20X8.

2   Acquisition of DCS

- 80% of the share capital of DCS could be acquired on 1 October 20X7 for a cash payment of $10.00 per share;
- DCS has 1,000,000 ordinary shares in issue;
- The cash would be raised by a rights issue to BAQ's existing shareholders. For the purposes of evaluation it can be assumed that the rights issue would take place on 1 October 20X7, that it would be fully taken up, that the market value of one share in BAQ on that date would be $5.36, and that the terms of the rights issue would be one new share for every five BAQ shares held at a rights price of $5.00;
- DCS's projected profit after tax for the year ending 31 March 20X8 is $860,000.

BAQ's profit after tax for the year ended 31 March 20X8 is projected to be $4.2 million. No changes in BAQ's share capital are likely to take place, except in respect of the possible acquisitions described above.

Required:

Calculate the group earnings per share that could be expected for the year ending 31 March 20X8 in respect of each of the acquisition scenarios outlined above.

(Total: 10 marks)

30 AGZ (NOV 08 EXAM)

AGZ is a listed entity. You are a member of the team drafting its financial statements for the year ended 31 August 20X8.

Extracts from the draft income statement, including comparative figures, are shown below:

	20X8	20X7
	$million	$million
Profit before tax	276.4	262.7
Income tax expense	85.0	80.0
Profit for the period	191.4	182.7

At the beginning of the financial year, on 1 September 20X7, AGZ had 750 million ordinary shares of 50¢ in issue. At that date the market price of one ordinary share was 87.6¢.

On 1 December 20X7, AGZ made a bonus issue of one new ordinary 50¢ share for every three held.

In 20X6, AGZ issued $75 million convertible bonds. Each unit of $100 of bonds in issue will be convertible at the holder's option into 200 ordinary 50¢ shares on 31 August 20Y2. The interest expense relating to the liability element of the bonds for the year ended 31 August 20X8 was $6.3 million (20X7 – $6.2 million). The tax effect related to the interest expense was $2.0 million (20X7 – $1.8 million).

There were no other changes affecting or potentially affecting the number of ordinary shares in issue in either the 20X8 or 20X7 financial years.

Required:

(a) **Calculate earnings per share and diluted earnings per share for the year ended 31 August 20X8, including the comparative figures.**   **(8 marks)**

(b) **Explain the reason for the treatment of the bonus shares as required by IAS 33 Earnings per Share.**   **(2 marks)**

(Total: 10 marks)

31 EPS (NOV 07 EXAM)

Earnings per share (EPS) is generally regarded as a key accounting ratio for use by investors and others. Like all accounting ratios, however, it has its limitations. You have been asked to make a brief presentation to CIMA students on the topic.

Required:

(a) **Explain why EPS is regarded as so important that the IASB has issued an accounting standard on its calculation.**   **(2 marks)**

(b) **Explain the general limitations of the EPS accounting ratio and its specific limitations for investors who are comparing the performance of different entities.**   **(8 marks)**

(Total: 10 marks)

32 CSA (MAY 10 EXAM)

On 1 January 20X9 CSA, a listed entity, had 3,000,000 $1 ordinary shares in issue. On 1 May 20X9, CSA made a bonus issue of 1 for 3.

On 1 September 20X9, CSA issued 2,000,000 $1 ordinary shares for $3.20 each. The profit before tax of CSA for the year ended 31 December 20X9 was $1,040,000. Income tax expense for the year was $270,000.

The basic earnings per share for the year ended 31 December 20X8 was 15.4 cents.

On 1 November 20X9 CSA issued convertible loan stock. Assuming the conversion was fully subscribed there would be an increase of 2,400,000 ordinary shares in issue. The liability element of the loan stock is $4,000,000 and the effective interest rate is 7%.

CSA is subject to income tax at a rate of 30%.

Required:

(a) Calculate the basic earnings per share to be reported in the financial statements of CSA for the year ended 31 December 20X9, including comparative, in accordance with the requirements of IAS 33 Earnings Per Share. **(4 marks)**

(b) Calculate the diluted earnings per share for the year ended 31 December 20X9, in accordance with the requirements of IAS 33 Earnings Per Share. **(3 marks)**

(c) Briefly explain why the bonus issue and issue at full market value are treated differently in arriving at basic earnings per share. **(3 marks)**

(Total: 10 marks)

33 LOP (NOV 10 EXAM)

LOP operates in the construction industry and prepares its financial statements in accordance with IFRS. It is listed on its local exchange. LOP is looking to expand its overseas operations by acquiring a new subsidiary. Two geographical areas have been targeted, Frontland and Sidcland. Entity A operates in Frontland and entity B operates in Sideland. Both entities are listed on their local exchanges.

The financial highlights for entities A, B and LOP are provided below for the last trading period.

	A	B	LOP
Revenue	$160m	$300m	$500m
Gross profit margin	26%	17%	28%
Net profit	9%	11%	16%
Gearing	65%	30%	38%
Average rate of interest available in the respective markets	5%	9%	8%
P/E ratio	11.6	15.9	16.3

Required:

(a) Analyse the information provided by the key financial indicators above and explain the impact that each entity would have on the financial indicators of LOP. **(7 marks)**

(b) Explain the limitations of using this type of analysis to decide on a potential takeover target. **(3 marks)**

(Total: 10 marks)

34 FGH (MAR 11 EXAM)

FGH has been trading for a number of years and is currently going through a period of expansion of its core business area.

The statement of cash flows for the year ended 31 December 20X0 for FGH is presented below.

Cash flows from operating activities	$000	$000
Profit before tax	2,200	
Adjustments for:		
Depreciation	380	
Gain on sale of investments	(50)	
Loss on sale of property, plant and equipment	45	
Investment income	(180)	
Interest costs	420	
	2,815	
Increase in trade receivables	(400)	
Increase in inventories	(390)	
Increase in payables	550	
Cash generated from operations	2,575	
Interest paid	(400)	
Income taxes paid	(760)	
Net cash from operating activities		1,415
Cash flows from investing activities		
Acquisition of subsidiary, net of cash acquired	(800)	
Acquisition of property, plant and equipment	(340)	
Proceeds from sale of equipment	70	
Proceeds from sale of investments	150	
Interest received	100	
Dividends received	80	
Net cash used in investing activities		(740)

Cash flows from financing activities

Proceeds of share issue	300	
Proceeds from long term borrowings	300	
Dividend paid to equity holders of the parent	(1,000)	
	‾‾‾‾‾	
Net cash used in financing activities		(400)
		‾‾‾‾‾
Net increase in cash and cash equivalents		275
Cash and cash equivalents at the beginning of the period		110
		‾‾‾‾‾
Cash and cash equivalents at the end of the period		385
		‾‾‾‾‾

Required:

Analyse the above statement of cash flows for FGH, highlighting the key features of each category of cash flows. **(Total: 10 marks)**

35 FGH OPERATING SEGMENTS (MAY 11 EXAM)

The directors of FGH have agreed as part of their strategic plan to list the entity's shares on the local stock exchange.

At a recent board meeting, the directors discussed, in overview, the additional compliance that would be required upon listing. This included compliance with the requirements of IFRS 8 *Operating Segments* (IFRS 8). The managing director commented that adherence to the requirements of IFRS 8 would be time-consuming and costly due to the additional financial information that the entity would have to prepare.

Required:

(a) **Discuss whether the managing director's comment is accurate in respect of the operating segment analysis that is required in accordance with IFRS 8.** **(4 marks)**

(b) (i) **Explain why the information that is presented for operating segments is likely to be highly relevant to investors.**

  (ii) **Discuss the potential limitations of operating segment analysis as a tool for comparing different entities.** **(6 marks)**

(Total: 10 marks)

36 BOB (SEP 11 EXAM)

Bob is a financial analyst whose job is to compare the financial performance of different entities which operate in the same sector, but which may be located at home or overseas. He uses the following four key performance indicators when undertaking this comparison:

- Gross margin

- Profit margin (profit for the year/ revenue)

- P/E ratio

- Return on capital employed

Required:

Discuss, with specific reference to the four ratios above, the extent to which entities within the same sector can be validly compared with each other. Include in your discussion the limitations of both, same sector and international comparison.

(Total: 10 marks)

DEVELOPMENTS IN EXTERNAL REPORTING

37 MNO (MAY 06 EXAM)

You are the assistant to the Finance Director of MNO, a medium-sized listed entity that complies with International Accounting Standards. One of MNO's directors has proposed the publication of an Operating and Financial Review (OFR) as part of the annual financial statements. Most of the directors know very little about the OFR, and the Finance Director has asked you to produce a short briefing paper on the topic for their benefit.

Required:

Write the briefing paper, which should discuss the following issues:

- **any relevant regulatory requirements for an OFR;**

- **the purpose and, in outline, the typical content of an OFR;**

- **the advantages and drawbacks of publishing an OFR from the entity's point of view.**

(Total: 10 marks)

38 ENVIRONMENTAL DISCLOSURES (NOV 07 EXAM)

It is becoming increasingly common for listed entities to provide non-financial disclosures intended to inform stakeholders about the business's environmental policies, impacts and practices. Supporters of such voluntary disclosures argue that stakeholders have a right to be informed about environmental issues in this way. However, there are also arguments against this type of disclosure.

Required:

Identify and explain the principal arguments against voluntary disclosures by businesses of their environmental policies, impacts and practices.

(Total: 10 marks)

39 ✓ INTELLECTUAL ASSETS (NOV 08 EXAM)

CIMA's Official Terminology defines intellectual capital as "knowledge which can be used to create value".

Currently, IFRS permit the recognition of only a limited range of internally generated intellectual assets including, for example, copyrights.

Required:

(a) **Explain the advantages that could be gained by entities and their stakeholders if the scope of IFRS were expanded to permit the recognition in the statement of financial position of a wider range of intellectual assets, such as know-how, the value of the workforce, and employee skills.** **(5 marks)**

(b) **Explain the principal reasons why IFRS do not currently permit the recognition in the statement of financial position of intellectual assets such as know-how, the value of the workforce, and employee skills.** **(5 marks)**

(Total: 10 marks)

40 IASB AND FASB (MAY 08 EXAM)

An important development in international accounting in recent years has been the convergence project between the IASB and the US standard setter, the Financial Accounting Standards Board (FASB).

Required:

(a) **Describe the objectives, and progress to date, of the convergence project, illustrating your response with examples of the work that has been successfully undertaken.** **(6 marks)**

(b) **Identify four continuing, and significant, areas of difference that exist between IFRS and US GAAP.** **(4 marks)**

(Total: 10 marks)

41 CONVERGENCE PROJECT (MAY 10 EXAM)

You are a trainee accountant with a large accountancy firm and a training day has been organised to update all technical staff on a range of topics across various technical disciplines.

You have been asked to prepare a brief report for inclusion in the course notes which will be distributed to all staff attending the training day. The report is to cover the recent attempts at convergence between IFRS and US GAAP.

Required:

Prepare the report, explaining the progress to date of the convergence project. Include four examples of areas of accounting where convergence has been achieved.

(Total: 10 marks)

42   STAFF RESOURCE (NOV 10 EXAM)

A relative of yours has retired recently from the business world and has decided to invest some of his money in the stock market. You have received an email from him asking for advice:

"I have set aside some funds and wish to make some investments in the stock market. There are a number of entities that have caught my attention and I have been comparing the performance and financial position using their latest financial statements.   The management commentary and chairman's statement for one entity in particular mentions staff being a key resource and a substantial asset."

Required:

Discuss why the narrative elements of financial statements are likely to include comments about staff resource being a key asset and the issues of recognition that prevent such assets from being included in the statement of financial position.

(Total: 10 marks)

43   HUMAN CAPITAL (MAR 11 EXAM)

A friend who likes to invest in the stock market made the following statement to you recently, "I don't invest in entities that operate in service or knowledge-based industries because their financial statements don't really reflect the true value of the entity. This makes it difficult for me to make informed decisions about whether to invest or not."

Required:

(a)   **Discuss why an investor may arrive at the conclusion that the financial statements of entities operating in service and knowledge based industries are not useful for making investment decisions.**   **(5 marks)**

(b)   **Explain the recognition criteria that prevent human capital being recognised as an asset in the financial statements.**   **(5 marks)**

(Total: 10 marks)

44   BNM (MAY 11 EXAM)

BNM is a knowledge-based business which relies on key personnel and internally generated intellectual capital to generate revenue. BNM is listed on a local exchange. The directors believe that the information provided by the annual financial report fails to provide a complete picture of the activities and economic environment in which BNM operates. They are keen to ensure that current and potential investors are aware of the intellectual property that is a primary resource in the business. The business has cultivated key customer relationships and as a result has secured four large contracts that will run for at least the next three years.

The directors of BNM consider themselves to be socially and environmentally aware and have made efforts to improve the entity's reputation as a good corporate citizen. They are considering including some form of additional narrative disclosure within the next annual report.

Required:

(a)   **Discuss the potential advantages that could be gained by BNM if it included voluntary narrative disclosures within the annual report.**   **(6 marks)**

(b)   **Discuss the potential drawbacks of voluntary disclosures being included in annual reports.**   **(4 marks)**

(Total: 10 marks)

45   **SRT (SEPT 11 EXAM)**

SRT is an entity quoted on its local stock exchange which is engaged in environmentally sensitive operations. A number of its competitors provide extensive disclosures in their external reports about their environmental policies, impacts and practices, albeit on a voluntary basis.

Required:

(a)   **Discuss the pressures for extending the scope of external reports prepared by entities to include voluntary disclosures about their environmental policies, impacts and practices.**   **(4 marks)**

(b)   **Discuss the potential advantages AND disadvantages to SRT of providing voluntary environmental disclosures.**   **(6 marks)**

(Total: 10 marks)

Section 2

SECTION B-TYPE QUESTIONS

GROUP FINANCIAL STATEMENTS

46 AC, BD AND CF (MAY 09 EXAM)

AC is a listed entity that has made several investments in recent years, including investments in BD and CF. The financial assistant of AC has prepared the accounts of AC for the year ended 31 December 20X8. The financial assistant is unsure of how the investments should be accounted for and is not sufficiently experienced to prepare the consolidated financial statements for the AC group.

The summarised statements of financial position of AC, BD and CF are given below.

Summarised statements of financial position

	AC	BD	CF
	$000	$000	$000
Assets			
Non-current assets			
Property, plant and equipment	25,700	28,000	15,000
Investments	34,300	–	–
Current assets	17,000	14,000	6,000
	77,000	42,000	21,000
Equity and liabilities			
Equity			
Share capital ($1 ordinary shares)	30,000	20,000	8,000
Revaluation reserve	3,000	1,000	1,000
Other reserves	1,000	–	–
Retained earnings	22,000	9,000	9,000
	56,000	30,000	18,000
Non-current liabilities	6,000	4,000	–
Current liabilities	15,000	8,000	3,000
	77,000	42,000	21,000

Additional information:

1   Investments

AC acquired 14 million $1 ordinary shares in BD on 1 March 20X3 for $18 million. At the date of acquisition BD had retained earnings of $3 million and a balance of $1 million on revaluation reserve.

On 1 July 20X8, AC acquired a further 20% stake in BD for $7 million. BD made profit of $1.6 million in the year to 31 December 20X8 and profits are assumed to accrue evenly throughout the year.

AC acquired 40% of the $1 ordinary share capital of CF on 1 February 20X5 at a cost of $7 million. The retained earnings of CF at the date of acquisition totalled $6 million.

The remaining investment relates to an available for sale investment. The investment has a market value of $2.6 million at 31 December 20X8. The financial assistant was unsure of how this investment should be treated, so the investment is included at its original cost.

2   CF revalued a property during the year resulting in a revaluation gain of $1 million. There were no other revaluations of property, plant and equipment in the year for the other entities in the group. All revaluations to date relate to land, which is not depreciated in accordance with group policy.

3   During the period, AC sold goods to CF with a sales value of $800,000. Half of the goods remain in inventories at the year end. AC made 25% profit margin on all sales to CF.

4   An impairment review was performed in the period and it was estimated that the investment in CF was impaired by $420,000.

5   It is group policy to value the non-controlling interest at acquisition at the proportionate share of the fair value of the net assets.

Required:

(a)   Explain how each of the three investments held by AC should be accounted for in the consolidated financial statements.   (5 marks)

(b)   Prepare the consolidated statement of financial position of the AC group as at 31 December 20X8.   (20 marks)

                                          (Total: 25 marks)

47 ✓ AT (MAY 07 EXAM)

AT holds investments in three other entities. The draft income statements for the four entities for the year ended 31 March 20X7 are as follows:

	AT	BU	CV	DW
	$000	$000	$000	$000
Revenue	2,450	1,200	675	840
Cost of sales	(1,862)	(870)	(432)	(580)
Gross profit	588	330	243	260
Distribution costs	(94)	(22)	(77)	(18)
Administrative expenses	(280)	(165)	(120)	(126)
Interest received	–	2	–	–
Finance costs	(26)	–	–	–
Profit before tax	188	145	46	116
Income tax	(40)	(50)	(12)	(37)
Profit for the period	148	95	34	79

Notes

Note 1: Investments in BU, CV and DW

Several years ago AT purchased 75% of the ordinary shares of BU. On 30 September 20X6 it purchased a further 5% of BU's ordinary shares. In 20X3 AT, together with two other investor entities, set up CV. Each of the three investors owns one-third of the ordinary shares in CV. All managerial decisions relating to CV are made jointly by the three investor entities. On 1 January 20X7, AT purchased 35% of the ordinary shares in DW. AT exerts significant influence over the management of DW, but does not control the entity.

Note 2: Intra-group trading

BU supplies inventories to AT, earning a gross profit margin of 20% on such sales. During the financial year ended 31 March 20X7, BU supplied a total of $80,000 at selling price to AT. Of these items, 25% remained in AT's inventories at the year end. AT supplies a range of administrative services to BU, at cost. $12,000 is included in BU's administrative expenses, and in AT's revenue, in respect of such services supplied during the year ended 31 March 20X7.

Note 3:

The group has a policy of adopting proportional consolidation wherever permitted by International Financial Reporting Standards. The group values non-controlling interests at fair value at the date of acquisition.

Note 4:

Revenue and profits accrue evenly throughout the year, unless otherwise stated.

Note 5: Finance costs

The finance costs in AT's income statement are in respect of short-term bank borrowings only. Finance costs in respect of its long-term borrowings have not yet been included, and an appropriate adjustment must be made. On 1 April 20X4, AT issued bonds at par in the amount of $1,000,000. Issue costs were $50,000. The bonds carry a coupon rate of interest of 5% each year, payable on the last day of the financial year. The interest actually paid on 31 March 20X7 has been debited to a suspense account, which is included under current assets in AT's draft statement of financial position. The bonds will be repaid on 31 March

20X9 at a premium of $162,000. The effective interest rate associated with the bonds is 9%, and the liability is measured, in accordance with IAS 39 Financial Instruments: Recognition and Measurement, at amortised cost.

Note 6: Financial asset

From time to time BU uses available cash surpluses to make short term investments in financial assets. Such assets are 'held-for-trading' and are invariably sold within a few months. At 31 March 20X7, BU held 4,000 shares in a listed entity, EX. The shares had been purchased on 20 January 20X7 at a price of 1332¢ per share. At 31 March 20X7, the market price per share was 1227¢. No adjustment has been made to the draft income statement above in respect of this financial asset.

Required:

Prepare the consolidated income statement for the AT group for the financial year ended 31 March 20X7. Show full workings.

Note: 8 marks are available for the adjustments in respect of notes 5 and 6.

Work to nearest $100. For the purposes of this question it is not necessary to make any adjustments to income tax.

(Total: 25 marks)

48   PURPLE

Below are the statements of financial position as at 30 September 20X6 of four entities, all of whom prepare their financial statements in accordance with International Accounting Standards:

	Purple	Red	Blue	Cyan
	$000	$000	$000	$000
Non-current assets				
Tangible assets	23,410	6,640	5,900	6,000
Investments	15,420	10,200	1,000	–
Current assets				
Inventory	14,975	7,560	3,870	4,240
Receivables	12,680	6,350	3,275	5,600
Bank	6,925	4,465	2,230	1,125
	73,410	35,215	16,275	16,965
Equity				
Share capital	30,000	10,000	5,000	8,000
Retained earnings	21,320	12,925	6,200	2,465
Non-current liabilities	10,000	5,000	1,500	2,500
Current liabilities				
Payables	9,640	5,800	2,835	2,880
Taxation	2,450	1,490	740	1,120
	73,410	35,215	16,275	16,965

Notes:

1   Purple acquired a 60% shareholding in Red on 1 October 20X2 for $11,000,000 when Red's retained earnings were $3,750,000.

2   Red acquired a 70% shareholding in Blue on 1 January 20X6 for $10,200,000. Blue's profit for the year ended 30 September 20X6 is $1,200,000.

3   Purple acquired 2.4 million shares in Cyan on 1 October 20X4 for $3,000,000 when Cyan's retained earnings were $1,110,000.

4   When Purple acquired its shareholding in Red it was determined that Red's land had a fair value of $1,000,000 in excess of its carrying value. Also, inventory with a carrying value of $2,000,000 was deemed to have a fair value of $2,400,000. All of this inventory had been sold by 30 September 20X6.

5   During the period from 1 January 20X6 to 30 September 20X6, Red sold goods to both Purple and Blue at a mark-up of 20% on cost. The value of goods included in closing inventories are:

    Purple $3,600,000

    Blue $1,230,000

6   At 30 September 20X6 Purple owed $2,150,000 and Blue owed $1,500,000 to Red. Red's total intercompany receivables figure at year end was $3,950,000.

7   By the year-end, it was determined that goodwill arising on the acquisition of Red had been impaired by 10% of its original value. There are no impairments in respect of Blue or Cyan. It is group policy to value the non-controlling interest at acquisition at the proportionate share of the fair value of the net assets.

Required:

Prepare the consolidated statement of financial position of the Purple group as at 30 September 20X6.

(Total: 25 marks)

49   AX (NOV 07 EXAM)

AX, a listed entity, is planning to acquire several smaller entities. In order to raise the cash for its programme of acquisitions, it has recently sold part of its stake in a subsidiary, CY, and has raised $10 million in a bond issue.

Summarised statements of financial position for AX, CY and the other member of the Group, EZ, at 31 October 20X7 are given below:

	AX $000	CY $000	EZ $000
Assets			
Non-current assets			
Property, plant and equipment	20,000	8,900	5,000
Investment in subsidiaries (notes 1 & 2)	15,500	–	–
	35,500	8,900	5,000
Current assets	34,500	9,500	4,700
	70,000	18,400	9,700

Equity and liabilities

Equity

Called up share capital ($1 shares)	20,000	4,000	3,000
Retained earnings	18,000	7,000	3,000
	38,000	11,000	6,000
Non-current liabilities	–	2,400	1,000
Current liabilities	18,000	5,000	2,700
Suspense account (notes 1 & 3)	14,000	–	–
	70,000	18,400	9,700

Notes:

(1)   The investment in 80% of CY's ordinary share capital was purchased several years ago for $8 million when CY's retained earnings were $3.5 million. There has been no change since then in the amount of CY's share capital, and goodwill has remained unimpaired. No adjustments to fair value of CY's net assets were made either at acquisition or subsequently.

AX has a policy of valuing non-controlling interests at fair value at acquisition. The fair value of NCI on acquisition was $1.75 million.

On 31 October 20X7 AX sold one-quarter of its shareholding in CY to an unconnected party for $4 million. This amount has been debited to cash and credited to the suspense account. It is estimated that a tax liability of $400,000 will arise in respect of the profit on disposal of the investment; no provision for this liability has been made in the statement of financial position above.

(2)   The investment in 100% of EZ's ordinary share capital was purchased on 30 April 20X5 for $7.5 million when EZ's retained earnings were $1.5 million. Goodwill has remained unimpaired since the date of acquisition.

Upon acquisition a revaluation exercise was carried out. Plant and equipment in EZ with a book value of $1 million was revalued to $1.5 million. There were no other adjustments in respect of fair value. The revaluation is treated as a consolidation adjustment only: EZ continues to recognise non-current assets at depreciated historic cost. The remaining useful life of the plant and equipment at 30 April 20X5 was estimated to be five years, of which 30 months had elapsed by 31 October 20X7.

(3)   AX issued $10 million of 5% convertible bonds on 31 October 20X7. The bonds were issued in units of $1,000 and are repayable on 31 October 20Y0. However, each bond is convertible into 250 ordinary shares at any time until maturity at the option of the bondholder. The market rate for similar, non-convertible, bonds is 7%. It can be assumed that there were no issue costs. The $10 million raised by the issue was debited to cash and credited to the suspense account.

Required:

(a)   **Explain the appropriate accounting treatment to record the issue of convertible bonds, discussing the reasons for the approach that is adopted by International Financial Reporting Standards for this type of financial instrument.** **(5 marks)**

(b)   **Prepare the consolidated statement of financial position for the AX group at 31 October 20X7.** **(20 marks)**

(Total: 25 marks)

50   AZ (MAY 06 EXAM)

The statements of financial position of AZ and two entities in which it holds substantial investments at 31 March 20X6 are shown below:

	AZ		BY		CX	
	$000	$000	$000	$000	$000	$000
Non-current assets:						
Property, plant and equipment	10,750		5,830		3,300	
Investments	7,650		–		–	
		18,400		5,830		3,300
Current assets:						
Inventories	2,030		1,210		1,180	
Trade receivables	2,380		1,300		1,320	
Cash	1,380		50		140	
		5,790		2,560		2,640
		24,190		8,390		5,940
Equity:						
Called up share capital ($1 shares)		8,000		2,300		2,600
Preferred share capital		–		1,000		–
Reserves		10,750		3,370		2,140
		18,750		6,670		4,740
Current liabilities:						
Trade payables	3,770		1,550		1,080	
Income tax	420		170		120	
Suspense account	1,250		–		–	
		5,440		1,720		1,200
		24,190		8,390		5,940

Notes:

Note 1 – Investments by AZ in BY

Several years ago AZ purchased 80% of BY's ordinary share capital for $3,660,000 when the reserves of BY were $1,950,000. Group policy is to measure non-controlling interests at fair value at acquisition and the fair value of a 20% holding at this date was $900,000. There has been no subsequent impairment. The fair value of the non-controlling interest in BY was $900,000.

At the same time as the purchase of the ordinary share capital, AZ purchased 40% of BY's preferred share capital at par. The remainder of the preferred shares are held by several private investors.

Note 2 – Investment by AZ in CX

Several years ago AZ purchased 60% of CX's ordinary share capital for $2,730,000 when the reserves of CX were $1,300,000. The fair value of the non-controlling interest in CX at acquisition was $1,900,000.

On 1 October 20X5, AZ disposed of 520,000 ordinary shares in CX, thus losing control of CX's operations. However, AZ retains a significant influence over the entity's operations and policies. The proceeds of disposal, $1,250,000, were debited to cash and credited to a suspense account. No other accounting entries have been made in respect of the disposal. An investment gains tax of 30% of the profit on disposal will become payable by AZ within the 12 months following the reporting date of 31 March 20X6, and this liability should be accrued.

The fair value of the remaining holding in CX after selling the shares on 1 October 20X5 was $2,000,000.

CX's reserves at 1 April 20X5 were $1,970,000. The entity's profits accrued evenly throughout the year.

Note 3 – Additional information

No fair value adjustments were required in respect of assets or liabilities upon either of the acquisitions of ordinary shares. The called up share capital of both BY and CX has remained the same since the acquisitions were made.

Note 4 – Intra-group trading

During the year ended 31 March 20X6, BY started production of a special line of goods for supply to AZ. BY charges a mark-up of 20% on the cost of such goods sold to AZ. At 31 March 20X6, AZ's inventories included goods at a cost of $180,000 that had been supplied by BY.

Required:

(a)   Calculate the profit or loss on disposal after tax of the investment in CX that will be disclosed in:

    (i)   AZ's own financial statements;

    (ii)   the AZ group's consolidated financial statements.   **(6 marks)**

(b)   Calculate the consolidated reserves of the AZ group at 31 March 20X6.   **(5 marks)**

(c)   Prepare the consolidated statement of financial position of the AZ group at 31 March 20X6.   **(14 marks)**

Full workings should be shown.   **(Total: 25 marks)**

51 AJ (MAY 05 EXAM)

AJ is a law stationery business. In 20X2, the majority of its board of directors was replaced. The new board decided to adopt a policy of expansion through acquisition. The statements of financial position at 31 March 20X5 of AJ and of two entities in which it holds substantial investments are shown below:

Parent _A Subsidiary_ _Associate_

	AJ	AJ	BK	BK	CL	CL
	$000	$000	$000	$000	$000	$000
Non-current assets:						
Property, plant and equipment	12,500		4,700		4,500	
Investments	18,000		–		1,300	
		30,500		4,700		5,800
Current assets:						
Inventories	7,200		8,000		–	
Trade receivables	6,300		4,300		3,100	
Financial assets	–		–		2,000	
Cash	800		–		900	
		14,300		12,300		6,000
		44,800		17,000		11,800
Equity:						
Called up share capital ($1 shares)		10,000		5,000.		2,500
Reserves		14,000		1,000		4,300
		24,000		6,000		6,800
Non-current liabilities:						
Loan notes		10,000		3,000		–
Current liabilities:						
Trade payables	8,900		6,700		4,000	
Income tax	1,300		100		600	
Short-term borrowings	600		1,200		400	
		10,800		8,000		5,000
		44,800		17,000		11,800

Notes to the statements of financial position:

Note 1 – Investment by AJ in BK

On 1 April 20X2, AJ purchased $2 million loan notes in BK at par.

Financial Asset:
loan + receivable
FV → amortised cost

On 1 April 20X3, AJ purchased 4 million of the ordinary shares in BK for $7.5 million in cash, when BK's reserves were $1.5 million.

$\frac{4,000}{5,000} = 80\%$ _Subsidiary_

At the date of acquisition of the shares, BK's property, plant and equipment included land recorded at a cost of $920,000. At the date of acquisition, the fair value of the land was $1,115,000. No other adjustments in respect of fair value were required to BK's assets and liabilities upon acquisition. BK has not recorded the fair value in its own accounting records.

Adjust

_920,000 ↑ 1,115,000_

y/E 31/3/X5

Note 2 – Investment by AJ in CL

1,000
2500
Associate ?
Equity
Account

On 1 October 20X4, AJ acquired 1 million shares in CL, a book distributor, when the reserves of CL were $3.9 million. The purchase consideration was $4.4 million. Since the acquisition, AJ has had the right to appoint one of the five directors of CL. The remaining shares in CL are owned principally by three other investors.

No fair value adjustments were required in respect of CL's assets or liabilities upon acquisition.

Note 3 – Goodwill on consolidation

impairment

Group policy is to value non-controlling interests at fair value at acquisition. The fair value of the non-controlling interest in BK at 1 April 20X3 was $1.8 million. During March 20X5, an impairment review was carried out. As a result, the goodwill in respect of, BK is now impaired by 10%.

Note 4 – Intra-group trading

BK → AJ
1,000 X 25%.

BK supplies legal books to AJ. On 31 March 20X5, AJ's inventories included books purchased at a total cost of $1 million from BK. BK's mark-up on books is 25%.

Required:

(a) Explain, with reasons, how the investments in BK and CL will be treated in the consolidated financial statements of the AJ group. **(5 marks)**

(b) Prepare the consolidated statement of financial position for the AJ group at 31 March 20X5. **(20 marks)**

Full workings should be shown. **(Total: 25 marks)**

52 EAG (MAY 08 EXAM)

Extracts from the consolidated financial statements of the EAG Group for the year ended 30 April 20X8 are as follows:

EAG Group: Consolidated income statement for the year ended 30 April 20X8

	$ million
Revenue	30,750.0
Cost of sales	(26,447.5)
	————
Gross profit	4,302.5
Distribution costs	(523.0)
Administrative expenses	(669.4)
Finance cost	(510.9)
Share of profit of associate	1.6
Profit on disposal of associate	3.4
	————
Profit before tax	2,604.2
Income tax	(723.9)
	————
Profit for the period	1,880.3
	————

	$ million
Profit Attributable to	
Equity holders of the parent	1,652.3
Non-controlling interests	228.0
	1,880.3

EAG Group: Statement of financial position at 30 April 20X8

	20X8		20X7	
	$ million	$ million	$ million	$ million
ASSETS				
Non-current assets				
Property, plant & equipment	22,225.1		19,332.8	
Goodwill	1,662.7		1,865.3	
Intangible assets	306.5		372.4	
Investment in associate	–		13.8	
		24,194.3		21,584.3
Current assets				
Inventories	5,217.0		4,881.0	
Trade receivables	4,633.6		4,670.0	
Cash	62.5		88.3	
		9,913.1		9,639.3
TOTAL ASSETS		34,107.4		31,223.6
EQUITY AND LIABILITIES				
Equity				
Share capital	4,300.0		3,600.0	
Retained earnings	14,643.7		12,991.4	
		18,943.7		16,591.4
Non-controlling interest		2,010.5		1,870.5
Non-current liabilities				
Long-term borrowings		6,133.9		6,013.0
Current liabilities				
Trade payables	5,579.3		5,356.3	
Short-term borrowings	662.4		507.7	
Income tax	777.6		884.7	
		7,019.3		6,748.7
TOTAL EQUITY & LIABILITIES		34,107.4		31,223.6

Notes:

1. Depreciation of $2,024.7 million was charged in respect of property, plant and equipment in the year ended 30 April 20X8.

2. On 1 January 20X8 EAG disposed of the investment in associate for $18 million. The share of profit in the income statement relates to the period from 1 May 20X7 to 31 December 20X7. A dividend was received from the associate on 1 June 20X7. There were no other disposals, and no acquisitions, of investments in the accounting period.

3. Goodwill in one of the group's subsidiaries suffered an impairment during the year. The amount of the impairment was included in cost of sales. It is group policy to measure non-controlling interest at acquisition at the proportionate share of the fair value of the net assets.

4. The long-term borrowings are measured at amortised cost. The borrowing was taken out on 1 May 20X6, and proceeds of $6,000 million less issue costs of $100,000 were received on that date. Interest of 5% of the principal is paid in arrears each year, and the borrowings will be redeemed on 30 April 20Y1 for $6.55 million. All interest obligations have been met on the due dates. The effective interest rate applicable to the borrowings is 7%. The finance cost in the income statement includes interest in respect of both the long-term and the short-term borrowing. Short-term borrowing comprises overdrafts repayable on demand.

5. Amortisation of 25% of the opening balance of intangibles was charged to cost of sales. A manufacturing patent was acquired for a cash payment on 30 April 20X8.

6. An issue of share capital at par was made for cash during the year.

7. Dividends were paid to non-controlling interests during the year, but no dividend was paid to the equity holders of the parent entity.

Required:

Prepare the consolidated statement of cash flows of the EAG Group for the financial year ended 30 April 20X8. The statement of cash flows should be presented in accordance with the requirements of IAS 7 Statements of Cash Flows, and using the indirect method. Notes to the financial statement are NOT required, but full workings should be shown.

(Total: 25 marks)

53 ⎷ DX AND EY (NOV 08 EXAM)

On 1 November 20X3, DX invested in 100% of the share capital of EY, a new entity incorporated on that date. EY's operations are located in a foreign country where the currency is the Franc. DX has no other subsidiaries.

The summary financial statements of the two entities at their 31 October 20X8 year-end were as follows:

Summary income statements for the year ended 31 October 20X8

	DX	EY
	$000	Franc 000
Revenue	3,600	1,200
Cost of sales, other expenses and income tax	(2,800)	(1,000)
Profit for the period	800	200

Summary statements of changes in equity for the year ended 31 October 20X8

	DX	EY
	$000	Franc 000
Brought forward at 1 November 20X7	5,225	1,500
Profit for the period	800	200
Dividends	(200)	–
Carried forward at 31 October 20X8	5,825	1,700

Summary statements of financial position at 31 October 20X8

	DX	EY
	$000	Franc 000
Property, plant and equipment	5,000	1,500
Investment in EY	25	–
Current assets	4,400	2,000
	9,425	3,500
Share capital	1,000	50
Retained earnings	4,825	1,650
Current liabilities	3,600	1,800
	9,425	3,500

Relevant exchange rates were as follows:

1 November 20X3	1$ = 2.0 francs
31 October 20X7	1$ = 2.3 francs
31 October 20X8	1$ = 2.7 francs
Average rate for year ended 31 October 20X8	1$ = 2.6 francs

Required:

(a) Explain the meaning of the term "functional currency" as used by IAS 21 *The Effects of Changes in Foreign Exchange Rates*, and identify THREE factors that an entity should consider in determining its functional currency. **(4 marks)**

(b) Prepare:

    (i) the summary consolidated statement of comprehensive income for the year ended 31 October 20X8 (including a calculation that shows how the exchange gain or loss for the year has arisen); **(12 marks)**

    (ii) the summary consolidated statement of financial position at 31 October 20X8. **(6 marks)**

(c) Prepare the summary consolidated statement of changes in equity for the year to 31 October 20X8. **(3 marks)**

    Work to the nearest $. **(Total: 25 marks)**

54 AD, BE AND CF (NOV 06 EXAM)

The statements of financial position of three entities, AD, BE and CF at 30 June 20X6, the reporting date of all three entities, are shown below:

	AD		BE		CF	
	$000	$000	$000	$000	$000	$000
Assets						
Non-current assets						
Property, plant and equipment	1,900		680		174	
Financial assets						
Investments in equity shares	880		104		–	
Other (see note 3)	980		–		–	
		3,760		784		174
Current assets						
Inventories	223		127		60	
Trade receivables	204		93		72	
Other financial asset (see note 4)	25		–		–	
Cash	72		28		12	
		524		248		144
		4,284		1,032		318

Equity and liabilities

Equity

Called up share capital ($1 shares)	1,000		300		100	
Reserves	2,300		557		122	
		3,300		857		222
Non-current liabilities		600		–		–
Current liabilities						
Trade payables	247		113		84	
Income tax	137		62		12	
		384		175		96
		4,284		1,032		318

Additional information

Note 1 – Investment by AD in BE

AD acquired 80% of the ordinary shares of BE on 1 July 20X3 for $880,000 when BE's reserves were $350,000. Goodwill continues to be unimpaired. It is group policy to measure the non-controlling interest at fair value at acquisition and the fair value of the non-controlling interest in BE on 1 July 20X3 was $200,000.

Note 2 – Investment by BE in CF

BE acquired 40% of the ordinary shares of CF on 1 January 20X6 for $104,000. BE appoints one of CF's directors and, since the acquisition, has been able to exert significant influence over CF's activities. CF's reserves at the date of acquisition were $102,000.

Note 3 – Non-current financial asset

AD's other non-current financial asset is a debenture with a fixed interest rate of 5%. AD invested $1 million in the debenture at par on its issue date, 1 July 20X4. The debenture is redeemable at a premium on 30 June 20X8; the applicable effective interest rate over the life of the debenture is 8%. The full annual interest amount was received and recorded by AD in June 20X5 and June 20X6, and the appropriate finance charge was recognised in the financial year ended 30 June 20X5. However, no finance charge has yet been calculated or recognised **in respect of the financial year ended 30 June 20X6**.

Note 4 – Current financial asset

The current financial asset of $25,000 in AD represents a holding of shares in a major listed company. AD maintains a portfolio of shares held for trading. At 30 June 20X6, the only holding in the portfolio was 4,000 shares in DG, a major listed company with 2.4 million ordinary shares in issue. The investment was recognised on its date of purchase, 13 May 20X6, at a cost of 625¢ per share. At 30 June 20X6, the fair value of the shares had risen to 670¢ per share.

Note 5 – Intra-group trading

BE supplies goods to both AD and CF. On 30 June 20X6, CF held inventories at a cost of $10,000 that had been supplied to it by BE. BE's profit margin on the selling price of these goods is 30%.

On 30 June 20X6, AD's inventories included no items supplied by BE. However, BE's receivables on 30 June 20X6 included $5,000 in respect of an intra-group balance relating to the supply of goods to AD. No equivalent balance was included in AD's payables because it had made a payment of $5,000 on 27 June 20X6, which was not received and recorded by BE until after the year end.

Required:

(a) **Explain the accounting treatment in the statement of financial position and income statement for the financial assets described in notes 3 and 4 above, as required by IAS 39 Financial Instruments: Recognition and Measurement.** **(5 marks)**

(b) **Prepare the consolidated statement of financial position for the AD Group at 30 June 20X6.** **(20 marks)**

(Total: 25 marks)

55 SOT, PB AND UV (MAY 10 EXAM) *Walk in the footsteps of a top tutor*

The statements of comprehensive income for three entities for the year ended 30 September 20X9 are presented below:

	SOT	PB	UV
	$000	$000	$000
Revenue	6,720	6,240	5,280
Cost of sales	(3,600)	(3,360)	(2,880)
Gross profit	3,120	2,880	2,400
Administrative expenses	(760)	(740)	(650)
Distribution costs	(800)	(700)	(550)
Investment income	80	–	–
Finance costs	(360)	(240)	(216)
Profit before tax	1,280	1,200	984
Income tax expense	(400)	(360)	(300)
Profit for the year	880	840	684
Other comprehensive income			
Actuarial gains on defined benefit pension plan	110	–	40
Tax effect of other comprehensive income	(30)	–	(15)
Other comprehensive income for the year, net of tax	80	–	25
Total comprehensive income for the year	960	840	709

Additional information

1   SOT acquired 160,000 of the 200,000 $1 issued ordinary share capital of PB on 1 May 20X9 for $2,800,000. The reserves of PB at 1 May 20X9 were $2,050,000. A year end impairment review indicated that goodwill on acquisition of PB was impaired by 10%. The group policy is to charge impairment losses to administrative expenses. The group policy is to value the non-controlling interest at the proportionate share of the fair value of the net assets at the date of acquisition.

The fair value of the net assets acquired was the same as the book value with the exception of property, plant and equipment, which was higher by $960,000. The uplift in value related to a depreciable property with an estimated total useful life of 50 years. At the date of acquisition PB had owned and used this property for 10 years. The group policy is to charge depreciation on buildings to administrative expenses on a monthly basis from the date of acquisition to the date of disposal.

2   SOT disposed of 40,000 $1 ordinary shares of UV on 1 July 20X9 for $960,000. SOT had acquired 75,000 of the 100,000 $1 issued ordinary share capital of UV for $980,000 on 1 November 20X6, when the balance on reserves was $1,020,000. The fair value of the shareholding retained at 1 July 20X9 was $792,000. There was no evidence of goodwill having been impaired since the date of acquisition. The reserves of UV at 1 October 20X8 were $1,300,000.

3   PB paid a dividend of $100,000 on 1 September 20X9 and SOT has recorded its share in investment income.

4   SOT holds several available for sale investments, and accounts for these in accordance with IAS 39 Financial Instruments: recognition and measurement. Gains on subsequent measurement of $46,000 occurred in the year. The financial controller, however is unsure how this should be presented within the statement of comprehensive income and so has yet to include it.

5   SOT also disposed of an available for sale investment during the year to 30 September 20X9 for $630,000, when the carrying value of the investment was $580,000. The gain on disposal of $50,000 is included in administrative expenses. Previously recognised gains associated with this investment of $40,000 still remain in other reserves.

Assume that all income and gains for the three entities accrue evenly throughout the year.

Ignore any further tax impact of available for sale investments.

Round all figures to the nearest $000.

Required:

Prepare the consolidated statement of comprehensive income for the SOT group for the year ended 30 September 20X9.

(Total: 25 marks)

56   ROB (NOV 10 EXAM)

The statements of financial position for ROB and PER as at 30 September 20X2 are provided below:

	ROB	PER
	$000	$000
ASSETS		
Non-current assets		
Property, plant and equipment	22,000	5,000
Available for sale investment (note 1)	4,000	–
	26,000	5,000
Current assets		
Inventories	6,200	800
Receivables	6,600	1,900
Cash and cash equivalents	1,200	300
	14,000	3,000
Total assets	40,000	8,000
EQUITY AND LIABILITIES		
Equity		
Share capital ($1 equity shares)	20,000	1,000
Retained earnings	7,500	5,000
Other components of equity	500	–
Total equity	28,000	6,000
Non-current liabilities		
5% Bonds 20X5 (note 2)	3,900	–
Current liabilities	8,100	2,000
Total liabilities	12,000	2,000
Total equity and liabilities	40,000	8,000

Additional information

1   ROB acquired a 15% investment in PER on 1 May 20X0 for $600,000. The investment was classified as available for sale and the gains earned on it have been recorded within other reserves in ROB's individual financial statements. The fair value of the 15% investment at 1 April 20X2 was $800,000.

On 1 April 20X2, ROB acquired an additional 60% of the equity share capital of PER at a cost of $2,900,000. In its own financial statements, ROB has kept its investment in PER as an available for sale asset recorded at its fair value of $4,000,000 as at 30 September 20X2.

2   ROB issued 4 million $1 5% redeemable bonds on 1 October 20X1 at par. The associated costs of issue were $100,000 and the net proceeds of $3.9 million have been recorded within non-current liabilities. The bonds are redeemable at $4.5 million on 30 September 20X5 and the effective interest rate associated with them is approximately 8.5%. The interest on the bonds is payable annually in arrears and the amount due has been paid in the year to 30 September 20X2 and charged to the income statement.

3   An impairment review was conducted at the year end and it was decided that the goodwill on the acquisition of PER was impaired by 10%.

4   It is the group policy to value non-controlling interest at fair value at the date of acquisition. The fair value of the non-controlling interest at 1 April 20X2 was $1.25 million.

5   The profit for the year of PER was $3 million, and profits are assumed to accrue evenly throughout the year.

6   PER sold goods to ROB for $400,000. Half of these goods remained in inventories at 30 September 20X2. PER makes 20% margin on all sales.

7   No dividends were paid by either entity in the year to 30 September 20X2.

Required:

(a)   **Explain how the investment in PER should be accounted for in the consolidated financial statements of ROB, following the acquisition of the additional 60% shareholding.** **(5 marks)**

(b)   **Prepare the consolidated statement of financial position as at 30 September 20X2 for the ROB Group.** **(20 marks)**

(Total: 25 marks)

57   ERT (MAR 11 EXAM)

The statements of financial position for ERT and BNM as at 31 December 20X0 are provided below:

	ERT	BNM
	$000	*$000*
ASSETS		
Non-current assets		
Property, plant and equipment	12,000	4,000
Available for sale investment (note 1)	4,000	–
	16,000	4,000
Current assets		
Inventories	2,200	800
Receivables	3,400	900
Cash and cash equivalents	800	300
	6,400	2,000
Total assets	22,400	6,000

EQUITY AND LIABILITIES

Equity

Share capital ($1 equity shares)	10,000	1,000
Retained earnings	7,500	4,000
Other reserves	200	–
Total equity	**17,700**	**5,000**
Non-current liabilities		
Long term borrowings	2,700	–
Current liabilities	2,000	1,000
Total liabilities	**4,700**	**1,000**
Total equity and liabilities	**22,400**	**6,000**

Additional information

1   ERT acquired a 75% investment in BNM on 1 May 20X0 for $3,800,000. The investment has been classified as available for sale in the books of ERT. The gain on its subsequent measurement as at 31 December 20X0 has been recorded within other reserves in ERT's individual financial statements. At the date of acquisition BNM had retained earnings of $3,200,000.

2   It is the group policy to value non-controlling interest at fair value at the date of acquisition. The fair value of the non-controlling interest at 1 May 20X0 was $1,600,000.

3   As at 1 May 20X0 the fair value of the net assets acquired was the same as the book value with the following exceptions:

The fair value of property, plant and equipment was $800,000 higher than the book value. These assets were assessed to have an estimated useful life of 16 years from the date of acquisition. A full year's depreciation is charged in the year of acquisition and none in the year of sale.

The fair value of inventories was estimated to be $200,000 higher than the book value. All of these inventories were sold by 31 December 20X0.

On acquisition ERT identified an intangible asset that BNM developed internally but which met the recognition criteria of IAS 38 *Intangible Assets*. This intangible asset is expected to generate economic benefits from the date of acquisition until 31 December 20X1 and was valued at $150,000 at the date of acquisition.

A contingent liability, which had a fair value of $210,000 at the date of acquisition, had a fair value of $84,000 at 31 December 20X0.

4   An impairment review was conducted at 31 December 20X0 and it was decided that the goodwill on the acquisition of BNM was impaired by 20%.

5   ERT sold goods to BNM for $300,000. Half of these goods remained in inventories at 31 December 20X0. ERT makes 20% margin on all sales.

6   No dividends were paid by either entity in the year ended 31 December 20X0.

Required:

(a)   **Explain how the fair value adjustments identified above will impact *BOTH* the calculation of goodwill on the acquisition of BNM *AND* the consolidated financial statements of the ERT group for the year ended 31 December 20X0.**   **(7 marks)**

(b)   **Prepare the consolidated statement of financial position as at 31 December 20X0 for the ERT Group.**   **(18 marks)**

     (Total: 25 marks)

58   A, B AND C (MAY 11 EXAM)

Extracts from the financial statements of A, its subsidiary, B and its associate, C for the year to 30 September 20X5 are presented below:

Summarised statement of comprehensive income

	A	B	C
	A$000	B$000	A$000
Revenue	4,600	2,200	1,600
Cost of sales and operating expenses	(3,700)	(1,600)	(1,100)
Profit before tax	900	600	500
Income tax	(200)	(150)	(100)
Profit for the year	700	450	400
Other comprehensive income:			
Revaluation of property, plant and equipment	200	120	70
Total other comprehensive income	200	120	70
Total comprehensive income	900	570	470

Statement of financial position

	A	B	C
	A$000	B$000	A$000
Assets			
Non-current assets			
Property, plant and equipment	7,000	4,000	2,000
Investment in B	5,200		
Investment in C	900		
	13,100	4,000	2,000
Current assets	3,000	2,000	1,000
Total assets	16,100	6,000	3,000

Equity and liabilities

Share capital	2,000	1,000	1,000
Reserves	12,100	3,500	1,500
	14,100	4,500	2,500
Current liabilities	2,000	1,500	500
Total equity and liabilities	16,100	6,000	3,000

Additional information

1   The functional currency of both A and C is the A$ and the functional currency of B is the B$.

2   A acquired 80% of B on 1 October 20X2 for A$5,200,000 when the reserves of B were B$1,800,000. The investment is held at cost in the individual financial statements of A.

3   A acquired 40% of C on 1 October 20X0 for A$900,000 when the reserves of C were A$700,000. The investment is held at cost in the individual financial statements of A.

4   No impairment to either investment has occurred to date.

5   The group policy is to value the non-controlling interest at fair value at the date of acquisition. The fair value of the non-controlling interest of B at 1 October 20X2 was B$600,000.

6   Relevant exchange rates are as follows:

1 October 20X2	A$/B$0.5000
30 September 20X4	A$/B$0.7100
30 September 20X5	A$/B$0.6300
Average rate for year ended 30 September 20X5	A$/B$0.6500

SoFP ← 30 September 20X5

1/5. ← Average rate for year ended 30 September 20X5

Required:

Prepare the consolidated statement of comprehensive income for the A Group for the year ended 30 September 20X5 and the consolidated statement of financial position as at that date.

(Total: 25 marks)

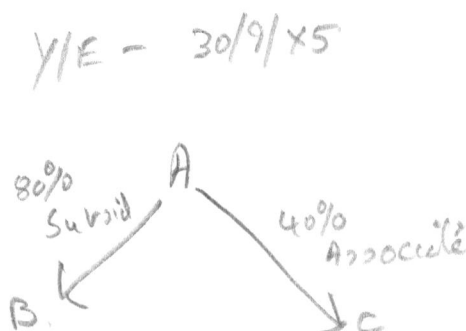

Y/E – 30/9/X5

80% Subsid / A \ 40% Associate
B ←   ↓ C

59   AB (SEP 11 EXAM)

The statement of financial position for the AB Group as at 30 June 20X1 and its comparative for 20X0 are shown below:

	20X1 $000	20X0 $000
ASSETS		
Non-current assets		
Property, plant and equipment	51,100	44,400
Goodwill	8,000	7,200
Investment in associate	24,400	23,400
Held to maturity asset	6,200	6,000
	89,700	81,000
Current assets		
Inventories	34,800	36,000
Receivables	28,200	26,400
Cash and cash equivalents	10,200	12,300
	73,200	74,700
Total assets	162,900	155,700
EQUITY AND LIABILITIES		
Equity attributable to owners of the parent		
Share capital ($1 ordinary shares)	36,000	30,000
Share premium	8,400	–
Revaluation reserve (note 3)	1,250	–
Retained earnings	21,850	20,100
	67,500	50,100
Non-controlling interests	19,500	18,300
Total equity	87,000	68,400
Non-current liabilities		
Long term borrowings	41,100	53,400
Provision for deferred tax	900	600
	42,000	54,000
Current liabilities		
Payables	32,100	30,600
Income tax	1,800	2,700
	33,900	33,300
Total liabilities	75,900	87,300
Total equity and liabilities	162,900	155,700

The statement of total comprehensive income for the AB Group for the year ended 30 June 20X1 is shown below:

	$000
Revenue	36,000
Cost of sales	(25,200)
Gross Profit	10,800
Distribution costs	(1,200)
Administrative expenses	(3,780)
Investment income (note 4)	320
Finance costs (note 5)	(1,350)
Share of profit of associate	1,500
Profit before tax	6,290
Income tax expense	(1,800)
Profit for the year	4,490
Other comprehensive income:	
Revaluation gain on PPE	1,450
Share of associate's OCI (net of tax)	120
Tax on OCI	(250)
Other comprehensive income for the year	1,320
Total comprehensive income	5,810
Profit for the year attributable to:	
Owners of parent	3,880
Non-controlling interests	610
	4,490
Total comprehensive income attributable to:	
Owners of parent	5,130
Non-controlling interests	680
	5,810

Additional information

1   There were no disposals of property, plant and equipment in the year. Depreciation charged in arriving at profit was $3,100,000.

2   AB acquired 70% of the ordinary share capital of XY on 1 January 20X1 for a cash consideration of $500,000 plus the issue of 1 million $1 ordinary shares in AB, which had a deemed value of $3.95 per share at the date of acquisition. The fair values of the net assets acquired on 1 January 20X1 were as follows:

	$000
Property plant and equipment	2,400
Inventories	3,600
Receivables	2,000
Cash and cash equivalents	200
Payables	(3,800)
	4,400

AB made no other purchases or sales of investments in the year. The group policy is to value the non-controlling interests at acquisition at its proportionate share of the fair value of the net assets.

3   The revaluation reserve consists of the revaluation gains of the parent plus the parent's share of its subsidiaries' and associates' revaluation gains, all net of relevant tax.

4   The held to maturity investment is measured at amortised cost. The investment income included in profit for the year was $320,000. The actual interest received based upon the coupon rate was $120,000.

5   Finance costs include interest on long-term borrowings. The effective rate equated to the coupon rate and all interest due was paid in the year.

Required:

Prepare the consolidated statement of cash flows for the AB Group for the year ended 30 June 20X1 in accordance with IAS 7 *Statement of Cash Flows*. Use the indirect method for calculating cash flows from operating activities.

(Total: 25 marks)

ISSUES IN RECOGNITION AND MEASUREMENT

60   TYD (MAY 07 EXAM)

You are the accounting adviser to a committee of bank lending officers. Each loan application is subject to an initial vetting procedure, which involves the examination of the application, recent financial statements, and a set of key financial ratios.

The key ratios are as follows:

•   Gearing (calculated as debt/debt + equity, where debt includes both long- and short-term borrowings);

•   Current ratio;

•   Quick ratio;

•   Profit margin (using profit before tax).

Existing levels of gearing are especially significant to the decision, and the committee usually rejects any application from an entity with gearing of over 45%.

The committee will shortly meet to conduct the initial vetting of a commercial loan application made by TYD, an unlisted entity. As permitted by national accounting law in its country of registration, TYD does not comply in all respects with International Financial Reporting Standards. The committee has asked you to interview TYD's finance director to determine areas of non-compliance. As a result of the interview, you have identified two significant areas for examination in respect of TYD's financial statements for the year ended 30 September 20X6.

1   Revenue for the period includes a sale of inventories at cost to HPS, a banking institution, for $85,000, which took place on 30 September 20X6. HPS has an option under the contract of sale to require TYD to repurchase the inventories on 30 September 20X8, for $95,000. TYD has derecognised the inventories at their cost of $85,000, with a charge to cost of sales of this amount. The inventories concerned in this transaction, are, however, stored on TYD's premises, and TYD bears the cost of insuring them.

2   Some categories of TYD's inventories are sold on a sale or return basis. The entity's accounting policy in this respect is to recognise the sale at the point of despatch of goods. The standard margin on sales of this type is 20%. During the year ended 30 September 20X6, $100,000 (in sales value) has been despatched in this way. The finance director estimates that approximately 60% of this value represents sales that have been accepted by customers; the remainder is potentially subject to return.

The financial statements of TYD for the year ended 30 September 20X6 are as presented below. (Note: at this stage of the analysis only one year's figures are considered).

TYD: Income statement for the year ended 30 September 20X6

	$000
Revenue	600
Cost of sales	450
Gross profit	150
Operating expenses	63
Finance costs	17
Profit before tax	70
Income tax expense	25
Profit for the period	45

TYD: Statement of changes in equity for the year ended 30 September 20X6

	Share capital $000	Retained earnings $000	Total $000
Balances at 1 October 20X5	100	200	300
Profit for the period		45	45
Balances at 30 September 20X6	100	245	345

TYD: Statement of financial position at 30 September 20X6

	$000	$000
Assets		
Non-current assets:		
Property, plant and equipment		527
Current assets:		
Inventories	95	
Trade receivables	72	
Cash	6	
		173
		700
Equity and liabilities		
Equity:		
Share capital	100	
Retained earnings	245	
		345
Non-current liabilities:		
Long-term borrowings		180
Current liabilities:		
Trade and other payables	95	
Bank overdraft	80	
		175
		700

Required:

Prepare a report to the committee of lending officers that:

(i) discusses the accounting treatment of the two significant areas identified in the interview with the FD, with reference to the requirements of International Financial Reporting Standards (IFRS) and to fundamental accounting principles;

(8 marks)

(ii) calculates any adjustments to the financial statements that are required in order to bring them into compliance with IFRS (ignore tax); **(5 marks)**

(iii) analyses and interprets the financial statements, calculating the key ratios before and after adjustments, and makes a recommendation to the lending committee on whether or not to grant TYD's application for a commercial loan. **(12 marks)**

(Total: 25 marks)

61 NED AND ABC (NOV 08 EXAM) *Walk in the footsteps of a top tutor*

Ned is a recently appointed non-executive director of ABC Corp, a listed entity. ABC's corporate governance arrangements permit non-executives to seek independent advice on accounting and legal matters affecting the entity, where they have any grounds for concern. Ned has asked you, an independent accountant, for advice because he is worried about certain aspects of the draft financial statements for ABC's year ended 30 September 20X8.

The ownership of most of ABC's ordinary share capital is widely dispersed, but the three largest institutional shareholders each own around 10% of the entity's ordinary shares. In meetings with management, these shareholders have made it clear that they expect improvements in the entity's performance and position. ABC appointed a new Chief Financial Officer (CFO) at the start of the 20X7/X8 financial year, and the board has set ambitious financial targets for the next five years.

The 20X7/X8 targets were expressed in the form of three key accounting ratios, as follows:

- Return on capital employed (profit before interest as a percentage of debt + equity): 7%

- Net profit margin (profit before tax as a percentage of revenue): 5%

- Gearing (long-term and short-term debt as a percentage of the total of debt + equity): below 48%

The draft financial statements include the following figures:

	$
Revenue	31,850,000
Profit before interest	2,972,000
Interest	1,241,000
Equity	22,450,800
Debt	18,253,500

The key ratios, based on the draft financial statements, are as follows:

Return on capital employed	7.3%
Net profit margin	5.4%
Gearing	44.8%

Ned's copies of the minutes of board meetings provide the following relevant information:

1 On 1 October 20X7 ABC sold an item of plant for $1,000,000 to XB, an entity that provides financial services to businesses. The carrying value of the plant at the date of sale was $1,000,000. XB has the option to require ABC to repurchase the plant on 1 October 20X8 for $1,100,000. If the option is not exercised at that date, ABC will be required under the terms of the agreement between the entities to repurchase the plant on 1 October 20X9 for $1,210,000. ABC has continued to insure the plant and to store it on its business premises. The sale to XB was recognised as revenue in the draft financial statements and the asset was derecognised.

2 A few days before the 30 September 20X8 year end, ABC entered into a debt factoring agreement with LM, a factoring business. The terms of the agreement are that ABC is permitted to draw down cash up to a maximum of 75% of the receivables that are covered under the factoring arrangement. However, LM is able to require

repayment of any part of the receivables that are uncollectible. In addition, ABC is obliged to pay interest at an annual rate of 10% on any amounts it draws down in advance of cash being received from customers by LM. As soon as the agreement was finalised, ABC drew down the maximum cash available in respect of the $2,000,000 receivables it had transferred to LM as part of the agreement. This amount was accounted for by debiting cash and crediting receivables.

3   In October 20X7, ABC issued 2,000,000 $1 preference shares at par. The full year's dividend of 8% was paid before the 30 September 20X8 year end, and was recognised in the statement of changes in equity. The preference shares are redeemable in 20Y5, and the entity is obliged to pay the dividend on a fixed date each year. The full $2,000,000 proceeds of the issue were credited to equity capital.

Required:

(a)   Discuss the accounting treatment of the three transactions, identifying any errors that you think have been made in applying accounting principles with references, where appropriate, to IFRS. Prepare the adjustments that are required to correct those errors and identify any areas where you would require further information.

(15 marks)

(b)   Calculate the effect of your adjustments on ABC's key accounting ratios for the year ended 30 September 20X8.   **(7 marks)**

(c)   Explain, briefly, the results and the implications of your analysis to the non-executive director.   **(3 marks)**

(Total: 25 marks)

FINANCIAL STATEMENT ANALYSIS

62 TEX (NOV 08 EXAM)   *Walk in the footsteps of a top tutor*

You are assistant to the Chief Financial Officer (CFO) of SWW, a large fashion retailer. SWW's merchandise is sourced from many different suppliers around the world. SWW's senior management has a business policy of building lasting relationships with suppliers either by investing in their shares, or by making loans to them at favourable rates of interest.

A request has recently been received from a supplier, TEX, for a loan of $25 million to allow it to invest in up to date machinery. The directors of TEX claim that the investment will result in efficiency improvements which, in the short to medium term, will allow it to reduce prices to its customers. SWW is a major customer of TEX, buying approximately 10% of TEX's annual output of cotton clothing.

In support of the application, TEX's CFO has supplied a one page report on the state of the business, and a statement of financial position and income statement for the year ended 30 September 20X8. The 20X8 figures are unaudited. TEX has not paid a dividend in the last five years. TEX's shares are listed on a local stock exchange, although the entity's founding family has retained a minor holding. TEX's functional and presentation currency is the $, and its financial statements are prepared in accordance with IFRS.

The financial statements supplied by TEX are as follows.

TEX: Consolidated income statement for the year ended 30 September 20X8

	20X8 $million	20X7 $million
Revenue	256.3	281.7
Cost of sales	(226.6)	(243.1)
Gross profit	29.7	38.6
Selling and distribution costs	(9.2)	(8.9)
Administrative expenses	(18.7)	(15.6)
Finance costs	(5.4)	(6.2)
Share of losses of associate	(1.3)	(6.8)
(Loss)/profit before tax	(4.9)	1.1
Income tax expense	1.5	(0.4)
(Loss)/profit for the period	(3.4)	0.7
Attributable to:		
Equity holders of parent	(3.2)	0.6
Non-controlling interest	(0.2)	0.1
	(3.4)	0.7

Handwritten annotations: "Prices of suppliers parties.", "up.", "Not sustainable.", "up.", "reduced", "loss.", "—"

TEX: Consolidated statement of financial position at 30 September 20X8

	20X8 $million	20X8 $million	20X7 $million	20X7 $million
ASSETS				
Non-current assets:				
Property, plant and equipment		221.4		227.3
Investment in associate		13.8		15.1
Available for sale investments		2.6		4.8
		237.8		247.2
Current assets:				
Inventories	132.4		125.6	
Trade and other receivables	51.7		58.2	
Cash	–		4.8	
		184.1		188.6
Total assets		421.9		435.8

Handwritten annotations: "liquidity", "No cash!", "up", "down", "no cash"

EQUITY AND LIABILITIES
Equity

Share capital ($1 shares)	25.0		25.0
Retained earnings and other reserves	103.2		106.2
Non-controlling interest	13.7		13.9
		141.9	145.1

Non-current liabilities:

Long-term borrowings	57.2		67.1	*down*
Deferred tax	18.0		25.8	
Defined benefit obligation	26.0		24.2	
		101.2	117.1	

Current liabilities:

Trade and other payables	150.1		161.2	
Borrowings	28.7		12.4	*up*
		178.8	173.6	
		421.9	435.8	

\ More expensive to service.

Required:

Produce a report to the CFO of SWW that:

(a) analyses and interprets the information given above from the point of view of SWW as a potential lender; **(20 marks)**

(b) describes the areas of uncertainty in the analysis and the nature of any additional information that will be required before a lending decision can be made. **(5 marks)**

Note: Up to 8 marks are available in part (a) for the calculation of relevant accounting ratios.

(Total: 25 marks)

63 ELB (MAY 09 EXAM)   *— Paper industry*

cost of expansion

ELB is an entity that manufactures and sells paper and packaging. For the last two years, the directors have pursued an aggressive policy of expansion. They have developed several new products and market share has increased.

ELB is finalising its financial statements for the year ended 31 December 20X8. These will be presented to the Board of Directors at its next meeting, where the results for the year will be reviewed.

The statement of financial position at the year end and income statement for the year, together with comparatives, are presented below:

Statement of financial position at 31 December

	20X8		20X7	
	$000	$000	$000	$000
Assets				
Non-current assets				
Property, plant and equipment		25,930		17,880
Investments – available for sale		6,200		5,400
		32,130		23,280
Current assets				
Inventories	4,500		3,600	
Trade receivables	4,300		5,200	
Cash and cash equivalents	–		120	
		8,800		8,920
Total assets		40,930		32,200
Equity and liabilities				
Equity				
Share capital ($1 ordinary shares)	10,000		10,000	
Revaluation reserve (Note 1)	4,200		1,100	
Other reserves (Note 2)	1,800		1,000	
Retained earnings	7,460		4,200	
		23,460		16,300
Non-current liabilities				
Term loan	6,000		6,000	
6% bonds 20Y0 (Note 3)	5,400		5,200	
		11,400		11,200
Current liabilities				
Trade and other payables	5,800		4,700	
Short term borrowings	270		–	
		6,070		4,700
Total equity and liabilities		40,930		32,200

Income statement for the year ended 31 December

	20X8	20X7
	$000	$000
Revenue	34,200	28,900
Cost of Sales	(24,000)	(20,250)
Gross Profit	10,200	8,650
Operating Costs	(5,120)	(3,300)
Finance costs	(520)	(450)
Profit before tax	4,560	4,900
Income tax	(1,300)	(1,400)
Profit for the period	3,260	3,500

(handwritten annotations: "increased sales" next to Revenue, "up" near Cost of Sales, and an arrow pointing at Operating Costs)

Note 1

The movement on the revaluation reserve relates to property, plant and equipment that was revalued in the year.

Note 2

The movement on other reserves relates to the gains made on the available for sale investments.

Note 3

The bonds are repayable on 1 July 20Y0. As part of their review, the directors will discuss certain key ratios that form part of the banking covenants in respect of the borrowing facilities as well as reviewing the performance in the year. The key ratios for the covenants include:

- Gearing (debt/equity) target is 50%
- Interest cover target is 9.5 times
- Current ratio target is 1.5 : 1
- Quick ratio target is 1.1 : 1

You are the assistant to the Chief Financial Officer of ELB and you have been asked to perform a preliminary review of, and prepare a commentary on, the year end figures. These comments will form part of the financial presentation to the board.

Required:

(a) Calculate the ratios required as part of the review of covenants and any other ratios that are relevant to assess the financial performance and position of ELB.

(8 marks)

(b) Prepare a report that explains the financial performance and position of ELB for presentation to the Board of Directors, including reference to the banking covenants. (12 marks)

(c) Identify, and briefly describe, any other points that should be added to the meeting agenda for the Board of Directors to discuss in respect of the future financing of ELB. (5 marks)

(Total: 25 marks)

64 BHG (MAY 08 EXAM)

BHG is a successful listed entity that designs and markets specialist business software. BHG's directors have decided to adopt a policy of expansion into overseas territories through the acquisition of similar software businesses possessing established shares of their domestic markets. BHG's aim is to obtain control, or at the minimum, significant influence (represented by at least 40% of issued share capital) of investee entities. Target investee entities are likely to be listed entities in their own countries, but the acquisition of unlisted entities is not ruled out.

You are a senior accountant in BHG, and you have been asked by the Chief Financial Officer (CFO) to establish a set of key accounting ratios for use in:

1   the initial appraisal of potential acquisitions;

2   on-going appraisal following acquisitions.

The ratios will be used as part of a suite of quantitative and non-quantitative measurements to compare businesses with each other. The CFO has suggested that it would be appropriate to identify no more than 5-7 key financial ratios.

One of your assistants has suggested a list of 5 key accounting ratios as suitable for both initial and on-going appraisal and comparison. She has provided reasons to support the case for their inclusion as key ratios.

1   Earnings per share: 'one of the most important investor ratios, widely used by all classes of investor to assess business performance'.

2   Dividend yield: 'this ratio provides a very useful measurement that allows comparison with yields from other equity and non-equity investments'.

3   Gearing: 'this is of critical importance in determining the level of risk of an equity investment'.

4   Gross profit margin: 'allows investors to assess business performance, and is of particular use over several accounting periods within the same organisation. It is also very useful for comparing performances between businesses'.

5   Asset turnover ratios: 'allow the investor to compare the intensity of asset usage between businesses, and over time'.

Required:

(a)   **Discuss the extent to which each of the 5 suggested accounting ratios is likely to be useful to BHG for both initial and on-going appraisal and comparison, and the extent to which your assistant's assessments of the value of the ratios are justified.**
                                                                                    (15 marks)

(b)   **Explain the problems and limitations of accounting ratio analysis in making inter-firm and international comparisons.**   **(10 marks)**

                                                                            (Total: 25 marks)

65   DAS (NOV 07 EXAM)

DAS, a listed entity, is engaged in house-building activities. It was listed a little over two years ago and it prepares its financial statements in compliance with International Financial Reporting Standards.

A business associate of yours is thinking about applying for a job as human resource manager at DAS. The job advertisement promises a 'great future in a rapidly expanding business'. She was made redundant when her last employer went into liquidation, and she is looking for a new role with a more stable and prosperous employer. She has obtained DAS's recently published financial statements for the year ended 31 August 20X7 and would like your advice on the entity's prospects for the future.

DAS provides several potentially useful voluntary disclosures about the nature of its business and its current work in progress. In the year ended 31 August 20X6 DAS sold 1,080 new houses. During the financial year ended 31 August 20X7, a major part of the entity's efforts were directed towards the development for housing on the site of a former hospital. This was DAS's largest project to date. By the year end most of the houses on site were nearly complete, and a few were ready for sale. The site contains 225 houses, which are expected to sell for between $425,000 and $600,000 each. DAS's directors consider that the development scheme has been successful; by the year end 100 of the available houses had been reserved by buyers who paid a 10% deposit. None of the hospital site house transactions had been completed by 31 August 20X7, although the Chief Executive's report noted that there were several completions during September and October 20X7. DAS sold 675 other houses during the year ended 31 August 20X7.

DAS's statement of financial position at 31 August 20X7 and an income statement for the year then ended, together with comparatives, follow:

DAS: Statement of financial position at 31 August 20X7

	20X7		20X6	
	$ million	$ million	$ million	$ million
Assets				
Non-current assets				
Property, plant and equipment		9.3		9.8
Current assets				
Inventories	270.5		275.0	
Trade and other receivables	3.2		3.7	
Cash	–		2.8	
	————		————	
		273.7		281.5
		————		————
TOTAL ASSETS		283.0		291.3
		————		————

Equity and liabilities

Equity

Called up share capital ($1 shares)	8.2		8.2	
Other reserves	16.3		16.3	
Retained earnings	61.9		54.7	
		86.4		79.2
Non-current liabilities				
Long-term borrowings		114.7		112.0
Current liabilities				
Loans and borrowings	52.6		75.4	
Trade and other payables	29.3		24.7	
		81.9		100.1
TOTAL EQUITY & LIABILITIES		283.0		291.3

DAS: Income statement for the year ended 31 August 20X7

	20X7	20X6
	$ million	$ million
Revenue	157.9	243.0
Cost of sales	(126.5)	(192.7)
Gross profit	31.4	50.3
Expenses	(9.2)	(8.6)
Finance costs	(12.2)	(13.4)
Profit before tax	10.0	28.3
Income tax expense	(2.8)	(8.9)
Profit for the period	7.2	19.4

Notes:

(1)   DAS's policy is to recognise revenue from the sale of houses upon legal completion of the transaction.

(2)   Most of the house-building work is undertaken by sub-contractors; DAS retains only a small direct labour force. Payments to sub-contractors are included as part of property under construction in inventories until such time as the houses are sold.

(3)   Inventories comprise the following:

	20X7	20X6
	$ million	$ million
Land held for development	130.0	210.0
Property under construction	140.5	65.0
	270.5	275.0

(4)   The statement of changes in equity (not given above) shows that no dividend was paid in the period of a little over two years since DAS was listed.

(5)   Deposits paid by buyers are included in trade and other payables.

(6)   Economic conditions are generally buoyant and house prices during 20X6 and 20X7 have risen at a rate significantly in excess of the general rate of inflation. Bank interest rates in respect of low risk lending have been running at between 5% and 6% throughout the two-year period covered by the financial statements shown above.

Required:

Write a report to your business associate that analyses and interprets the information given above. The report should explain the extent to which DAS can be considered to meet her requirements for a 'stable and prosperous' employer.

Up to 8 marks are available for the calculation and explanation of relevant accounting ratios.

(Total: 25 marks)

66   PJ GAMEWRITERS (NOV 05 EXAM)

You are assistant to the Finance Director (FD) of OPQ, a well-known retailer of music, video and games products. OPQ's profit margins are under increasing pressure because of the entry of online retailers into the market. As part of their response to this challenge, OPQ's directors have decided to invest in entities in the supply chain of their most popular products. They are currently considering the acquisition of the business that supplies some of its best-selling computer games, PJ Gamewriters (PJ). The FD has asked you, as a preliminary step, to examine the most recent financial statements of the entity.

PJ was established six years ago by twin brothers, Paul and James, who had recently graduated in computing. Their first business success was a simulated empire building game; this has continued to bring in a large proportion of PJ's revenue. However, they have also been successful in a range of other games types such as combat simulations, golf and football management games. The business has grown rapidly from year to year, and by 20X5 it employed ten full-time games writers. Manufacture and distribution of the software in various formats is outsourced, and the business operates from office premises in a city centre. PJ bought the freehold of the office premises in 20X2, and its estimated market value is now $900,000, nearly $350,000 in excess of the price paid in 20X2. Apart from the freehold building, the business owns few non-current assets.

The equity shares in PJ are owned principally by Paul, James and their parents, who provided the initial start-up capital. Paul and James are the sole directors of the business. A small proportion of the shares (around 8%) is owned by five of the senior software writers. PJ is now up for sale as the principal shareholders wish to realise the bulk of their investment in order to pursue other business interests. It is likely that about 90% of the shares will be for sale. The copyrights of the games are owned by PJ, but no value is attributed to them in the financial statements.

PJ's income statement and summarised statement of changes in equity for the year ended 31 July 20X5, and statement of financial position at that date (all with comparatives) are as follows:

PJ: Income statement for the year ended 31 July 20X5

	20X5	20X4
	$000	$000
Revenue	2,793	2,208
Cost of sales (see note below)	(1,270)	(1,040)
Gross profit	1,523	1,168
Operating expenses	(415)	(310)
Profit from operations	1,108	858
Interest receivable	7	2
Profit before tax	1,115	860
Income tax expense	(331)	(290)
Profit for the period	784	570

Note: Cost of sales comprises the following:	2005	2004
	$000	$000
Games writers' employment costs	700	550
Production costs	215	160
Directors' remuneration	200	200
Other costs	155	130
	1,270	1,040

PJ: Summarised statement of changes in equity for the year ended 31 July 20X5

	20X5	20X4
	$000	$000
Opening balance	703	483
Profit for the period	784	570
Dividends	(500)	(350)
Closing balance	987	703

PJ: Statement of financial position at 31 July 20X5

	20X5		20X4	
	$000	$000	$000	$000
Non-current assets:				
Property, plant and equipment		610		620
Current assets:				
Inventories	68		59	
Trade receivables	460		324	
Cash	216		20	
		744		403
		1,354		1,023
Equity:				
Share capital	60		60	
Retained earnings	927		643	
		987		703
Current liabilities:				
Trade and other payables	36		30	
Income tax	331		290	
		367		320
		1,354		1,023

Required:

(a) **Prepare a report on the financial performance and position of PJ Gameswriters, calculating and interpreting any relevant accounting ratios.** **(17 marks)**

(b) **Explain the limitations of your analysis, identifying any supplementary items of information that would be useful.** **(8 marks)**

(Total: 25 marks)

67 BZJ (MAY 06 EXAM)

Higher
NC Assets

You advise a private investor who holds a portfolio of investments in smaller listed companies. Recently, she has received the annual report of the BZJ Group for the financial year ended 31 December 20X5. In accordance with her usual practice, the investor has read the Chairman's statement, but has not looked in detail at the figures. Relevant extracts from the Chairman's statement are as follows:

Dep costs ↑
net profit
margin ?

'Following the replacement of many of the directors, which took place in early March 20X5, your new board has worked to expand the group's manufacturing facilities and to replace non-current assets that have reached the end of their useful lives. A new line of storage solutions was designed during the second quarter and was put into production at the beginning of September. Sales efforts have been concentrated on increasing our market share in respect of storage products, and in leading the expansion into Middle Eastern markets. *← mktg costs or low prices → GP margin ? & admin costs.*

Debt/equity ?
interest cover
|
increased
expense
|
impact on
profit,

The growth in the business has been financed by a combination of loan capital and the issue of additional shares. The issue of 300,000 new $1 shares was fully taken up on 1 November 20X5, reflecting, we believe, market confidence in the group's new management. Dividends have been reduced in 20X5 in order to increase profit retention to fund the further growth planned for 20X6. The directors believe that the implementation of their medium- to long-term strategies will result in increased returns to investors within the next two to three years.'

The group's principal activity is the manufacture and sale of domestic and office furniture. Approximately 40% of the product range is bought in from manufacturers in other countries.

Extracts from the annual report of the BZJ Group are as follows:

BZJ Group: Consolidated statement of comprehensive income for the year ended 31 December 20X5

	20X5	20X4
	$000	$000
down → Revenue	120,366	121,351
Cost of sales	(103,024)	(102,286)
Gross profit	17,342	19,065
Operating expenses	(11,965)	(12,448)
Profit from operations	5,377	6,617
Interest payable *much higher →*	(1,469)	(906)
Profit before tax	3,908	5,711
Income tax expense	(1,125)	(1,594)
Profit for the period	2,783	4,117
Other comprehensive income	*drop significant*	
Surplus on revaluation of properties	2,000	–
Total comprehensive income	4,783	4,117

Attributable to:

Equity holders of the parent (2,460 + 2,000)	4,460	3,676
Non-controlling interest	323	441
	4,783	4,117

BZJ Group: Summarised consolidated statement of changes in equity for the year ended 31 December 20X5 (attributable to equity holders of the parent)

	Accum. profit $000	Share capital $000	Share premium $000	Reval. reserve $000	Total 20X5 $000	Total 20X4 $000
Opening balance	18,823	2,800	3,000		24,623	21,311
Total comprehensive income for the period	2,460			2,000	4,460	3,676
Issue of share capital		300	1,200		1,500	–
Dividends paid 31/12	(155)				(155)	(364)
Closing balance	21,128	3,100	4,200	2,000	30,428	24,623

BZJ Group: Consolidated statement of financial position at 31 December 20X5

	20X5 $000	$000	20X4 $000	$000
Non-current assets:				
Property, plant & equipment	40,643		21,322	
Goodwill	1,928		1,928	
Trademarks and patents	1,004		1,070	
		43,575		24,320
Current assets:				
Inventories	37,108		27,260	
Trade receivables	14,922		17,521	
Cash	–		170	
		52,030		44,951
		95,605		69,271
Equity:				
Share capital ($1 shares)	3,100		2,800	
Share premium	4,200		3,000	
Revaluation reserve	2,000		–	
Accumulated profits	21,128		18,823	
		30,428		24,623
Non-controlling interest		2,270		1,947
Total equity		32,698		26,570

[Handwritten annotations: "increase", "down.", "No cash?!", "belter credit terms?", "in line with build up for sales?", "or not reaching expectations?", "Fully taken up"]

u.p.

Non-current liabilities:		
Interest-bearing borrowings	26,700	16,700
Current liabilities:		*shrewd*
		money margin
Trade and other payables	31,420	24,407 *o ?*
Income tax	1,125	1,594 *cannot pay?*
Short-term borrowings	3,662	–
	_____	_____
	36,207	26,001
	_____	_____
	95,605	69,271
	_____	_____

Required:

(a) Calculate the earnings per share figure for the BZJ Group for the years ended 31 December 20X5 and 20X4, assuming that there was no change in the number of ordinary shares in issue during 20X4. **(3 marks)**

(b) Produce a report for the investor that:

    (i) analyses and interprets the financial statements of the BZJ Group, commenting upon the group's performance and position; and **(17 marks)**

    (ii) discusses the extent to which the Chairman's comments about the potential for improved future performance are supported by the financial statement information for the year ended 31 December 20X5. **(5 marks)**

(Total: 25 marks)

68 BSP (MAY 07 EXAM)

revenue?

cost
GP ?

marketing
cos up?

BSP, a listed entity, supplies, installs and maintains burglar alarm systems for business clients. As a response to increased competition and falling margins in the burglar alarm market, the entity's directors decided, towards the end of 20X5, to extend its operations into the provision of fire alarm and sprinkler systems. A training programme for staff was undertaken in the early months of 20X6 at a cost of around $200,000. An aggressive marketing campaign, costing $250,000, was launched at the same time. Both costs were incurred and settled before the 31 March 20X6 year end. BSP commenced its new operations with effect from the beginning of its financial year on 1 April 20X6.

Share issue

financed
through
Sale

BSP's cash resources were at a low level in early 20X6, so, in order to finance the costs of the new operation and the necessary increase in working capital to fund the new operations, BSP made a new issue of shares. The issue took place in May 20X6. During March 20X7, BSP disposed of its two overseas subsidiaries in order to concentrate on operations in its home market. Both were profitable businesses and therefore sold for an amount substantially in excess of carrying value. These subsidiaries accounted for almost 10% of group sales during the 20X6/20X7 financial year.

As the finance director's assistant you have been responsible for the preparation of the draft financial statements, which have been circulated to the directors in advance of a board meeting to be held later this week.

The marketing director, who was appointed in June 20X6, has sent you the following e-mail:

'When I did my university course in marketing I studied a module in finance and accounting, which covered the analysis of financial statements. Unfortunately, it was a long time ago, and I've forgotten quite a lot about it.

I'm puzzled by the statement of cash flows, in particular. The income statement shows a loss, which is obviously bad news, especially as the budget showed a profit for the year. However, the cash resources of the business have actually increased by quite a large amount between March 20X6 and March 20X7. It is said that 'cash is king', so I'm assuming that the poor profitability is a short-term problem while the new operation settles down.

As you know, we almost managed to achieve our sales targets in both the fire and burglar alarm sectors for the year, (although of course we did have to offer some customers special discounts and extended credit as inducements). I'm assuming, therefore, that the lack of profitability is a problem of cost control.

It would be really helpful if you could provide me with a brief report, in advance of this week's meeting, which tells me what this statement of cash flows means. You could include ratios, provided that you show how they are calculated.'

The consolidated statement of cash flows for the year ended 31 March 20X7 (with comparative figures for 20X6) is as follows:

BSP: Consolidated statement of cash flows for the year ended 31 March 20X7

	20X7 $000	20X7 $000	20X6 $000	20X6 $000
Cash flows from operating activities				
(Loss)/profit before tax		(453)	306	
Adjustments for:				
Depreciation		98	75	
Foreign exchange loss		22	37	
Profit on sale of investments		(667)	–	
Interest expense		161	45	
		(839)	463	
Increase in inventories		(227)	(65)	
Increase in receivables		(242)	(36)	
Increase in payables		62	12	
Cash generated/ (consumed) from operations		(1,246)	374	
Interest paid		(157)	(42)	
Tax paid		(38)	(55)	
Net cash (outflow)/inflow from operating activities		(1,441)	277	

Cash flows from investing activities

Proceeds from sale of investments	2,320		–
Purchase of property, plant and equipment	(661)		(425)
Income from associates	23		26
Net cash inflow/(outflow) from investing activities		1,682	(399)

Cash flows from financing activities

Proceeds from issue of share capital	850		–
Dividends paid	–		(200)
Net cash inflow/(outflow) from financing activities		850	(200)
Net increase/(decrease) in cash		1,091	(322)
Cash at start of period		27	349
Cash at end of period		1,118	27

Sales price 0

Static .

← *alot of cash*

Additional information:

Revenue in the 20X5/X6 financial year was $12.11 million. In the 20X6/X7 financial year, total revenue was $12.32 million, $10.93 million of which arose in respect of the sale of burglar alarms.

Inventories at the start of the 20X5/X6 financial year were $591,000, and receivables were $1,578,000. There was no increase in long-term borrowings throughout the two year period covered by the statement of cash flows above.

Required:

Analyse and interpret the information given, and produce a report to the marketing director. The report should explain the difference between cash and profit, and should discuss the business's profitability and working capital position. It should also discuss, to the extent possible from the information given, the prospects for BSP's future.

(Total: 25 marks)

69   FJK (MAY 08 EXAM)

Several years ago, on leaving university, Fay, Jay and Kay set up a business, FJK, designing and manufacturing furniture for sale to retailers. When FJK was established, Fay and Jay each took 45% of the share capital, with Kay holding the remaining 10%. This arrangement has remained unchanged. Fay and Jay have always worked full-time in the business and remain its sole directors. Kay's role was initially part-time, but after the first two years she transferred to full-time work in her own consultancy business. Her contribution to FJK in recent years has been limited to occasionally providing advice. The relationship between the three shareholders has remained good, but all three are so busy that Kay rarely meets the others. FJK has been successful, and in February of each year, with the exception of 20X8, has paid a substantial dividend to its three shareholders.   *missing information*

Kay's consultancy business has also been successful and she now employs 20 staff. You are Kay's financial adviser.

During 20X6, the two directors decided to expand FJK's international sales, by establishing sales forces in two neighbouring countries. By early 20X7, orders were starting to come in from the new countries. The expansion strategy has been very successful. Last week, Kay attended a meeting with Fay and Jay, to discuss the future of FJK. Fay and Jay explained that the business now requires more capital in order to fund further expansion, and the *investment* purpose of the meeting with Kay was to request her to inject capital of $250,000 into the business.

Kay was provided with a draft income statement for the year ended 31 March 20X8 and a statement of financial position at that date (given below). The draft statements are unaudited, but the figures are not expected to change, except for the income tax expense *Possible increase* figure for 20X8. FJK's accountant has not yet completed a tax calculation and so the 20X7 figure of $164,000 has been used as an estimate. No statement of changes in equity has been provided, but the only movements on it would be in respect of a revaluation of property, plant and equipment that took place during the year, and the movement on *property revaluation* retained earnings for profit for the period.

Kay, who has a reasonably good understanding of financial statements, is impressed by the *will lower* revenue and profit growth. However, she has asked you, as her financial adviser, to look at *Profits* the figures, in order to identify possible risks and problem areas. *increase admin cost.*

FJK: Draft income statement for the year ended 31 March 20X8

	20X8	20X7
	$000	$000
Revenue ↑	5,973	3,886
Cost of sales	(4,318)	(2,868)
Gross profit	1,655	1,018
Distribution costs	(270)	(106)
Administrative expenses	(320)	(201)
Profit from operations	1,065	711
Finance costs	(97)	(40) *— caused by loan increase*
Profit before tax	968	671
Income tax expense	(164)	(164)
Profit for the period	804	507

FJK: Draft statement of financial position at 31 March 20X8

	20X8		20X7	
	$000	$000	$000	$000
ASSETS				
Non-current assets				
Property, plant and equipment		3,413		1,586
Current assets				
Inventories	677		510	
Trade and other receivables	725		553	
Cash	–		12	
		1,402		1,075
TOTAL ASSETS		4,815		2,661
EQUITY AND LIABILITIES				
Equity				
Called up share capital ($1 shares)	1		1	
Retained earnings	2,166		1,362	
Revaluation reserve	167		–	
		2,334		1,363
Non-current liabilities				
Long-term borrowings		763		453
Current liabilities				
Loans and borrowings	327		103	
Trade and other payables	1,227		578	
Income tax	164		164	
		1,718		845
TOTAL EQUITY & LIABILITIES		4,815		2,661

(handwritten annotations: "Liquidity issue", arrows pointing to Property plant and equipment, Cash, Retained earnings, Non-current liabilities, and Trade and other payables)

Required:

Prepare a report for Kay that:

(a) analyses and interprets the draft financial statements and discusses FJK's performance and position. **(19 marks)**

(b) discusses possible risks and problem areas revealed by the financial statements, and the actions that the directors could take to address these risks and problems. **(6 marks)**

(Up to 8 marks are available for the calculation of relevant accounting ratios).

(Total: 25 marks)

70   RG (NOV 09 EXAM)

RG, a listed entity, invested significantly in one of its many operating segments in 20X8, by acquiring property, plant and equipment and developing a new distribution network in an attempt to increase market share. The network has been put in place (distribution costs have been incurred within the set budget) and a new sales team has been hired and has just recently completed its product training. The first orders from the new customers were received in June 20X9 and were higher than expected.

Extracts from the financial statements for RG for the year ended 30 June 20X9 are presented below.

Income statement for the year ended 30 June 20X9 for the RG group

	20X9	20X8
	$m	$m
Revenue	576	573
Cost of sales	(422)	(428)
Gross profit	154	145
Distribution costs	(56)	(40)
Administrative expenses (including profit on disposal of investments)	(37)	(22)
Finance costs	(6)	(8)
Share of profit of associate	5	–
Profit before tax	60	75
Income tax expense	(15)	(14)
Profit for the period	45	61
Attributable to:		
Equity holders of the parent	37	52
Non Controlling interest	8	9
	45	61

Statement of Comprehensive Income for the year ended 30 June 20X9 for the RG group

	20X9	20X8
	$m	$m
Profit for the year	45	61
Other comprehensive Income:		
Gains on available for sale investments	6	–
Transfer of gains on disposal	(4)	–
Total comprehensive Income	47	61
Attributable to:		
Equity holders of parent	39	52
Non controlling interest	8	9
	47	61

Statement of changes in equity

	Share capital	Share premium	Other reserves	Retained earnings	Non control-ling interest	Total
	$m	$m	$m	$m	$m	$m
1 July 20X8	80	4	8	372	11	475
Total comprehensive income	–	–	2	37	8	47
Dividends	–	–	–	(50)	(5)	(55)
Issue of share capital	30	18	–	–	–	48
30 June 20X9	110	22	10	359	14	515

Statement of Financial Position as at 30 June 20X9

expected

	20X9	20X8
ASSETS	$m	$m
Non-current assets		
Property, plant and equipment	371	346
Investment in associate	85	–
Available for sale investments	65	140
	521	486
Current assets		
Inventories	133	82
Receivables	109	76
Cash and cash equivalents	12	137
	254	295
Total assets	775	781
EQUITY AND LIABILITIES		
Attributable to the equity shareholders of the parent:		
Called up share capital ($1 shares)	110	80
Share premium	22	4
Other reserves	10	8
Retained earnings	359	372
	501	464
Non controlling interest	14	11
Total equity	515	475

liquidity issue. *up.* *up.*

− Profitability
− Liquidity
− Gearing

−EPS
− Dividend cover
− PE ratio.

SECTION B-TYPE QUESTIONS : **SECTION 2**

fallen.

Non-current liabilities		
Long term loan	154	205
Current liabilities		
Trade payables	91	87
Income tax payable	15	14
	——	——
	106	101
	——	——
Total equity and liabilities	775	781
	——	——

u p slightly.

A close friend of yours has inherited a portfolio of investments which includes a holding in RG. He is contemplating whether to retain or sell his shareholding. As he does not have a financial background he is looking for your advice.

investment

In his email to you he appeared to be focusing his initial conclusions on the decreased profitability of the business but wanted your opinion on the profitability and financial health of RG. He also wants your thoughts on its future prospects.

Prof

He mentioned that he had had a quick look at the segmental information provided in the financial statements but was confused by the volume of numerical information and was questioning whether a review of the segmental information was relevant for his purposes. To help with your review he has sent through extracts from the financial statements, shown above, but has not provided any segmental information.

Required:

(a) Prepare a report that analyses the financial performance and position of RG to assist your friend in his decision making. (8 marks are available for the calculation of relevant ratios.) **(21 marks)**

(b) Briefly discuss how useful segmental analysis could be in the analysis of RG's financial statements. **(4 marks)**

(Total: 25 marks)

71   KER (MAY 10 EXAM)

A friend is seeking advice on one of his investments, KER. KER manufactures stationery supplies. The entity appointed a new Chairman in 20X8 and since then has been implementing an expansion strategy aimed at pursuing new markets with its existing product base.

expansion funds?

The Chairman's report included in the 20X9 annual report announces the success of the expansion plan, citing increased revenues and profits as evidence of the entity's success, and noting that the entity has invested in non-current assets to ensure revenue continues to increase. Your friend is intending to retain his investment in KER based on the positive chairman's report but has asked you to consider the financial information to assess whether the figures support the chairman's claims.

where's in cost Jron ?

The statement of financial position as at 31 December 20X9 and its comparative is shown below:

	20X9	20X8	
ASSETS	$m	$m	
Non-current assets			
Property, plant and equipment	480	404	↑
Investment in associate	177	–	– new investment
Available for sale investments	150	140	
	807	544	
Current assets			
Inventories	up 145	65	more stock
Receivables	247	134	
Cash and cash equivalents	No cash –	22	
	392	221	
Total assets	1,199	765	
EQUITY AND LIABILITIES			
Equity			
Share capital	100	100	
Revaluation reserve	74	32	significant
Other reserves	32	22	
Retained earnings	↑ 457	333	
Total equity	663	487	
Non-current liabilities			
Loans	400	210	gearing
Current liabilities			
Payables	99	68	taking longer to pay
Overdraft	overdraft! 37	–	
	136	68	
Total liabilities	536	278	
Total equity and liabilities	1,199	765	

The statement of comprehensive income for the year ended 31 December 20X9 and its comparative is shown below:

	20X9 $m	20X8 $m
Revenue	1,430	1,022
Cost of sales	(1,058)	(705)
Gross profit	372	317
Administrative expenses	(74)	(62)
Distribution costs	(158)	(100)
Finance costs	(60)	(30)
Share of profit of associate	80	–
Profit before tax	160	125
Income tax expense	(40)	(33)
Profit for the year	120	92
Other comprehensive income:		
Revaluation gain on property, plant and equipment	45	15
Gains on Available for sale investments	16	6
Tax effects of other comprehensive income	(14)	(5)
Other comprehensive income for the year, net of tax	47	16
Total Comprehensive income for the year	167	108

(handwritten annotations: "improved revenue", "higher cos", "up.", "good. without His problems? reliant.", "expected with expansion double.")

Required:

(a) Analyse the financial performance and financial position of KER for the year to 31 December 20X9 and comment on the Chairman's claims on expansion (8 marks are available for the calculation of relevant ratios). **(20 marks)**

(b) Differences in accounting policies and estimates can affect the comparison of financial statements of two or more entities. Discuss three examples of where such differences could affect comparability between entities. **(5 marks)**

(Total: 25 marks)

72   GD (NOV 10 EXAM)

GD is an entity that operates in the packaging industry across a number of different markets and activities. GD has applied to the financial institution where you are employed, for a long term loan of $150 million. Your immediate supervisor was working on the report and recommendation in response to GD's request, but has fallen ill and you have been asked to complete the analysis and prepare the supporting documentation for the next management meeting to discuss applications for lending.

Extracts from the consolidated financial statements of GD are provided below:

Statement of financial position as at 30 June

	20X1 $m	20X0 $m
ASSETS		
Non-current assets		
Property, plant and equipment	548	465
Goodwill	29	24
	577	489
Current assets		
Inventories	146	120
Receivables	115	125
Held for trading investments	31	18
Cash and cash equivalents	–	41
	292	304
Total assets	869	793
EQUITY AND LIABILITIES		
Equity attributable to owners of the parent		
Share capital ($1 shares)	120	120
Revaluation reserve	18	–
Retained earnings	293	183
	431	303
Non-controlling interest	65	61
Total equity	496	364
Non-current liabilities		
Long term loans	90	180
Current liabilities		
Payables	185	160
Bank overdraft	50	–
Income tax payable	48	89
	283	249
Total liabilities	373	429
Total equity and liabilities	869	793

Statement of comprehensive income for the year ended 30 June

	20X1	20X0
	$m	$m
Revenue	1,200	1,400
Cost of sales	(840)	(930)
Gross profit	360	470
Distribution costs	(40)	(45)
Administrative expenses	(130)	(120)
Finance costs	(11)	(15)
Profit before tax	179	290
Income tax expense	(50)	(85)
PROFIT FOR THE YEAR	129	205
Other comprehensive income		
Revaluation of property	18	–
Total comprehensive income (net of tax)	147	205
Profit for the year attributable to:		
Owners of the parent	121	195
Non-controlling interest	8	10
	129	205
Total comprehensive income attributable to:		
Owners of the parent	139	195
Non-controlling interest	8	10
	147	205

Handwritten annotations: "revenue down", "Profit down", "Profit down", "includes deduction of gains from gains in HFT investment"

Additional information

1   In August 20X0, a new competitor entered one of GD's markets and pursued an aggressive strategy of increasing market share by undercutting GD's prices and prioritising volume sales. The directors had not anticipated this as GD had been the market leader in this area for the past few years. *[handwritten: Competitor.]*

2   The minutes from the most recent meeting of the Board of Directors state that the directors believe they can implement a new strategy to regain GD's market position in this segment, providing long term funding can be secured. GD acquired a subsidiary during the year as part of the new strategy and revenue is forecast to increase by the second quarter of 20X2. *[handwritten: information about subsidiary? / New subsidiary acquired.]*

3   A meeting is scheduled with GD's main suppliers to discuss a reduction in costs for bulk orders.

4   The existing long-term loan is due to be repaid on 1 August 20X2.

5   Gains of $9 million generated by the held for trading investments have been offset against administrative expenses.

Required:

(a)   **Analyse the financial performance and financial position of GD and recommend whether or not GD's application for borrowing should be considered further**

        Note: 8 marks are available for the calculation of relevant ratios.   (21 marks)

(b)   **Explain what further information might be useful in assessing the future prospects of GD and its ability to service a new long term loan.   (4 marks)**

                                                                        (Total: 25 marks)

73   DFG (MAR 11 EXAM)

A friend has approached you looking for some advice. He has been offered the position of Sales Director within an entity, DFG, which supplies the building trade. He commented that he had reviewed the information on DFG's website and there were lots of positive messages about the entity's future, including how it had secured a new supplier relationship in 20X1 resulting in a significant improvement in margins.

He has been offered a lucrative remuneration package to implement a new aggressive sales strategy, but has been with his current employer for six years and wants to ensure his future would be secure. He has provided you with the finalised financial statements for DFG for the year ended 31 December 20X1, with comparatives.

The financial statements for DFG are provided below:

Statement of financial position at 31 December

	20X1	20X0
	$m	$m
ASSETS		
Non-current assets		
Property, plant and equipment	254	198
Investment in associate	24	–
	278	198
Current assets		
Inventories	106	89
Receivables	72	48
Cash and cash equivalents	–	6
	178	143
Total assets	456	341

EQUITY AND LIABILITIES
Equity

Share capital ($1 equity shares)	45	45
Retained earnings	146	139
Revaluation reserve	40	–
Total equity	231	184
Non-current liabilities		
Long term borrowings	91	91
Current liabilities		
Trade and other payables	95	66
Short term borrowings	39	–
	134	66
Total liabilities	225	157
Total equity and liabilities	456	341

Statement of comprehensive income for the year ended 31 December

	20X1	20X0
	$m	$m
Revenue	252	248
Cost of sales	(203)	(223)
Gross profit	49	25
Distribution costs	(18)	(13)
Administrative expenses	(16)	(11)
Share of profit of associate	7	–
Finance costs	(12)	(8)
Profit before tax	10	(7)
Income tax expense	(3)	2
Profit for the year	7	(5)
Other comprehensive income:		
Revaluation gain on PPE	40	–
Total other comprehensive income	40	–
Total Comprehensive income for the year	47	(5)

Additional information

1   **Long term borrowings**

The long term borrowings are repayable in 20X3.

2   **Contingent liability**

The notes to the financial statements include details of a contingent liability of $30 million. A major customer, a house builder, is suing DFG, claiming that it supplied faulty goods. The customer had to rectify some of its building work when investigations discovered that a building material, which had recently been supplied by DFG, was found to contain a hazardous substance. The initial assessment from the lawyer is that DFG is likely to lose the case although the amount of potential damages could not be measured with sufficient reliability at the year-end date.

3   **Revaluation**

DFG decided on a change of accounting policy in the year and now includes its land and buildings at their revalued amount. The valuation was performed by an employee of DFG who is a qualified valuer.

Required:

(a)   Analyse the financial performance of DFG for the year to 31 December 20X1 and its financial position at that date AND briefly discuss SFG's suitability as a secure employer for your friend *(8 marks are available for the calculation of relevant ratios).*   (20 marks)

(b)   Explain the potential limitations of using traditional ratio analysis as a means of decision making, using DFG's situation to illustrate your answer.   (5 marks)

(Total: 25 marks)

74   CVB (MAY 11 EXAM)

A friend has recently inherited some money and has approached you seeking investment advice. She has an interest in fashion and has decided to invest in the fashion retail sector. She has performed some initial research which concentrated on the social and economic policies of a number of entities. She has selected a listed entity, CVB, for potential investment as she was particularly impressed with the fact that they had recently introduced a new line of fair-trade clothing.

She has asked that you help with a review of the financial information before she makes her final decision to invest. CVB's current share price is $1.25 per share, which is 40% lower than at the same time last year.

The financial statements for CVB are provided below:

Consolidated statement of financial position as at 30 September

	20X1 $m	20X0 $m
ASSETS		
Non-current assets		
Property, plant and equipment	262	235
Investment in associate	14	16
	276	251
Current assets		
Inventories	140	87
Trade and other receivables	75	63
Cash and cash equivalents	–	9
	215	159
Held for sale assets	4	–
Total assets	495	410
EQUITY AND LIABILITIES		
Equity attributable to owners of the parent		
Share capital	30	30
Share premium	48	48
Retained reserves	179	164
	257	242
Non-controlling interest	16	14
Total equity	273	256
Non-current liabilities		
Long-term borrowings	55	58
Deferred tax provision	5	1
	60	59
Current liabilities		
Trade and other payables	144	95
Short-term borrowings	18	–
	162	95
Total liabilities	222	154
Total equity and liabilities	495	410

Consolidated statement of comprehensive income for the year ended 30 September

	20X1	20X0
	$m	$m
Revenue	453	412
Cost of sales	(305)	(268)
Gross profit	148	144
Sales and marketing costs	(66)	(60)
Administrative expenses	(62)	(64)
Finance costs	(8)	(5)
Share of (loss)/profit of associate	(2)	3
Profit before tax	10	18
Income tax expense	(2)	(5)
Profit for the year	8	13
Other comprehensive income:		
Revaluation gains from property (net of tax)	14	–
Total Comprehensive income for the year	22	13
Profit for the year attributable to:		
Equity holders of the parent	7	11
Non-controlling interest	1	2
	8	13
Total comprehensive income attributable to:		
Equity holders of the parent	21	11
Non-controlling interest	1	2
	22	13

Required:

(a) Analyse and prepare a report on the financial performance and financial position of CVB *(8 marks are available for the calculation of relevant ratios).* **(20 marks)**

(b) Explain what further financial information may assist your friend in deciding whether or not to invest in CVB. **(5 marks)**

(Total: 25 marks)

75 LKJ (SEP 11 EXAM)

LKJ has expanded during the last year and from 1 October 20X0 has been supplying a new range of products, some of which are simply cheaper versions of existing products and some of which are completely new. This has resulted in LKJ increasing its market share and creating a more mixed customer base. The directors have been looking at ways that fixed overheads can be cut and following a review last year, outsourced its payroll requirements, which led to a significant drop in administrative expenses.

In the past, LKJ has been known as a cash-rich business and a regular payer of dividends. However a recent cash shortage meant that a cash dividend was not possible in the year ended 30 April 20X1. Therefore, in lieu of paying a dividend, LKJ made a 1 for 2 bonus issue on 1 January 20X1.

The financial statements of LKJ are provided below:

Statement of financial position as at 30 April

	20X1 $m	20X0 $m
ASSETS		
Non-current assets		
Property, plant and equipment	554	418
Investment in associate	140	–
Available for sale investments	300	280
	994	698
Current assets		
Inventories	290	130
Receivables	468	263
Cash and cash equivalents	–	144
	758	537
Total assets	1,752	1,235
EQUITY AND LIABILITIES		
Equity		
Share capital ($1 equity shares)	300	200
Revaluation reserve	130	64
Other reserves	76	44
Retained earnings	789	739
Total equity	1,295	1,047

Non-current liabilities

Long-term borrowings	200	60
Current liabilities		
Payables	199	128
Short-term borrowings (overdraft)	58	–
	257	128
Total liabilities	457	188
Total equity and liabilities	1,752	1,235

Statement of comprehensive income for the year ended 30 April

	20X1	20X0
	$m	$m
Revenue	2,630	2,022
Cost of sales	(2,058)	(1,505)
Gross profit	572	517
Administrative expenses	(114)	(163)
Distribution costs	(288)	(203)
Finance costs	(20)	(6)
Share of profit of associate	80	–
Profit before tax	230	145
Income tax expense	(70)	(63)
Profit for the year	160	82
Other comprehensive income:		
Revaluation gain on property, plant and equipment	80	25
Gains on available for sale investments	32	12
Tax effects of other comprehensive income	(24)	(15)
Other comprehensive income for the year, net of tax	88	22
Total Comprehensive income for the year	248	104

LKJ has submitted an application for long-term borrowing to the finance company that you work with. You are to prepare a report that analyses the financial performance and position of LKJ for review by your supervisor. Your supervisor encourages his employees to make an initial recommendation as to whether or not the application should be given further consideration.

Required:

(a) Prepare a report that analyses the financial performance of LKJ for the year ended 30 April 20X1 and its financial position at that date. *(8 marks are available for the calculation of relevant ratios).* **(20 marks)**

(b) (i) Explain how the bonus issue in the year will impact the calculation of the earnings per share of LKJ for inclusion in its financial statements for the year ended 30 April 20X1.

(ii) Calculate the basic earnings per share for LKJ for the year ended 30 April 20X1 and the comparative figure for 20X0 that would appear in the 20X1 financial statements. **(5 marks)**

(Total: 25 marks)

DEVELOPMENTS IN EXTERNAL REPORTING

76   FW (MAY 05 EXAM)   *Walk in the footsteps of a top tutor*

FW is a listed entity involved in the business of oil exploration, drilling and refining in three neighbouring countries – Aye, Bee and Cee. The business has been consistently profitable, creating high returns for its international shareholders. In recent years, however, there has been an increase in environmental lobbying in FW's three countries of operation. Two years ago, an environmental group based in Cee started lobbying the government to take action against FW for alleged destruction of valuable wildlife habitats in Cee's protected wetlands and the displacement of the local population. At the time, the directors of FW took legal advice, on the basis of which they assessed the risk of liability at less than 50%. A contingent liability of $500 million was noted in the financial statements to cover possible legal costs, compensation to displaced persons and reinstatement of the habitats, as well as fines.

FW is currently preparing its financial statements for the year ended 28 February 20X5. Recent advice from the entity's legal advisers has assessed that the risk of a successful action against FW has increased, and must now be regarded as more likely than not to occur. The board of directors has met to discuss the issue. The directors accept that a provision of $500 million is required, but would like to be informed of the effects of the adjustment on certain key ratios that the entity headlines in its annual report. All of the directors are concerned about the potentially adverse effect on the share price, as FW is actively engaged in a takeover bid that would involve a substantial share exchange. In addition, they feel that the public's image of the entity is likely to be damaged. The chief executive makes the following suggestion:

'Many oil businesses now publish an environmental and social report, and I think it may be time for us to do so. It would give us the opportunity to set the record straight about what we do to reduce pollution, and could help to deflect some of the public attention from us over this law suit. In any case, it would be a good public relations opportunity; we can use it to tell people about our equal opportunities programme. I was reading about something called the Global Reporting Initiative (GRI). I don't know much about it, but it might give us some help in structuring a report that will get the right message across. We could probably pull something together to go out with this year's annual report.'

The draft financial statements for the year ended 28 February 20X5 include the following information relevant for the calculation of key ratios. All figures are before taking into account the $500 million provision. The provision will be charged to operating expenses.

	$m
Net assets (before long-term loans) at 1 March 20X4	9,016
Net assets (before long-term loans) at 28 February 20X5	10,066
Long-term loans at 28 February 20X5	4,410
Share capital + reserves at 1 March 20X4	4,954
Share capital + reserves at 28 February 20X5	5,656
Revenue	20,392
Operating profit	2,080
Profit before tax	1,670
Profit for the period	1,002

The number of ordinary shares in issue throughout the years ended 29 February 20X4 and 28 February 20X5 were 6,000 million shares of 25¢ each.

FW's key financial ratios for the 20X4 financial year (calculated using the financial statements for the year ended 29 February 20X4) were:

- Return on equity (using average equity): 24.7%

- Return on net assets (using average net assets): 17.7%

- Gearing (debt as a percentage of equity): 82%

- Operating profit margin: 10.1%

- Earnings per share: 12.2¢ per share

Required:

In your position as assistant to FW's chief financial officer produce a briefing paper that:

(a) analyses and interprets the effects of making the environmental provision on FW's key financial ratios. You should take into account the possible effects on the public perception of FW;   (12 marks)

(b) identifies the advantages and disadvantages to FW of adopting the chief executive's proposal to publish an environmental and social report;   (7 marks)

(c) describes the THREE principal sustainability dimensions covered by the GRI's framework of performance indicators.   (6 marks)

(Total: 25 marks)

77   BCA (NOV 09 EXAM)

BCA is a multinational entity and part of its business is the operation of power stations. Minimising pollution is of primary concern to the entity and therefore it has contracts with CAD, a relatively new and innovative entity, to undertake regular monitoring of the output of potentially hazardous gases from the stations.

CAD utilises sophisticated equipment that is highly sensitive to many gases. The equipment and related software were developed by CAD using innovative techniques created by the Chief Scientific Officer (CSO) who has extensive expertise in gas sensing and laser physics. A number of CAD's products have been patented. As the CSO is considered to be a vital part of the entity's ongoing success, CAD required her to sign a nine month contract. This contract prevents her from developing similar products for anyone else for a further 12 months. The CSO was also given a bonus this year, as the development of new technology helped to secure a lucrative four year contract with a new customer. It is likely to bring additional revenues from existing contracts over the next couple of years. The CSO has an equity stake in the business as does the Chief Executive.

Despite having another three key contracts, similar to the one with BCA, CAD is struggling financially and is desperately in need of investment. CAD is having difficulty raising finance as it has very few tangible assets on which security can be offered.

The directors of CAD have approached the board of BCA to ask for investment and have indicated that they would be willing to give up their controlling interest in CAD if the entity's future, and their own, could be secured.

Summary financial information is provided below:

Income statement for the year ended 30 September 20X9 for CAD

	20X9	20X8
	$000	$000
Revenue	4,330	3,562
Cost of sales	(3,702)	(2,810)
Gross profit	628	752
Other operating expenses	(465)	(580)
Finance costs	(13)	(2)
Profit before tax	150	170
Income tax expense	(42)	(45)
Profit for the period	108	125

Statement of financial position as at 30 September 20X9 for CAD

	20X9 $000	20X8 $000
ASSETS		
Non-current assets		
Property, plant and equipment	52	78
Intangible assets	89	38
	141	116
Current assets		
Inventories	125	72
Trade receivables	1,091	587
Cash and cash equivalents	58	318
	1,274	977
Total assets	1,415	1,093
EQUITY AND LIABILITIES		
Equity attributable to equity owners of the parent		
Share capital ($1 ordinary shares)	4	4
Retained earnings	539	431
Total equity	543	435
Non-current liabilities		
Provisions	62	173
Current liabilities		
Trade and other payables	687	485
Short term borrowings	123	–
Total current liabilities	810	485
Total Liabilities	872	658
Total equity and liabilities	1,415	1,093

Required:

(a)   Prepare a preliminary report for the board of BCA, highlighting the key considerations of CAD as a potential target for acquisition. Your report should include discussion of the key challenges that CAD faces and whether these would change if BCA were to acquire CAD. (5 marks are available for relevant ratios that can aid your discussion.)   **(15 marks)**

(b)   (i)   Explain why there is increasing pressure to extend the scope of corporate reporting and why this may result in an increase in narrative reporting.

                                                                                                    (4 marks)

      (ii) Discuss why a report, similar to the UK's Operating and Financial Review, might be helpful to potential investors in CAD.   **(6 marks)**

                                                                                          (Total: 25 marks)

Section 3

ANSWERS TO SECTION A-TYPE QUESTIONS

GROUP FINANCIAL STATEMENTS

1   ST (MAY 06 EXAM)

Consolidated income statement for the year ended 31 January 20X6

	$000
Revenue (W2)	3,490
Cost of sales (W3)	(2,266)
	——
Gross profit	1,224
Operating expenses (450 + 375 + (50% × 74))	(862)
	——
Profit from operations	362
Finance cost (16 + 12 − 6% x 100 i/co)	(22)
	——
Profit before tax	340
Income tax expense (45 + 53 + (50% × 26))	(111)
	——
Profit for the period	229
	——
Attributable to:	
Equity holders of the parent	196
Non-controlling interests (30% × 110)	33
	——
	229
	——

Workings

(W1) **Group structure**

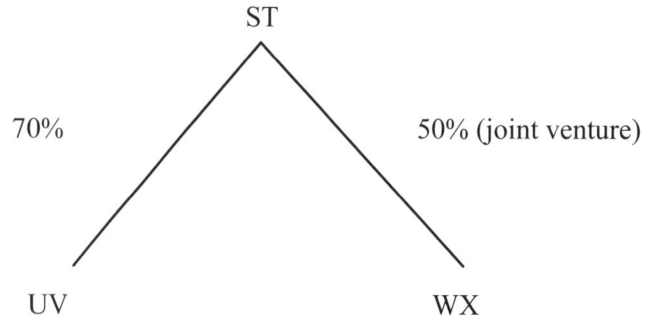

(W2) **Revenue**

	$000	$000
ST		1,800
UV		1,400
WX	600	
Less: intra group sales	(20)	
	580	
Group share (50%)		290
		3,490

(W3) **Cost of sales**

	$000	$000
ST	1,200	
Less: intra-group sales (50% × 20)	(10)	
	1,190	
UV		850
WX	450	
Plus provision for unrealised profit (20,000 × ½ × 20%)	2	
	452	
Group share (50%)		226
		2,266

2   HOME AND FOREIGN (NOV 06 EXAM)

Consolidated income statement for the year ended 31 July 20X6

	$000
Revenue (3,000 + 270.8 (W2) − 20.8 (W3))	3,250
Cost of sales (2,400 + 229.2 (W2) − 20.8 (W3))	(2,608.4)
Gross profit	641.6
Distribution costs (32 + 17.1 (W2))	(49.1)
Administrative expenses (168 + 36.2 (W2) + 1.9 (W4) − 1.3 (W5))	(204.8)
Finance costs (15 + 4.2 (W2))	(19.2)
Profit before tax	368.5
Income tax (102 − 4.2 (W2))	(97.8)
Profit for the period	270.7

Workings

(W1) **Group structure**

Home has owned 100% of Foreign throughout the year.

(W2) **Translation of income statement of Foreign**

	Crowns 000	Rate	$000
Revenue	650	2.4	270.8
Cost of sales	(550)	2.4	(229.2)
Gross profit	100		41.6
Distribution costs	(41)	2.4	(17.1)
Administrative expenses	(87)	2.4	(36.2)
Finance costs	(10)	2.4	(4.2)
Loss before tax	(38)		(15.9)
Income tax	10	2.4	4.2
Loss for the period	(28)		(11.7)

(W3) **Intra group sales**

Intra-group sales were $20.8k (50k ÷ 2.4).

(W4) **Impairment of goodwill**

	Crowns 000
Cost of investment	204
Less: net assets acquired (100%) (1 + 180)	(181)
	23
Impairment (20% × 23)	4.6
Impairment in dollars (4.6 ÷ 2.4)	1.9

(W5) **Exchange difference in accounts of Home**

	$000
At 1 June 20X6 (32 ÷ 1.5)	21.3
At 31 July 20X6 (32 ÷ 1.6)	(20.0)
Gain on outstanding payable	1.3

3   SGB (MAY 09 EXAM)

Consolidated income statement for the year ended 31 December 20X8

		$000
Revenue (8,200 + (9/12 x 3,600))		10,900
Cost of sales (4,300 + (9/12 x 1,900))		(5,725)
Gross profit		5,175
Distribution costs (1,200 + (9/12 x 800))		(1,800)
Administrative expenses (800 + (9/12 x 600))		(1,250)
Profit from operations		2,125
Gain on disposal (W2)		737
Share of profit of associate (W7)		15
Profit before tax		2,877
Tax (600 + (9/12 x 100))	675	
Tax on gain on disposal (W6)	225	(900)
Profit for the period		1,977
Attributable to:		
Non-controlling interests (20% x S's PAT)		
20% x 9/12 x 200		30
Parent shareholders (β)		1,947
		1,977

Workings

(W1) Group structure

SGB
|
|
FMA

1.6m/2m = 80%
20X6

	Shares	Holding	Status
20X6	1.6m	80%	Subsidiary
1 October 20X8 disposal	(1m)		
31 December 20X8	0.6m	30%	Associate

(W2) Gain on disposal

		$000
Proceeds		2,500
Fair value of retained interest		1,200
		3,700
Less: carrying value of sub disposed of		
Net assets at disposal (W3)	3,300	
Unimpaired goodwill (W4)	384	
Less: NCI at disposal (W5)	(721)	
		(2,963)
Group gain on disposal		737

(W3) Net assets of FMA

	Acquisition	Disposal
	$000	$000
Share capital	2,000	2,000
Retained earnings	1,000	
1,150 + (200 x 9/12)		1,300
	3,000	3,300

(W4) Goodwill at disposal date

	$000
Parent's investment	2,800
Fair value of non-controlling interest	680
Less: Fair value of net assets acquired (W3)	(3,000)
Goodwill on acquisition	480
Impairment (20% x 480)	(96)
Goodwill at disposal	384

(W5) **NCI at disposal date**

	$000
Fair value at acquisition	680
Share of post-acquisition reserves	
20% x (3,300 – 3,000 (W3))	60
Share of goodwill impairment	
20% x 96 (W4)	(19)
	___
Goodwill at disposal	721
	___

(W6) **Parent gain on disposal**

	$000
Proceeds	2,500
Less: 1m/1.6m x 2,800	(1,750)
	___
	750
	___
Tax charge at 30%	225
	___

(W7) **Share of profit of associate**

	$000
FMA's PAT x 3/12 x 30%	
200 x 3/12 x 30%	15
	___

4 AAY (MAY 08 EXAM)

Key answer tips

Start by drawing up the table for the statement of changes in equity with headings and line descriptions. The dividends should be dealt with first as they are most straightforward. Then work through the information you are given in the question and put items into workings. The provision for unrealised profit was complicated as you had to deal with a PUP in opening inventory. Remember that an adjustment needs to be made *on consolidation only* at each year end.

AAY Group consolidated statement of changes in equity

	Attributable to equity holders of parent	Non-controlling interest	Total
	$000	$000	$000
Balance brought forward (W1,2)	690,780	28,660	719,440
Profit for the period (W4)	99,140	4,360	103,500
Dividends	(18,000)		(19,200)
(20% x 6,000)		(1,200)	
Balance carried forward	771,920	31,820	803,740

Workings

(W1) **Balance brought forward**

		$000
AAYs balance b/f		662,300
Share of BBZs post acquisition reserves		
80% x ((143,700 − 400 (PUP (W3))) − 107,700)		28,480
		690,780

(W2) **Non-controlling interest b/f**

		$000
Value at acquisition 20% x 107,700		21,540
Share of post acquisition reserves		
20% x ((143,700-400 (PUP (W3))) − 107,700)		7,120
		28,660

(W3) **Provision for unrealised profit**

		$000
Opening inventory	2m x 25/125	400
Closing inventory	3m x 25/125	600
Increase in provision in current year		200

(W4) **Profit for the year**

	$000	$000
BBZ profit per question	22,000	
Less: PUP (W3)	(200)	
	21,800	
NCI: 20% x 21,800		4,360
Group: AAY's profit	81,700	
Plus: 80% x 21,800	17,440	
		99,140

5 ✓ AB, GH, JK & LM (MAY 10 EXAM)

Key answer tips

The question tests the treatment of investments in consolidated accounts but in a narrative style. The examiner would have been looking for you to write a couple of points on each investment, setting out the key rules on what to report. You then need to illustrate the accounting treatment using the financial information given. An attempt at each investment would have been vital.

(a)   **Investment in AB**

DF holds 90% of the ordinary share capital and therefore, in accordance with IAS 27 *Consolidated and Separate Financial Statements*, is presumed to be able to exercise control over AB's operating and financial policies. AB is a subsidiary of DF and should be fully consolidated in the group financial statements.

Investment in GH

The 40% investment in GH is presumed, in accordance with IAS 28 *Investment in Associates*, to give DF the ability to exercise significant influence over GH and will be accounted for using equity accounting. On acquisition, the investment is recognised at cost and in subsequent periods at cost of $2 million plus group share of any post-acquisition gains and losses.

Investment in JK

In accordance with IFRS 5 *Non-current assets held for sale and discontinued operations*, DF need not consolidate JK if it intends to resell the investment within 12 months of acquisition. Since it is being actively marketed it can be assumed that the requirements of IFRS 5 have been met. JK will not be consolidated, instead the cost of the investment will be included separately on the consolidated statement of financial position under "Assets held for resale".

Investment in LM

IFRS 3 *Business combinations* requires goodwill on acquisition to be calculated at the date control is gained. The second acquisition gives DF a 55% holding and therefore control over LM. The simple investment will be derecognised and the 55% holding will be fully consolidated as a subsidiary in the group financial statements. The goodwill will be calculated as the cost of the 40% acquired in October 2009 plus the fair value of the previously held interest of 15%, compared with the fair value of the net assets at the date of acquisition, 1 October 2009.

(b) The 90% acquired for $6 million had a fair value of $6.12m ($6.8m x 90%) and so DF acquired a bargain purchase. The $120,000 should be written off to profit or loss in the year of acquisition and to retained earnings in subsequent years. The fair value uplift will result in an additional $25,000 (($6.8m - $5.8m)/40 years) in depreciation chargeable to consolidated profit or loss (only $12,500 in year of acquisition as subsidiary acquired half way through year). The cumulative depreciation should be deducted from consolidated retained earnings. The consolidated non-current assets will be increased by the net amount (the uplift less accumulated depreciation).

Examiner's comments

This question was well answered by most candidates. Most identified the subsidiary, associate and dealt with the step acquisition, although missed the final mark that related to incorporating the FV of the existing investment in the goodwill calculation. The more difficult point on IFRS 5 was generally missed with many suggesting that it was a financial instrument, held for trading rather than held for sale. Many candidates commented on the treatment of goodwill but few had worked out that in fact this acquisition resulted in a bargain purchase.

---

6 ✓ MX (MAY 10 EXAM)

(i) Goodwill

	$
Parent's investment	1,750,000
Fair value of non-controlling interest	320,000
Less fair value of net assets acquired (W1)	(1,885,000)
Goodwill on acquisition and reporting date	185,000

(ii) Consolidated retained earnings

	$
100% AB	3,200,000
80% CD post acquisition (1,996,333 – 1,885,000) (W1)	89,066
	3,289,066

(iii) Non-controlling interest

	$
Fair value at the date of acquisition	320,000
20% share of CD post acquisition (1,996,333 – 1,885,000) (W1)	22,267
	342,267

Workings

(W1) **Net assets of FZ**

	Acquisition $	*Disposal* $
Share capital	1,000,000	1,000,000
Retained earnings	920,000	1,100,000
Fair value adjustments:		
Property ($745k – $680k)	65,000	65,000
Contingent liability	(100,000)	(100,000)
Depreciation on fair value adjustments:		
Property ($65k / 5 yrs x 8/12)		(8,667)
Provision for unrealised profit		
300k x 20%		(60,000)
	1,885,000	1,996,333

Examiner's comments (extract)

This question was well attempted by many candidates. UK candidates in particular were well-prepared for the new approach to adopt when non-controlling interest is valued at fair value on acquisition, and scored full marks. Only the calculation of NCI caused problems – a number of candidates presented a hybrid calculation of NCI at FV and then added to this NCI's share of total net assets.

---

7 AB, CD & EF (NOV 10 EXAM)

The consolidated income statement for AB Group for the year ended 30 June 20X9:

(all amounts in the workings are in $000, unless stated otherwise)	$000
Revenue (2,000 + 1,500)	3,500
Cost of sales (1,200 + 1,000)	(2,200)
Gross profit	1,300
Distribution costs (400 + 120)	(520)
Administration expenses (240 + 250 + 30 (W1) + 20 (W2))	(540)
Share of profit of associate (W3)	13
Profit before tax	253
Income tax expense (50 + 40)	(90)
Profit for the year	163
Attributable to:	
Equity holders of the parent	155
Non-controlling interest (W5)	8

Workings

(W1) Goodwill impairment

	$000
Consideration transferred	4,100
Non-controlling interest at fair value	1,100
Fair value of the net assets acquired	(5,000)
Goodwill	200
15% impairment	30

(W2) Additional depreciation on fair value adjustment

	$000
Fair value adjustment on depreciable assets	240
Remaining useful life of assets	12 years
Annual depreciation charged to group admin expenses	20

(W3) Share of profit of associate

	$000
Profit after tax of EF	100
Pro-rata from date of acquisition – 9 months	75
Less unrealised profit on sales to AB (W4)	(10)
	65
20% group share	13

(W4) Unrealised profit on inventories

	$000
Sales value of goods in inventories at year end (80 x ½)	40
Unrealised profit at 25% margin	10

(W5) Non-controlling interest

	$000
Profit for the year for CD (as reported)	90
Additional depreciation on fair value uplift	(20)
Goodwill impairment	(30)
	40
20% NCI share	8

Examiner's comments

This question was well answered by the majority of candidates with many getting full marks. By far the most common mistake was treating the intercompany transfer of goods as a transaction between the subsidiary and the parent, followed closely by the failure to eliminate the intercompany dividend.

---

8 KL, LM & NP (MAR 11 EXAM)

The consolidated income statement for the KL Group for the year ended 31 December 20X1:

	$000
(All workings in $000)	$000
Revenue (4,000 + 1,500 − 140)	5,360
Cost of sales (2,300 + 1,000 − 140 + 14 (W4))	(3,174)
Gross profit	2,186
Distribution costs (900 + 120)	(1,020)
Administrative expenses (350 + 150 + 60 (W1) + 40 (W2))	(600)
Share of profit of associate (W3)	12
Profit before tax	578
Income tax expense (250 + 80)	(330)
Profit for the year	248

Attributable to:

Equity holders of the parent	237
Non-controlling interest (W5)	11
	248

Workings

(W1) **Goodwill impairment**

	$000
Consideration transferred	8,200
Non-controlling interest at fair value	2,200
Fair value of the net assets acquired	(10,000)
Goodwill at acquisition	400
15% impairment in 20X1	60

(W2) **Additional depreciation on fair value adjustment**

	$000
Fair value adjustment on depreciable assets	240
Remaining useful life of assets	6 years
Annual depreciation charged to group admin expenses	40

(W3) **Share of profit of associate**

	$000
Profit after tax of NP	120
Pro-rata from date of acquisition – 3 months	30
40% group share	12

(W4) **Unrealised profit on inventories**

	$000
Sales value of goods in inventories at year end (140 x ½)	70
Unrealised profit at 20% margin	14

(W5) **Non-controlling interest**

	$000
Profit for the year for LM (as reported)	150
Additional depreciation on fair value uplift (W2)	(40)
Goodwill impairment (W1)	(60)
Unrealised profit in inventories (W4)	(14)
	36
30% NCI share	11

9   RBE (MAY 11 EXAM)

(a)   The additional 20% purchase by RBE results in an increase in the controlling interest held in the subsidiary, DCA. No further goodwill is calculated on the additional purchase as goodwill is only calculated at the date control was gained in accordance with IFRS 3. However, at the date of the additional purchase (1 October 20X0) the value of NCI needs to be established. The proportion "sold" will be transferred from NCI to parent's equity within the SOCIE. The difference between that value and the consideration transferred is included in parent's equity as an "adjustment to parent equity" on acquisition.

(b)   **Statement of changes in equity for the year ended 31 December 20X0**

	Attributable to equity holders of parent	Non-controlling interest	Total
	$000	$000	$000
Balance at the start of the year	3,350	650	4,000
TCI for the year (W1)	1,350	150	1,500
Share issue (2m x $1.30)	2,600		2,600
Dividends	(200)	(30) (W2)	(230)
Adjustment to NCI for additional purchase of DCA shares (W3)		(503)	(503)
Adjustment to parent's equity (W3)	(37)		(37)
Balance at the end of the year	7,063	267	7,330

Workings

(W1) **TCI for the year**

	$000
NCI share of total comprehensive income of DCA $600,000	8,200
NCI at 30% x $600,000 x 9/12 months	135
NCI at 10% x $600,000 x 3/12 months	15
NCI share of TCI	150

Therefore parent share of TCI of DCA is $600k – $150k = $450,000

Total TCI attributable to equity holders of parent is $900k + $450k = $1,350,000

(W2) **NCI share of dividend paid April 20X0 by DCA**

= 30% x $100k = $30,000

(W3) **Value of NCI transferred**

Value of NCI at 1 October 20X0 is $650k + $135k (W1) – $30k (W2) = $755,000

Therefore the value transferred is $755k x 2/3 = $503,333

Adjustment to parent's equity	$000
Consideration transferred	540
Value of non-controlling interest transferred	(503)
Adjustment to parent equity	37

Examiner's comments

Part (a) of the question was reasonably well done with many candidates identifying that this was a piecemeal acquisition. Having correctly discussed the impact, however they failed to then apply this in part (b) with many ignoring the impact of the transfer when preparing the SOCIE. Only the minority attempted to calculate the adjustment to parent's equity. Many failed also to recognise that the parent column would only include the dividend paid to those shareholders.

10   SD (SEP 11 EXAM)

(i)   **Goodwill non acquisition (calculated at date control gained – on 1 July 20X0)**

	$000	$000
Consideration transferred for 60% of shares		3,250
Non-controlling interest at fair value at 1 July 20X0		1,960
Less fair value of net assets acquired:		
Share capital	1,000	
Retained earnings	2,760	
		(3,760)
Goodwill arising		1,450

(ii)   **Group retained earnings**

	$000
Retained earnings of SD at 30 June 20X1	9,400
60% x RE of KL from acquisition to 1 March 20X1	
60% x [($3,400k – $2,760k) x 8/12]	256
80% x ($640k x 4/12)	171
Adjustment to parent's equity (W1)	66
Group share of unrealised profit on inventories transferred	
80% x (40% x $750k x 25/125)	(48)
	9,845

(iii)   **Non-controlling interest**

	$000
On acquisition	1,960
Share of post-acquisition profits to 1 March 20X1	
40% x [($3,400k – $2,760k) x 8/12]	171
NCI value at disposal date	2,131
Disposal of 20% of 40% holding	(1,066)
	1,066
Share of profit for last 4 months	
20% x ($640k x 4/12)	43
Less NCI share of unrealised profit on inventories	
20% x (40% x $750k x 25/125)	(12)
NCI at reporting date	1,096

Tutorial note:

See end of solution for an alternative layout to the above using the standard SFP workings.

Workings

(W1) **Adjustment to parent's equity**

	$000
Value of NCI transferred to SD (20%/40%)	1,066
Consideration paid by SD	1,000
Adjustment to parent's equity (credit to RE)	66

Tutorial note:

A non-current assets working can help with the calculation of group retained earnings and NCI, particularly given the unrealised profit adjustment required to the subsidiary's reserves. See below for our standard net assets working and an alternative layout to the examiner's answer above.

Solution (extract) using standard SFP workings:

(ii) **Group retained earnings**

	$000
Retained earnings of SD at 30 June 20X1	9,400
Share of KL's post-acquisition reserves	
60% x 427 (W2)	256
80% x 153 (W2)	123
Adjustment to parent's equity (W1)	66
	9,845

(iii) **NCI**

	$000
Value at acquisition	1,960
Share of post-acquisition profits to date of transfer	
40% x 427 (W2)	171
NCI value at transfer date	2,131
Transferred to parent (2,131 x 20/40)	(1,066)
	1,065
Share of post-acquisition reserves from transfer to year end	
20% x 153 (W2)	31
NCI at reporting date	1,096

Working:

(W2) **Net assets of KL**

	Acquisition $000	Transfer $000	Year end $000
Share capital	1,000	1,000	1,000
Retained earnings	2,760	3,187	3,400
Unrealised profit on inventories 750k x 40% x 25/125			(60)
	3,760	4,187	4,340

Transfer takes place 4 months prior to year end, therefore difference between transfer date and year end retained earnings = ($3,400,000 – $2,760,000) x 4/12 = $213,333

The post-acquisition reserves are:

	$000
From acquisition to transfer (4,187 – 3,760)	427
From transfer to year end (4,340 – 4,187)	153

ISSUES IN RECOGNITION AND MEASUREMENT

11 CBA (NOV 06 EXAM)

Briefing Paper

To: The Directors of CBA

From: Financial Controller

Subject: Accounting for actuarial losses

IAS 19 *Employee Benefits* gives the option of three methods for accounting for actuarial gains and losses. They may be recognised in profit and loss (in the income statement) immediately or in part or they may be recognised outside profit and loss, in the statement of other comprehensive income.

Recognition in profit and loss immediately

It is possible to recognise actuarial gains or losses immediately in profit or loss provided that:

- the method adopted is systematic;
- the same method is adopted for both gains and losses; and
- the method is applied consistently from period to period.

Recognition in profit and loss using the 10% corridor

IAS 19 states that an entity must recognise a portion of an actuarial loss as an expense in the year if the net cumulative unrecognised actuarial gains and losses at the start of the period (1 October 20X5) exceed the greater of:

- 10% of the present value of the defined benefit liability (before deducting the plan assets) at that date; and

- 10% of the fair value of the plan assets at that date.

If unrecognised net losses fall outside these limits (known as the '10% corridor') the excess must be recognised in the income statement. The expense is spread over the expected average remaining working lives of the employees in the plan.

Recognition in the statement of other comprehensive income

IAS 19 also states that actuarial gains and losses may be recognised in the statement of other comprehensive income in the period in which they occur. If this policy is adopted it must be applied: consistently from period to period; for all an entity's defined benefit plans; and for all actuarial gains and losses.

It is also worth noting that the statement in which the losses are recognised must be a statement of other comprehensive income (a statement that does not show transactions with equity owners), not a statement of changes in equity.

Potential impact on the financial statements

The actuarial loss suffered in the current year will not affect the '10% corridor' limits for the year ended 30 September 20X6, because the calculation is based on the opening position (at 1 October 20X5). However, the corridor limits will probably be exceeded at 30 September 20X6 and therefore it is likely that at least part of the actuarial loss will have to be recognised in the year ended 30 September 20X7.

If the 10% corridor method is adopted, part of the actuarial loss will be recognised in the income statement. Profit for the year will be reduced and the defined benefit liability in the statement of financial position will be increased. However, the company will only have to recognise the amount by which cumulative losses exceed the '10% corridor' and this will be spread over the expected average remaining working lives of the employees. It is possible that the impact on the financial statements will not be material.

If the loss is recognised in full, the whole of the loss of $7.2 million will be recognised in the income statement or statement of other comprehensive income for the current year. Shareholders' equity will be reduced and the defined benefit liability will be increased by that amount. This accounting treatment has the advantage of being simple, but would probably lead to volatility in the statement of comprehensive income.

I hope that this information is helpful.

12   FDE (MAY 09 EXAM)

(a)   **Pension scheme expense for the income statement year ended 31 March 20X9**

	$m
Current service cost	7.8
Return on assets	
(8.219% x 73m)	(6)
Interest cost	10.2
Actuarial loss (W1)	0.08
	────
	12.08
	────

(b)   **Net pension scheme liability for the statement of financial position at 31 March 20X9**

	$m	$m
Closing liabilities	95	
Closing assets	(84)	
	────	
		11
Unrecognised actuarial losses (W2)		(9.52)
		────
Net pension liability		1.48
		────

(W1)   **Actuarial gain/ loss to be recognised in income statement year ended 31 March 20X9**

		$m
Unrecognised actuarial losses b/f		8.8
10% corridor: higher of		
10% x opening assets (73)	7.3	
10% x opening liabilities (80)	8	(8)
		────
Excess loss		0.8
		────
Spread over remaining average service life of employees of 10 years		0.08
		────

(W2)   **Unrecognised actuarial gains/ losses**

	$m
Unrecognised actuarial losses b/f	8.8
Actuarial loss arising in current year (W3)	0.8
Actuarial loss recognised in current year (W1)	(0.08)
	────
Unrecognised actuarial loss at 31 March 20X9	9.52
	────

(W3) **Actuarial gain/ loss in current year**

		$m
Opening liabilities	80	
Opening assets	(73)	7
	⎯	
Current service cost		7.8
Contributions		(8.8)
Return on assets		(6)
Interest cost		10.2
		⎯
		10.2
Actuarial loss (β)		0.8
		⎯
Closing liabilities	95	
Closing assets	(84)	
	⎯	11
		⎯

(c)   **Permitted alternative treatments**

IAS 19 currently permits faster recognition of the actuarial gains and losses through the income statement on a systematic basis. The full amounts of the actuarial gains/losses on both the pension scheme assets and obligations can be recognised in the period, but through equity. Recognition through retained earnings would minimise the effect on profit for the year and would be reported in the Statement of Other Comprehensive Income.

13   LMN (MAY 06 EXAM)

The economic substance of the arrangement between the two entities is determined by analysing the risks and benefits of the transaction. The entity that receives the benefits and bears the risks of ownership should recognise the vehicles as inventory. LMN, the motor vehicle dealer, appears to derive the following benefits:

- It is free to determine the nature of the inventory it holds, in terms of ranges and models;

- It is protected against price increases between the date of delivery to it and the date of sale because the price is determined at the point of delivery;

- It has access to the inventory for demonstration purposes.

LMN incurs the following costs and risks:

- IJK retains legal title to the goods, so in the case of dispute IJK would probably be entitled to recover its legal property;

- LMN is required to bear the cost of insuring the vehicles against loss or damage;

- Although LMN obtains the benefit of using vehicles for demonstration purposes a rental charge may become payable;

- If price reductions occur between the date of delivery and the date of sale, LMN will lose out because it will be required to pay the higher price specified upon delivery.

The analysis of the risks and benefits of the transaction does not produce a clear decision as to the economic substance of the arrangement between the two parties. IJK bears the substantial risk of incurring costs related to slow-moving or obsolete vehicles because LMN can return any vehicle to it, without incurring a penalty. This point alone is highly significant and may be sufficient to ensure that IJK, the manufacturer, should continue to recognise the vehicles in its own inventory. A further relevant point is that IJK is not paid until the point of sale to a third party, and thus it bears a significant financial risk involved in financing the inventory.

In respect of the sale of goods, IAS 18 *Revenue* requires that a sale should be recognised when the selling entity transfers to the buyer the significant risks and rewards of ownership of the goods. As noted above, significant risks and some of the rewards of ownership remain with the manufacturer, IJK, until such time as the goods are sold by the dealer to a third party. Therefore, revenue should be recognised by IJK only when a sale to a third party takes place.

14   GHK (MAY 09 EXAM)

(a)   Property sale

The asset should not be derecognised as there are conditions attached to the sale agreement which will result in GHK repurchasing the property at some later date and not necessarily at a price that reflects market conditions at that time. IAS 18 requires that the significant risks and rewards of the asset be transferred in order that a sale be recognised. GHK remains open to the main risk and potential reward associated with property, the downward or upward movement in its market value, and therefore no sale can be recognised.

The substance of the transaction is that GHK has borrowed $65 million using the property as security. The sale and subsequent gain must be reversed and the proceeds of the transaction shown as a financial liability. The increase of $2·5m in the repurchase price in the year represents the finance cost charged by the financial institution and should be recorded in the income statement. The property will be reinstated and depreciation charge for the year will be incorporated.

The correcting entries are:

		$m
Dr	Gain on sale (W1)	17
Dr	Property, plant and equipment (W1)	48
Cr	Loan liability	65

The loan received and correcting entries for the sale.

Dr	Finance cost	2.5
Cr	Loan liability	2.5

The finance cost for the year ended 31 January 20X9.

Dr	Depreciation charge (2% x $60m)	1.2
Cr	PPE – accumulated depreciation	1.2

The depreciation charge for the year ended 31 January 20X9.

(W1) **Gain on sale**

	$m	$m
Proceeds		65
Cost of asset	60	
Accumulated depreciation		
(2% x 10 years x 60)	(12)	
Carrying value at 1 Feb X8		(48)
Gain on sale		17

(b) **Share issue**

In accordance with IAS 32 the preference shares should be classified as non-equity shares and included in debt as the terms of the instrument contain an obligation to transfer economic benefit, by way of a dividend. The issue costs should be deducted from the proceeds received on issue and the dividend should be treated as a finance cost in the year and debited to the income statement.

The correcting entries are:

		$m
Dr	Equity	10
Cr	Share premium	0.05
Cr	Non-current liabilities	9.95

The correcting entry for recording the issue and issue costs.

		$m
Dr	Finance cost (income statement)	0.6
Cr	Retained earnings	0.6

The correcting recording of the non-equity dividend paid.

15 AZG (MAY 08 EXAM)

Key answer tips

The requirement for part (c) asked for extracts from the statement of financial position and income statement so ensure you format your answer correctly. Parts (a) and (b) were testing knowledge of derivatives in a straightforward manner if you have learned the definitions.

(a) A derivative is defined in IAS 39 as having all three of the following characteristics:

(i) Its value changes in response to the change in a specified interest or exchange rate, or in response to the change in a price, rating, index or other variable;

(ii) It requires no initial net investment; and

(iii) It is settled at a future date.

(b) IAS 39 requires that derivative financial instruments should be recognised as either financial assets or liabilities. They should be measured at fair value both on initial recognition and subsequently with any gains or losses being taken to the income statement.

(c) **AZG: extract from income statement for year ended 31 March 20X7**

	20X7	20X6
Gain on derivative	$73,891	$68,966

AZG: extract from statement of financial position as at 31 March 20X7

	20X7	20X6
Financial asset	$142,857	$68,966

Workings

1 Feb 20X6	Enter into contract; no value at inception
31 Mar 20X6	Year end rate 2.9
	(6m florins / 2.9) – (6m florins / 3) = $68,966 gain
31 Mar 20X7	Year end rate 2.8
	(6m florins / 2.8) – (6m florins / 3) = $142,857 gain
	Gain in 20X7 = $142,857 – $68,966 = $73,891

16 BGA (NOV 07 EXAM)

Key answer tips

Remember that the '10% corridor' is based on **opening** obligations and assets and opening unrecognised actuarial losses. Interest and the expected return on assets are also calculated on **opening** balances.

(a) **Calculation of actuarial gains or losses on pension scheme assets and liabilities for the year ended 31 October 20X7**

	$
Present value of obligation at 1 Nov 20X6	18,360,000
Current service cost	1,655,000
Benefits paid	(1,860,300)
Interest cost (6.5% x $18,360,000)	1,193,400
Actuarial gain (balancing figure)	(692,600)
Present value of obligation at 31 Oct 20X7	18,655,500

	$
Fair value of scheme assets at 1 Nov 20X6	17,770,000
Contributions paid in	997,000
Benefits paid	(1,860,300)
Expected return on assets (9.4% × 17,770,000)	1,670,380
Actuarial loss (balancing figure)	(159,900)
Fair value of scheme assets at 31 Oct 20X7	18,417,180

(b) **Actuarial gains and losses to be recognised for the year ended 31 October 20X7**

	$
'10% corridor' limits: higher of:	
10% of the PV of scheme obligations at 1 Nov 20X6	1,836,000
10% of the FV of the scheme assets at 1 Nov 20X6	1,777,000
Therefore the corridor limit is	$1,836,000

At 1 November 20X6 net unrecognised actuarial losses are $802,000. This is within the '10% corridor'.

Therefore no actuarial loss is recognised for the year.

17   DG (NOV 09 EXAM)

(a)   **Financial Instrument**

The held for trading investment should be classified as an asset held at fair value through profit or loss.

It is initially measured at fair value, in this case the cost of $1.75 million (500,000 shares x $3.50).   The transaction costs should not be included in the cost of the investment and should be written off to the income statement as an expense.

The investment is subsequently measured (at 30 June 20X9) at fair value of $1.825 million (500,000 shares x $3.65). The following adjustments are therefore required:

Dr Administrative expenses $15,000

      Cr FVPL Investment $15,000

Being the correction in respect of transaction costs

Dr FVPL Investment $75,000

      Cr Gain on investment (IS) $75,000

Being the gain on the investment being credited to the income statement

(b) **Financial Instrument**

The bond purchased by DG should be classified as a held to maturity investment as DB intends to hold it to redemption.

It is initially recorded at the net cost of $4.5 million and then subsequently measured at amortised cost using the effective interest rate. Only the interest received of $250,000 (5% x face value of $5 million) has been recorded in the income statement. The following adjustment is therefore required:

Dr   HTM asset $211,700

     Cr   Investment income $211,700

Being the additional investment income to be recognised in the income statement

Working:

B/fwd	Inv Income – 10.26% (IS)	Cash – 5%	C/fwd
	(effective rate)	*(Coupon rate)*	*(SFP)*
$000	$000	$000	$000
4,500	461.7	(250)	4,711.7

The investment will be held at $4.71 million and a further $211,700 ($461,700 - $250,000) will be credited to the income statement.

18   JK (MAY 10 EXAM)

(a)   The economic substance of the transaction is determined by analysing the risks and benefits of the transaction.

JK had access to the following benefits of ownership:

- Protected from price increases as prices are agreed at the point of delivery.

JK incurred the following costs and was subject to the following risks:

- Incurred the cost of insurance while vehicles were on display in its forecourt;

- Retained risk that price reductions were not passed on since price was agreed at point of delivery;

- SB retained legal title to vehicles so in the event of any dispute SB would probably be entitled to recover its legal property.

Initially therefore it appears that JK may hold the risks and rewards of the inventory. However, the significant risk, obsolescence, must be considered. JK can return the vehicles at any time without penalty and this would indicate that the risk of obsolescence is in fact with SB. As this is seen as the most significant risk, SB should continue to recognise the goods within its inventories.

(b)   SARs are an example of a cash-settled share-based transaction and, in accordance with IFRS 2 Share-based Payments, are initially measured at their fair value at grant date and subsequently re-measured to fair value at each year end. The liability is re-measured and any difference is charged to the income statement as an expense.

In the year to 30 November 20X8:

Eligible employees $(120 - 12 - 15) = 93$

Equivalent cost of SARs = 93 employees x 1,000 rights x FV $15 = $1,395,000

Allocate over 3 year vesting period $1,395,000 / 3 = $465,000 equivalent charge to the income statement in the first year.

In the year to 30 November 20X9:

Eligible employees $(120 - 12 - 8 - 10) = 90$

Equivalent cost of SARs = 90 employees x 1,000 rights x FV $17 = $1,530,000

Cumulative amount to be recognised as a liability = $1,530,000 x 2/3 = $1,020,000

Less amount previously recognised = $1,020,000 – $465,000 = $555,000

The expense will be recorded as:

Dr Income statement $555,000

Cr SoFP – Liability $555,000

Examiner's comments

Both parts of this question were answered very well, with many achieving full marks. This was extremely positive as this question was a test of application of skills – the ability to use technical knowledge and apply to a scenario. Those with lower marks in part (a) were guilty of repeating the question but not specifically relating the points to risk or reward of the parties involved. The most common mistakes in part (b) were not allocating the total liability over the 3 years and taking two-thirds in the second year – and crediting equity rather than liability.

---

19   **LBP (NOV 10 EXAM)**

(a)   **20Y0 equity balance required:**

$(600 - 20 - 25 - 15 - 20) = 520$ employees eligible

Total expected equivalent value = 520 x 500 options x $1.48 = $384,800

$384,800 x 3/4 years = $288,600

Previously recognised to 30 September 20X9:

$(600 - 20 - 25 - 40) = 515$ employees eligible

515 employees x 500 options x $1.48 = $381,100

$381,100 x 2/4 years = $190,550

Amount to be recognised in the income statement in 20Y0

= $98,050 ($288,600 – $190,550)

Recorded in 20Y0 financial statements:

Dr   Income statement – staff costs $98,050

    Cr   Equity – other reserves $98,050

(b) The sales director is incorrect, despite no cash changing hands, the share options are issued in exchange for employees providing services to LBP. Possibly the options have been given as a reward for service provided or in lieu of a pay rise or bonus which would otherwise have been paid in cash. As there is no direct wage cost, we instead must calculate an equivalent cost of receiving staff services and match this with the revenue that the staff helps to generate. We do this by estimating the value inherent in the options and allocating that over the period in which employees must remain with LBP, in this case 4 years.

The amount chargeable to the income statement is based on the fair value of the share options at the grant date. This is not subsequently re-measured as these share options represent an equity-settled share-based payment. The equivalent cost will be updated each year for those employees that are still eligible or expected to be eligible at the year end to ensure that the amount charged reflects the amount that is expected to vest.

Examiner's comments

This question was reasonably well answered. Most made good attempts at the calculations and even those that got a bit muddled on the employee numbers at least displayed an appreciation of the principle of calculating the amount to be recognised to date less the amount to be recognised for 2009. Strangely many calculated the charge for 20X8 which was not required as the total for 20X9 was cumulative. The most common error in part (a) was crediting a liability in the statement of financial position rather than equity.

Part (b) followed a regular F2 style which required explanation of recognition and measurement principles. Candidates are still failing to see that there are two distinct parts to this – many provided good explanations of why an expense should be recognised but few were able to articulate the principles of measurement – even those who had correctly applied it in part (a).

20   BCL (NOV 10 EXAM)

(a) At 31 July 2010 this instrument meets the definition of a derivative:

- Small or no initial investment.
- Its value is dependent on an underlying economic item; exchange rate.
- Its settlement will take place at some future date.

As a derivative it should be accounted for as an "asset or liability held at fair value through profit or loss". The value of the derivative instrument will be the difference between the value of the contract when settled compared with the cost of B$2m being purchased at the spot rate at the year-end date.

Cost of B$2m at a contracted rate of B$0.64 = A$3,125,000

Cost of B$2m at the forward rate of B$0.70 = A$2,857,143

The derivative results in a liability at the year-end date of A$267,857 (A$3,125,000 – A$2,857,143) as the contract has unfavourable terms when compared to the spot rate. The loss on derivative would be charged to the income statement in the year to 31 August 2010.

Recorded as:

Dr   Income statement (loss on derivative)   A$267,857

      Cr   Liabilities – derivatives   A$267,857

(b)   (i)   If the derivative was designated as a hedging instrument in a cash flow hedge then the loss of A$267,857 would be recognised in other comprehensive income until the related cash flow (hedged item) occurred, and shown as a loss in other comprehensive income in the year ended 31 August 2010. This ensures that the movements in the hedged item and the hedging item can be offset in the same accounting period.

(ii)   Statement of total comprehensive income for the year ended 31 August 2010

	A$
Profit for the year	1,000,000
Other comprehensive income:	
Loss on hedging item	(267,857)
Total comprehensive income	732,143

Examiner's comments

The main errors displayed in the answers were recording the B$2 million rather than just recognising the financial instrument which was the derivative; and recognising the gains through reserves in part (a) and then through profit or loss in part (b) – with explanation including reference to recycling, obviously confusing it with treatment of available for sale investments.

Candidates coped with part (b) better by providing reasonable explanations of matching/offsetting, etc and most managed to prepare the extract and were given credit for bringing their own figures forward from part (a).

---

21   JKL (MAR 11 EXAM)

(a)   **Share-based payment**

(i)   **20X7** $(300 - 25 - 40) \times 1,000 \times \$1.22 = \$286,700$ over 3 years = $95,567 charge for 20X7

20X8 $(200 - 25 - 15 - 20) \times 1,000 \times \$1.22 = \$292,800 \times 2/3$ years = $195,200 recognisable to date

Less amount recognised in 20X7 $195,200 – $95,567 = $99,633 charge for 20X8

Charge for 20X8 of $99,633 will be recorded as:

Dr   Income statement – staff costs $99,633

      Cr   Other reserves (equity) $99,633

Being the charge for share-based payment for the year ended 31 December 20X8

(ii)   Share-based payments that are to be settled in cash would be credited instead to liabilities in the statement of financial position and the liability would be re-measured using the fair value of the shares at each year-end date until the end of the vesting period.

(b) **Defined benefit pension plan**

(i) **Statement of financial position**

	$m
PV of plan liability	13.9
FV of plan assets	(13.1)
	0.8
Unrecognised actuarial losses	(0.5)
Net pension liability	0.3

(ii) IAS 19 *Employee benefits* permits actuarial gains or losses to be included in profit or loss (i.e. the income statement) in a way that recognises them faster than the corridor approach. Alternatively, an amendment to IAS 19 now allows the full amount of the gains or losses to be included in other comprehensive income in the year and charged to equity.

22 MNB (MAR 11 EXAM)

(a) (i) The held to maturity investment will be initially recorded at fair value plus transaction costs. It will be subsequently measured at each year-end at amortised cost using the effective interest rate.

(ii) **Held to maturity investment** – amortised cost using effective interest rate of 7.05%.

Year end	Opening balance $	Effective interest 7.05% $	Interest received $	Closing balance $
20X0	3,200,000	225,600	(180,000)	3,245,600

Investment income – Income from HTM investment $225,600

Non-current assets – Held to maturity investment $3,245,600

(b) **Held for trading investment**

Initial recording:

Dr Current asset investment $300,000
Cr Bank $300,000

Being the purchase of shares

Dr Income statement $12,000
Cr Bank $12,000

Being the write off of the transaction costs to the income statement as the investment is an asset held at fair value through profit or loss

Subsequent measurement

Dr Current asset investment $40,000
Cr Income statement – gain $40,000

Being the uplift in value and the recording of the gain in the income statement

23   EAU (MAY 11 EXAM)

(a)   **Calculation of the actuarial gain/losses in year to 31 December 20X8**

	FV of plan assets $000	PV of plan liabilities $000
Opening balance	2,600	2,900
Service cost		450
Interest cost (8% x $2,900,000)		232
Expected return (5% x $2,600,000)	130	
Past service cost		90
Benefits paid	(240)	(240)
Contributions	730	
	3,220	3,432
Actuarial gain on assets	**180**	
Actuarial loss on liabilities		**68**
Closing balance	3,400	3,500

(b)   SARs are an example of a cash-settled share-based transaction and, in accordance with IFRS 2 *Share-based payments*, are initially measured at fair value at the grant date and subsequently re-measured to fair value at each year-end. The liability is re-measured and any difference is charged to the income statement as an expense. (This explanation is not a required part of the answer but is included to aid understanding.)

20X7

Eligible employees (300 – 32 – 35) = 233

Equivalent cost of SARs = 233 employees x 1,000 rights x FV $8 = $1,864,000

Allocate over 3 year vesting period $1,864,000 / 3 = $621,333 equivalent charge to the income statement in the first year.

20X8

Eligible employees (300 – 32 – 28 – 10) = 230

Equivalent cost of SARs = 230 employees x 1,000 rights x FV $12 = $2,760,000

Cumulative amount to be recognised as a liability = $2,760,000 x 2/3 years = $1,840,000

Less amount previously recognised = $1,840,000 – $621,333 = $1,218,667

The expense will be recorded as:

> Dr   Staff costs $1,218,667
>
>   Cr   Liability $1,218,667

Examiner's comments

This question was answered very well with many scoring full marks. Those who lost their way often prepared the income statement calculation for pensions, which was not required, but generally it was evident that they knew how each item affected the assets and liabilities.

The most common mistakes in part (b) were failing to update the FV to $12, and forgetting to take one-third and two-thirds of the total calculated in each year.

---

24   QWE (MAY 11 EXAM)

(a)   **Convertible instrument**

A convertible instrument is considered part liability and part equity. IAS 32 requires that each part is measured separately on initial recognition. The liability element is measured by estimating the present value of the future cash flows from the instrument (interest and potential redemption) using a discount rate equivalent to the market rate of interest for a similar instrument with no conversion terms. The equity element is then the balance, calculated as follows:

	$
PV of the principal amount $10m at 7% redeemable in 5 years	
$10m x 0.713	7,130,000
PV of the interest annuity at 7% for 5 years	
(5% x $10m) x 4.100	2,050,000
	9,180,000
Equity element (balancing figure)	820,000
Total proceeds raised	10,000,000

The equity will not be re-measured, however the liability element will be subsequently re-measured at amortised cost using the effective interest rate of 7%. The total finance cost for the year ended 31 December 20X0 is $642,600 (7% x $9,180,000). The coupon rate of interest of 5% has already been charged to profit or loss in the year so a further $142,600 should be recorded:

Dr   Finance costs $142,600

    Cr   Non-current liability $142,600

(b)   **Preference shares**

The substance of the instrument is a debt instrument. IAS 32 requires that any instrument that contains an obligation to transfer economic benefit be classified as a liability. The cumulative nature of the returns on the preference shares means that the outflow of benefit is inevitable. The preference shares would then be classified as debt and would in fact increase the gearing of the entity.

Examiner's comments (extract)

Candidates have finally taken heed of my comments on how this area will be tested – concentrating on initial recognition and measurement and subsequent measurement. Part (a) was answered exceptionally well. The majority of candidates demonstrated that they grasped the principles of accounting for convertible instrument.

---

25   VB (SEP 11 EXAM)

(a)   **Financial instruments**

(i)   Available for sale (AFS) investment initially recorded at fair value plus transaction costs:

Dr   AFS investment   (40,000 shares x $2.68) $107,200

    Cr   Bank $107,200

Being initial recognition of AFS asset

Dr   AFS investment $5,360

    Cr   Bank $5,360

Being 5% commission paid on purchase

The investment is subsequently measured at the fair value of the shares with the gain or loss calculated as fair value of the investment less its carrying amount. This is a valuation exercise, not a transaction, so there is no need to account for commission when calculating the year end valuation [(40,000 x $2.96) – $112,560].

Dr   AFS investment $5,840

    Cr   Equity – other reserves $5,840

Being subsequent measurement of AFS asset

(ii)   In accordance with IAS 39, all derivative contracts are classified as fair value through profit and loss, therefore any gain or loss in the value of the derivative contract is taken directly to the income statement. Gains or losses on available for sale investments are normally recorded through other comprehensive income. However, as hedge accounting can be applied (because it has been designated as a hedge) then the gain/loss on both the investment (hedged item) and the derivative contract (hedging instrument) can be offset within the income statement. Hedge accounting (for this fair value hedge) ensures that the gain/loss on the AFS investment is taken to profit or loss and matched against the gain/loss on the hedging instrument.

(b)   **Share-based payment**

Year ended 31 July 20X1

(500 – 20 – 50) x 1,000 x $1.30 = $559,000 over 4 years

Charge for the year = $559,000 / 4 = $139,750

Year ended 31 July 20X2

(500 – 20 – 18 – 30) x 1,000 x $1.30 = $561,600

Recognisable to date = $561,000 x 2/4 = $280,800

Charge for year ended 31 July 20X2 = $280,800 – $139,750 = $141,050

Charge for the year ended 31 July 20X2 of $141,050 will be recorded as:

Dr   Income statement – staff costs $141,050

    Cr   Other reserves (equity) $141,050

Being charge for share-based payment for the year ended 31 July 20X2

26   OVS (SEP 11 EXAM)

(a)   Recognition of inventories

The economic substance of the arrangement is determined by analysing which party holds the significant risks and benefits of ownership of the vehicles.

Factors indicating that the risks and benefits of ownership are with OVS:

- OVS is responsible for insuring the vehicles whilst at their premises.

- OVS is able to use the vehicles for demonstration purposes and to move them between sites freely. However, this is slightly mitigated by the fact that there is a mileage limit (see later).

Factors indicating that the risks and benefits of ownership are with GH:

- OVS is free to return any vehicle free of charge within six months. This means that the most significant risk of obsolescence rests with GH.

- GH, by setting a mileage limit, is still effectively in control of the vehicles.

- Legal title remains with GH, hence should a dispute arise GH should be able to recover the vehicles.

OVS does hold some of the risks and rewards of ownership associated with the vehicles, however, the significant risk of obsolescence is held by GH. OVS can return the vehicles at any time without penalty and, as noted above, would indicate that the risk of obsolescence is in face with GH. As this is seen as the most significant risk, GH should continue to recognise the goods within its inventories.

(b)   Historical cost accounting

In times of increasing prices, historical cost accounting shows the following defects:

Revenues are stated at current values but are matched with costs incurred at an earlier date and therefore a reduced price. As a result, reported profits are overstated.

Current values of property, plant and equipment may be significantly higher than the carrying value (depreciated historic cost, if the cost model of IAS 16 is adopted). This will not only affect the statement of financial position but will impact profits via the depreciation charge. The depreciation charge based on the historic cost may be an unrealistic estimate of the consumption of the asset and again being artificially low will result in overstated profits.

Overstatement or understatement of profit can affect performance ratios that OVS is likely to be relying on in its assessment of RT, including return on capital employed, and profitability ratios.

FINANCIAL STATEMENT ANALYSIS

27   JKL

(a)   Basic earnings per share:

$$\frac{2,763,000}{6,945,922} = 39.8c$$

Diluted EPS:

$$\frac{2,858,200}{9,045,922} = 31.6c$$

Workings:

(W1)   Calculate the theoretical ex-rights price after the rights issue

	¢
4 shares × 145¢	580
1 share × 125¢	125
	——
Theoretical value of holding of 5 shares	705
	——
Theoretical ex-rights price of 1 share after rights issue: 705/5	141
	——

(W2)   Calculate bonus fraction

$$\frac{\text{Fair value of one share before rights issue}}{\text{Theoretical ex - rights price of one share (W1)}} = \frac{145}{141}$$

(W3)   Weighted average number of shares in issue in the year to 31 August 20X4

	Number of shares
1 September 20X3 – 1 February 20X4	
6,000,000 × 145/141 × 5/12	2,570,922
1 February 20X4 – 31 August 20X4	
7,500,000 × 7/12	4,375,000
	—————
	6,945,922
	—————

(W4)   Adjustment to earnings for calculation of diluted EPS

	$
Earnings	2,763,000
Add: Interest after tax	
(2,000,000 × 7%) × (1–0.32)	95,200
	—————
Diluted earnings	2,858,200
	—————

(W5) **Adjustment to number of shares for calculation of diluted EPS**

Note: Use the most advantageous (for loan stockholders) conversion rate.

	Number of shares
Weighted average shares in issue in year to 31 August 20X4 (W3)	6,945,922
Add: Dilutive effect 2,000,000/100 × 105	2,100,000
Diluted shares	9,045,922

(b) Much of the information contained in financial statements refers to events that have occurred in the past, and so it is of relatively restricted usefulness in making decisions. Diluted earnings per share, however, can be quite useful to investors and potential investors in that it incorporates some information about likely future events. Where potentially dilutive financial instruments have been issued, it is helpful to investors to be able to appreciate the impact full dilution would have upon the earnings of the business.

However, it should be appreciated that only some elements of the calculation relate to the future. One of the key elements of the calculation, the basic earnings for the period, relates to events that have already taken place and that may not be replicated in the future.

28 CB (MAY 05 EXAM)

Key answer tips

In part (b), remember to explain the significance of CB's P/E ratio, as well as the significance of the P/E ratio in general.

(a) **Earnings per share and price earnings ratio**

Earnings per share $\dfrac{725,000}{3,694,349} = 19.6c$

Price earnings ratio $\dfrac{625}{19.6} = 31.9$

Workings

(W1) **Theoretical ex-rights price and bonus fraction**

	$
4 shares x $7.50	30.00
1 share x 6.50	6.50
5 shares	36.50
Theoretical ex-rights price (36.50/5)	7.30

Bonus fraction: $\dfrac{7.50}{7.30}$

(W2) **Weighted average number of shares in issue for the year ended 31 January 20X5**

		Number
1 February 20X4 – 1 March 20X4	$3,000,000 \times 7.50/7.30 \times 1/12$	256,849
1 March 20X4 – 31 January 20X5	$3,750,000 \times 11/12$	3,437,500
		3,694,349

(b) **Significance of the price earnings ratio**

The price earnings ratio is a measure of how the stock market views the shares of an entity. A relatively high P/E usually suggests that the shares are regarded as a safe investment. Lower P/E suggests risk and volatility. However, it is unsafe to generalise too much. Where a listed entity has become a highly fashionable investment for some reason (for example, technology shares have in the past been regarded in this way from time to time) its high P/E ratio may help to mask a fundamental weakness.

CB's P/E is a little above the sector average indicating that it is probably regarded as a slightly less risky investment within its sector. Its competitor has a substantially higher P/E which, on the face of it, would suggest that it is regarded as a very sound investment, and that its shares are currently preferred by the market compared to those of CB.

29 BAQ (MAY 07 EXAM)

Key answer tips

Remember that group earnings are increased by the subsidiary's **post-acquisition** profits only.

Acquisition of CBR

Projected group earnings per share:

$$\frac{\$4,543,750}{8,150,000} = 55.8¢$$

Projected group earnings for year ended 31 March 20X8:

	$
BAQ	4,200,000
CBR: $(625,000 \times 110\% \times 6/12)$	343,750
	4,543,750

Weighted average number of ordinary shares in issue:

1 April 20X7 – 30 September 20X7 6/12 × 8,000,000	4,000,000
1 October 20X7 – 31 March 20X8 {[¾ × 400,000] + 8,000,000} × 6/12	4,150,000
	8,150,000

Acquisition of DCS

Projected group earnings per share:

$$\frac{\$4,544,000}{8,845,283} = 51.4¢$$

Projected group earnings for year ended 31 March 20X8:

	$
BAQ	4,200,000
DCS: (860,000 × 80% × 6/12)	344,000
	4,544,000

Weighted average number of ordinary shares in issue:

1 April 20X7 – 30 September 20X7 6/12 × 8,000,000 × 5.36/5.30 (W)	4,045,283
1 October 20X7 – 31 March 20X8 6/12 × 8,000,000 × 6/5	4,800,000
	8,845,283

Working

Theoretical ex-rights price

	$
5 × $5.36	26.80
1 × $5.00	5.00
6	31.80
TERP (31.80 / 6)	5.30

Therefore the bonus fraction is 5.36/5.30.

30   AGZ (NOV 08 EXAM)

> **Key answer tips**
>
> Read the question carefully to make sure you calculate both basic and diluted EPS for 20X8 AND comparatives.

(a)   **EPS and diluted EPS**

Year ended 31 August 20X8:

EPS

$$\frac{\text{Profit for the period attributable to ordinary shareholders}}{\text{Weighted average number of shares (W1)}} = \frac{191.4}{1000}$$

$$=19.1\text{c per share}$$

$$\text{Diluted EPS} = \frac{195.7\,(\text{W2})}{1000 + 150\,(\text{W3})} = \frac{195.7}{1150} = 17.0\text{c per share}$$

Year ended 31 August 20X7:

$$\text{EPS} = \frac{182.7}{750 \times 4/3} = \frac{182.7}{1000} = 18.3\text{c per share}$$

$$\text{Diluted EPS} = \frac{187.1\,(\text{W2})}{1000 + 150\,(\text{W3})} = \frac{187.1}{1150} = 16.3\text{c per share}$$

(W1)   **Weighted average number of shares**

750 m x 4/3 = 1,000m

(W2)   **Interest saving on convertible debt**

	20X8	20X7
Profit after tax	191.4	182.7
Interest saved		
6.3 – 2.0	4.3	
6.2 – 1.8		4.4
	195.7	187.1

(W3)   **Potential new shares**

$75m / $100 x 200 shares =   150m

(b)   **Bonus issue**

Bonus shares are issued for no consideration, and so there is no increase in resources associated with them. All other things being equal, no increase in earnings can be expected following a bonus issue; the effect is that the same amount of earnings is divided by a greater number of shares. In order to ensure continuing comparability, the bonus issue is adjusted for as if it had taken place at the beginning of the earliest period presented.

31   EPS (NOV 07 EXAM)

Key answer tips

Look carefully at the requirement; you must explain both general *and* specific limitations.

(a)   **The importance of EPS**

EPS is of particular importance because it is one of the component parts of the Price/Earnings ratio. P/E is used by investors to help them identify the relative riskiness of investments, and investments that are over-valued or under-valued by the stock market. Also, EPS is accorded great importance by investors, analysts and others as a key measurement of performance and as a basis for making decisions. It is principally for these reasons that some accounting standard setters, amongst them the IASB, have produced accounting standards regulating its calculation.

(b)   **Limitations of EPS**

The principal general limitations of EPS include the following:

- EPS is based on accounting figures, and can only be as reliable as those figures. Accounting figures may be subject to manipulation by using creative accounting techniques. Even where no malicious manipulation is intended, the figures are often imprecise because they involve the use of estimation.

- EPS is essentially a backward looking measure because it is based on accounting figures reporting on transactions and events that have already taken place. It is of limited use for predictive purposes, although, perhaps inevitably, it is used as an indicator of future performance.

- EPS, like all other accounting information published in the annual report of a business, is soon out of date. The P/E ratio calculation uses an up to date price figure, but where the price has been affected significantly by events after the reporting date, the mixing of a current price with an old earnings figure may be, essentially, meaningless.

The specific limitations of EPS for the purposes of making comparisons include the following:

- The number of shares in issue is rarely compatible between entities.

- In some instances, accounting standard permit a choice of accounting treatments. It is quite likely, therefore, that entities being compared with each other use different policies and/or bases for preparation of the financial statements. Where such policies and bases impact upon the profit figure, as will usually be the case, EPS figures are not strictly comparable.

- The problem of comparability is made worse where the entities being compared are subject to different sets of accounting standards.

- EPS is calculated on the basis of after tax figures. Where entities are subject to significantly differing rates of tax because they are based in different countries, the comparison is unrealistic.

32   CSA (MAY 10 EXAM)

> **Key answer tips**
>
> Read the question carefully to make sure you calculate both basic and diluted EPS for 20X9 AND comparatives. EPS is regularly examined and a topic that can catch unprepared candidates out. You need to make sure you understand the difference between basic and diluted EPS and the adjustments required when shares have been issued.

(a)   **Basic EPS**

Profit after tax ($1,040,000 – $270,000)		$770,000
Weighted average number of shares:		
At 1 January 20X9	3,000,000	
Bonus issue	1,000,000	
Full market price issue (2,000,000 x 4/12)	666,667	
	————	
	4,666,667	
Basic EPS for 20X9 $770,000 / 4,666,667		16.5 cents per share
Basic EPS for 20X8 restated 15.4 cents x bonus fraction of 3/4		11.6 cents per share

(b)   **Fully diluted EPS**

Reported profit after tax (as in part (a))		$770,000
Plus post-tax saving of finance costs (70% x 7% x $4m)		$196,000
		————
		$966,000
Weighted average number of shares:		
As reported in part (a)	4,666,667	
Dilution from potential share issue	2,400,000	
	————	
	7,066,667	
Fully diluted EPS $966,000 / 7,066,667		13.7 cents per share

(b) **Bonus issue**

A bonus issue does not raise any new finance and therefore the profit for the year will have been generated with the same level of resources throughout the year. As the issue results in no additional resources it is treated as if it had always been in existence. Comparative figures also need to be restated as if the bonus issue was made at the earliest reported period.

The issue at full market price brings additional resources, which will impact on profits from the date of issue. Therefore a weighted average number of shares is used to calculate EPS.

Examiner's comments

This area continues to pose problems for many candidates. Many did not deal correctly with the impact of the bonus issue on basic earnings per share and although most attempted to restate the comparative many applied an incorrect fraction. The diluted calculation was better dealt with – most candidates appreciating the need to revise both the numerator and denominator. The most common mistake in part (b) was time apportioning the 2.4 million shares that would be issued on conversion. The marks for part (c) were awarded for candidates that could articulate why the treatment was different rather than for a description of the accounting treatment that they had just applied.

---

33 LOP (NOV 10 EXAM)

(a) Entity A is considerably smaller than B in terms of revenue and would not impact LOP's revenue to the same extent. However A earns a considerably better gross profit margin at 26% as opposed to 17% for B. A's margin is closer to LOP's and would have a less negative impact. It maybe suggests that A has targeted a similar market to LOP, whereas B has focussed on revenue at the expense of margin – high volume / low margin strategy. Alternatively, it could indicate that the two entities classify costs differently between cost of sales and other operating costs – especially when we consider the difference in net profit margin.

Entity B earns a better net profit at 11% and would have less impact on LOP's net margin. A's figure of 9% appears very low with its GP at 26%. It could be that this is a smaller entity and not able to take advantage of economies of scale, has high fixed costs or has poor cost control. A has high gearing and the related finance costs are also having an impact on net profit.

The gearing of A would have a significant effect on the results of LOP as gearing is at 65% as opposed to B's gearing of 30% and LOP's 38%. However when we consider this together with the available lending rates, it perhaps suggests that the management of A have shrewdly capitalised on low lending rates and funded the entity through external finance. The low gearing of B however, probably gives room to increase borrowing if required in the future.

The P/E ratio is an important ratio for investors and LOP's ratio would be adversely affected by either acquisition. A's P/E ratio is considerably lower than B and LOP but it is difficult to make an assessment of the relevant risk of the entities when they are judged by different markets.

(b) The entities are listed on different exchanges and so may prepare their financial statements using different accounting standards. This will reduce the comparability of financial highlights. The ratios provided tell us nothing about the efficiency of the entities and the fit of management styles could be an important factor in a takeover situation. The entities could apply different accounting policies that could impact on the ratios, e.g. equity could be boosted by a revaluation of non-current assets which would reduce the gearing ratio and could mask an increase in borrowings.

Examiner's comments

Many candidates scored full marks on this question which was very encouraging. Poorer scripts included a lot of chat about the impact being positive or negative but offered no reason for why this may be the case, others wrongly assumed that for all ratios they could simply be added to the acquiring entity's ratio and divided by 2. Part (b) was very well answered and we offered a number of possibilities for valid points on limitations of using basic comparison of ratios in takeover situations.

---

34 FGH (MAR 11 EXAM)

FGH has managed to generate significant cash from operating activities which is a positive sign for any business wishing to be a going concern, particularly since it appears that FGH is expanding. In addition to the inflow of cash from trading, the directors have clearly made some good investment decisions as income of $180,000 has been included in the year and also profit of $50,000 has been earned from the sale of some of these investments.

It does look as if FGH needs to improve working capital as receivables have increased in the year and it looks like the entity has in turn withheld payment to payables with an increase of $550,000. The increase in receivables may be a deliberate attempt to secure new customers by offering them favourable credit terms but it is essential that good working capital management is not compromised. The increase in inventories has probably arisen in order to meet future expected demand from the expansion. It should also be noted that FGH has acquired a subsidiary during the year, although the effect of the subsidiary on the working capital balances will have been adjusted for in the completion of the statement of cash flows.

The expansion is shown in two areas of investment, with the acquisition of a subsidiary and in the purchase of property, plant and equipment. The sale of property, plant and equipment for $70,000 resulted in a loss of $45,000. It's possible that the expansion has resulted in the need for new equipment and hence management have taken the view to sell some of the old equipment whilst there is still a second hand market for it. The sale of investments for $150,000 has probably been undertaken in order to generate funds for the expansion. The only note of caution is that these investments seem to be profitable and hence given that a proportion has been sold during the year, future income from investments will be reduced.

It is clear from the cash flows from financing that FGH appears to have the backing of its shareholders. A share issue has been supported and the shareholders have been rewarded with a significant dividend in the year. . A good sign is that FGH has managed to fund the expansion without increasing the overall gearing of the business, as equal amounts of debt and equity have been raised as new finance. It indicates good stewardship of assets when long term expansion is financed by long term financing. FGH appear to have used a mixture of long term financing and retained earnings generated in the year, together with the sale of some investments to fund the expansion. However, this is not to the detriment of shareholders as they have still received a significant dividend during the year and it's possible that the new investments in a subsidiary and PPE will generate greater returns in the future than the investments which have been sold. In times of expansion, however, a more modest dividend may have negated the need for long term financing and the interest costs associated with it.

35 FGH OPERATING SEGMENTS (MAY 11 EXAM)

(a) IFRS 8 *Operating segments* requires that segmental information be provided by listed entities. Clearly FGH is looking to list and hence IFRS 8 will be applicable. The disclosures required are indeed extensive and should the information need to be compiled from scratch then this is likely to be time-consuming and costly.

However, the essence of IFRS 8 is that the entity should utilise information prepared for internal decision making. Therefore, in accordance with IFRS 8, it is the directors who decide which components of the business are reportable segments and these segments should be the individual parts of the business that the chief operating decision maker reviews in order to make financial and economic decisions. The entity will therefore already have prepared the financial information for these parts of the business for internal management purposes and so the costs of compliance should be minimal.

(b) (i) **Relevance to investors (advantages)**

In accordance with IFRS 8, the operating segment analysis will reflect the information used by the chief operating decision maker of the entity to make economic decisions about the business. Therefore, investors get to view what the decision makers within the entity think is important and also get an idea of how good/bad their decision making is. This will help investors to make investment decisions which are based upon their assessment of and confidence in the management team.

Many listed entities engage in varied activities and operating segment analysis could help explain the breakdown of the business activities and the principal risks affecting performance. This again will help investors to make decisions.

IFRS 8 also requires that entities provide information on major customers and a geographical split of results and resources. Again this information is likely to be relevant to investors as it provides detail which is not evident in the main financial statements.

Since 75% of total reported revenue must be covered by operating segment analysis, the information provided is likely to be highly relevant as it covers the majority of the business.

(ii) **Limitations**

Since it is management that decides on which segments are reported, no two entities will necessarily use the same criteria. Therefore there is a lack of comparability between entities.

There is also a risk that entities will conceal information by the way they define the reportable segments.

Examiner's comments

Part (a) was poorly answered with few candidates realising that the standard is intended to minimise cost and designed to embrace the reporting entity's own management information so the information is already likely to exist. Many candidates ignored the questions and chose to provide an exhaustive list of thresholds and percentages from IFRS 8.

Part (b) (i) was answered well but again in part (ii) candidates failed to answer the specifics of the question, instead listing generic limitations of financial analysis rather than those limitations that were specific to operating segment analysis as a tool for comparing entities.

---

36 BOB (SEP 11 EXAM)

Limitations of same sector comparison

The accounting policies that an entity selects can impact on ratios. For example an entity that revalues PPE will have higher depreciation charges than an entity that doesn't revalue, which will reduce the gross profit margin and lower the ROCE. Although IFRS is committed to reducing the alternative treatments, there is still an element of choice in, for example, measurement of PPE and accounting for joint ventures.

Entities could be operating at different ends of the sector – low price/high volume versus luxury items with high sales prices. This means that their profit margins are not likely to be comparable.

Many entities are classified as being in the same sector but some might have a range of activities within the business e.g. supermarkets now operate in food, retail clothing, and financial services – and are likely to have quite different margins.

The size of the entity could impact the margins. Larger entities may be benefiting from economies of scale which will improve profit margins.

The classification of costs such as depreciation between cost of sales and administrative costs could impact gross profit margins.

Business decisions like whether to lease PPE under operating or finance leases may reduce the comparability of two similar entities. The capital element of a finance lease would be included in the capital employed in the business, therefore reducing the ROCE, whereas an entity that leases equipment using operating lease will only have an expense included in the profit or loss but nothing in the SOFP.

The age of the business could impact on the P/E ratio, which is often an indication of how risky the market feels the entity is. A new entity with a minimum track record may have a lower P/E ratio than an established entity, regardless of the fact their activities and other ratios are similar.

P/E ratios are also often impacted by factors outside of the control of the entity e.g. factors influencing the market generally or macro-economic factors such as interest rate changes. This may reduce comparability as some entities will be impacted more than others.

Limitations of international comparisons

Preparing financial statements using different accounting standards is likely to have an impact on the financial ratios. Different measurement rules for major elements like PPE, inventories and provisions are likely to impact on profit margins and ROCE. In addition, differences in the tax regimes that entities are subject to would affect the comparison of the profit margin.

The entities being compared may also be operating in different economic environments with different cultural pressures – minimum wage, quotas or local taxes on goods shipped in or out of the country. This will affect the margins and in turn may reduce the ROCE.

Entities being compared may be listed on stock markets with quite different levels of liquidity. A small more illiquid market may have lower share prices as there is less activity in the market. This will in turn affect the P/E ratio reducing comparability between it and an entity listed on another market.

DEVELOPMENTS IN EXTERNAL REPORTING

37 MNO (MAY 06 EXAM)

> **Key answer tips**
>
> The answer below is comprehensive and you would not be expected to come up with this level of content in the exam. Remember, you're looking for 10 marks worth. The important thing is to cover all parts of the requirement.

Briefing Paper to the Directors of MNO

The Operating and Financial Review

Many international entities are choosing to expand the scope of their reporting in the form of an Operating and Financial Review (OFR). There is no formal regulatory requirement to publish such a review, although IAS 1 *Presentation of Financial Statements* encourages entities to present a financial review by management that would ideally cover some of the areas that are commonly covered by the OFR. Any such publication, however, would constitute a set of voluntary disclosures.

The principal source of guidance on the purpose and content of an OFR is the UK Accounting Standards Board (ASB) Reporting Statement of Best Practice which was issued in January 2006. However, this statement has no international application, except as a source of general guidance.

Internationally, the IASB have recently (December 2010) published their own practice statement on the international equivalent of the OFR, "Management Commentary".

The purpose of the OFR is to assist users, principally investors, in making a forward-looking assessment of the performance of the business by setting out management's analysis and discussion of the principal factors underlying the entity's performance and financial position.

Typically, an OFR would comprise some or all of the following:

- Description of the business and its objectives;

- Management's strategy for achieving the objectives;

- Review of operations;

- Commentary on the strengths and resources of the business;

- Commentary about such issues as human capital, research and development activities;

- Development of new products and services;

- Financial review with discussion of treasury management, cash inflows and outflows and current liquidity levels.

The publication of such a statement would have the following advantages for MNO:

- It could be helpful in promoting the entity as progressive and as eager to communicate as fully as possible with investors;

- It could be a genuinely helpful medium of communicating the entity's plans and management's outlook on the future;

- If the IASB were to introduce a compulsory requirement for management commentary by listed entities, MNO would already have established the necessary reporting systems and practices.

However, there could be some drawbacks:

- If an OFR is to be genuinely helpful to investors, it will require a considerable input of senior management time. This could be costly, and it may be that the benefits of publishing an OFR would not outweigh the costs;

- There is a risk in publishing this type of statement that investors will read it in preference to the financial statements, and that they may therefore fail to read or miss important information.

38 ENVIRONMENTAL DISCLOSURES (NOV 07 EXAM)

Key answer tips

The requirement says 'identify and explain' so the examiner is probably not expecting ten points for ten marks. You do, however, need to go into detail on at least some of them. Try to think of arguments against disclosure from the perspective of both users and preparers of the information.

Arguments against voluntary disclosures by businesses in respect of their environmental policies, impacts and practices might include the following principal points:

- The traditional view of the corporation is that it exists solely to increase shareholder wealth. In this view business executives have no responsibility to broaden the scope or nature of their reporting as doing so reduces returns to shareholders (because there is a cost associated with additional reporting).

- From a public policy perspective, if governments wish corporations and similar entities to bear the responsibility for their environmental impacts, they should legislate accordingly. In the absence of such legislation, however, businesses bear no responsibility for environmental impacts, and in consequence there is no reporting responsibility either.

- Voluntary disclosures of any type are of limited usefulness because they are not readily comparable with those of other entities. Therefore, it is likely that the costs of producing such disclosures outweigh the benefits to stakeholders.

- The audit of voluntary disclosures is not regulated. Even where such disclosures are audited, the scope of the audit may be relatively limited, and moreover, its scope may not be clearly laid out in the voluntary report. Voluntary reports are not necessarily, therefore, reliable from a stakeholder's point of view.

- Especially where voluntary disclosures are included as part of the annual report package, there is a risk of information overload: stakeholders are less able to identify in a very lengthy report the information that is relevant and useful to them.

- Voluntary disclosures by business organisations, because they are at best lightly regulated, may be treated by the organisation in a cynical fashion as public relations opportunities. The view of the business's activities could very well be biased, but it would be quite difficult for most stakeholders to detect such bias.

It is questionable whether voluntary disclosures about environmental policies, impacts and practices would meet the qualitative characteristics of useful information set out in the IASB's Framework. The key characteristics are: understandability, reliability, relevance and comparability. Voluntary environmental disclosures might well fail to meet any of these characteristics and, if this is the case, it is highly questionable whether or not they merit publication.

39 INTELLECTUAL ASSETS (NOV 08 EXAM)

> **Key answer tips**
>
> Try to consider this from a real life perspective. What advantages do you think would arise for your firm if they could recognize your own training as an asset on their statement of financial position? Why is this not likely to be possible within IFRS?

(a)   The recognition of intangible assets, and of intellectual capital assets in particular, has been much discussed in recent years. The traditional business model involving exploitation of physical assets in the form of tangible non-current assets and inventory is no longer so prevalent. For many service businesses, the most significant category of "asset" relates to the skills and talents of the people who work for them. If accounting regulation and practice permitted the recognition of such assets as part of the business statement of financial position, there could be some positive effects.

Under current accounting practice, the statements of financial position of many types of business recognise few intangible assets. Recognition of a wider range of assets would provide a more realistic view of the productive capacity of the business, which could be helpful to many categories of stakeholder. For example, existing and potential investors would find it easier to relate the flow of revenue to the "assets" that had produced it, thus improving understanding of the nature of the business and its ability to generate positive income streams.

A related point is that realistic analysis of financial statements would be much easier where a greater range of assets was recognised. Under current IFRS many of the standard accounting ratios make little sense because the recognised asset base is so low. Accounting ratios such as asset turnover, return on assets and return on capital employed are essentially meaningless in businesses that rely principally on intellectual capital assets. With full recognition of intellectual assets, comparisons between the productivity of different types of business would become more realistic.

From the point of view of the employee stakeholder group, recognition of intellectual assets would increase the prominence of the value they add to the organisation. Instead of being viewed as a cost to be borne by the business, the amounts incurred in remunerating and training employees could be seen as an investment by the business. If a formal valuation process were adopted in respect of individuals their status and prospects could be improved.

(b)   The principal problems relating to the recognition of intellectual assets are as follows:

- Intellectual assets such as know-how and skills do not usually fall into the *Framework* definition of as asset ("a resource controlled by the entity as a result of past events and from which future economic benefits are expected to flow to the entity").

- The problem is one of control: skills are in the possession of the individual employee who has the option to cease working for the entity and to take his or her skills elsewhere. Where resources cannot be controlled their value to the entity is questionable.

- Realistic measurement of intellectual assets presents a challenge that may well be insuperable in practice. Although some guidance is provided by market salary rates from which a capital value could in theory be extrapolated, any such values would necessarily be vague and imprecise. The difficulties in reaching realistic values would rule out valid inter-firm comparability.

- Finally, because of the problems of arriving at consistent and robust measurement techniques, there would be scope for creative accounting by the unscrupulous.

40   IASB AND FASB (MAY 08 EXAM)

Key answer tips

The convergence between IFRS and US GAAP is a topic the examiner is keen to focus upon as it is an extremely important current issue. The verb "describe" was used in the requirement so comprehension of the key features and progress that has been made was being sought. Only four differences were asked for in part (b) so don't expect more marks if you list out more differences.

(a)   In September 2002, FASB and IASB agreed to undertake a project with the objective of converging international standards and US GAAP, thus reducing the number of differences between the two sets of conventions. The 2002 agreement (the "Norwalk agreement") committed the two parties to making their existing standards fully compatible as soon as practicable, and to co-ordinating their future work programs. To date, the Boards have undertaken a short-term project to address, and where possible, remove some of the differences between standards. The longer term issues have been tackled by undertaking work jointly on the development of new standards.

A memorandum of understanding between FASB and IASB sets out a "Roadmap" of convergence between IFRS and US GAAP. This was aimed at removing the need for entities having prepared their financial statements using IFRS to prepare reconciliation to US GAAP in order to be listed on a US exchange. The requirement for the reconciliation has now been removed, ahead of the scheduled date and both parties announced their continued commitment to the process in 2009.

The convergence project has produced several tangible results, including the following:

- IFRS 5 *Non-Current Assets Held for Sale and Discontinued Operations*;
- IFRS 3 (revised) *Business Combinations*;
- IFRS 8 *Operating Segments*;
- The revision of IAS 1 Presentation of financial statements, and an agreement on common wording to be used in accounting standards.

(b) Many differences between US GAAP and IFRS continue to exist. Examples include:

- The general approach to IFRS is principles-based; whereas US GAAP follows a more prescriptive rules-based approach.

- Inventory cost: IFRS prohibits the use of the LIFO method of valuation, whereas it is permitted by US GAAP.

- Accounting for investments in joint ventures: IFRS permits the use of either proportionate consolidation (the preferred method) or the equity method. US GAAP permits only the equity method.

- Development costs: IFRS requires that development costs be capitalised, provided that a set of conditions are met. US GAAP stipulates that development costs must be written off when incurred.

NB: There are other relevant differences that would also earn marks.

41   CONVERGENCE PROJECT (MAY 10 EXAM)

Key answer tips

The convergence between IFRS and US GAAP is the biggest development in international reporting and so we can expect it to be tested time and again. The examiner is looking for an awareness of new standards that have been written as a direct result of the convergence project – you must be able to give examples.

Report on convergence project to date

The US has traditionally adopted a rules based approach to financial reporting standard setting, whereas the IASB's financial reporting standards are principles based. The US has, in light of a number of major corporate scandals, now accepted that a principles-based reporting framework is more appropriate to current corporate reporting needs.

In September 2002, the US standard setter, Financial Accounting Standards Board (FASB) and the IASB agreed to undertake a project to converge their accounting practices and aimed to reduce the number of differences between US GAAP and IFRS. The agreement, known as the Norwalk agreement, committed the two parties to making their existing standards fully compatible as soon as practicable, and to co-ordinate their future work programs to avoid future differences in approach. A short term project was undertaken to remove some of the differences between existing standards in order to achieve the first objective of the Norwalk agreement. In order, to meet the second, the two bodies have collaborated on the development of new and revised standards, and continue to do so.

A memorandum of understanding between FASB and IASB sets out a "Roadmap" of convergence between IFRS and US GAAP. This was aimed at removing the need for entities having prepared their financial statements using IFRS to prepare reconciliation to US GAAP in order to be listed on a US exchange. The requirement for the reconciliation has now been removed, ahead of the scheduled date and both parties announced their continued commitment to the process in 2009.

Projects undertaken jointly between FASB and IASB have produced the following:

- The issue of IFRS 5 Non-current assets held for sale and discontinued operations;

- IFRS 8 Operating segments;

- The revision of IAS 1 Presentation of financial statements, and an agreement on common wording to be used in accounting standards;

- The revision of IFRS 3 Business combinations.

There are a number of ongoing, longer term projects including the revising of the accounting framework set out in the Framework for the preparation and presentation of financial statements, income taxes and revenue recognition.

Examiner's comments (extract)

It was truly astonishing how unprepared many candidates were for this question. Section D of the syllabus carries a syllabus weighting of 10% and therefore will account for approximately 10% of the exam.

Prepared candidates sailed through this, many scoring full marks. The others stumbled through the question often highlighting the areas that were not yet converged – the complete opposite from the question being asked. The question style and topic could not have been a surprise so I can only conclude that candidates' had simply not studied the material.

---

42 STAFF RESOURCE (NOV 10 EXAM)

It is true that company financial statements will often include narrative information about staff as a key resource. However, under accounting regulation this resource is not shown as an asset in the statement of financial position for a number of reasons which are discussed below.

Narrative Reporting

Entities that depend on human resources to generate revenue often will have a relatively low level of capital investment. This often makes the statement of financial position look under capitalised and it is difficult to see where the value of the entity lies. Common ratios targeting efficiency and financial position, like return on capital employed and return on assets will not provide us with useful measures as the key assets of the business are not reflected in the financial statements.

For successful companies the gap between market capitalisation and book value of net assets can be considerable and it is therefore important for entities to inform the market of key personnel resource, processes or intellectual capital.

Recognition Issues

The recognition of assets requires certain criteria to be met; an asset must be "a resource controlled by an entity as a result of a past event and from which future economic benefit is expected to flow". This asset must then be capable of being reliably measured in order to be recognised in the statement of financial position.

Human resources are expected to generate future economic benefit for the entity, however the resource is one that cannot be controlled. Staff members are free to leave at any time taking their skills and intellectual capital with them.

Notwithstanding the issue of control, there are also a number of issues concerning the measurement of a staff resource as an asset. The cost of staff is their training costs and remuneration. It could be argued that training costs have an on-going benefit and therefore could be capitalised, however, remuneration relates to a service provided by the staff in that year and therefore should be taken to the income statement as a period cost. It is possible to value assets on a fair value basis, however, for staff this would involve establishing future cash flows and discounting to present value. It is difficult to see how this could be achieved on a reliable basis due to the estimation required.

Staff resource therefore fails the recognition criteria for an asset and cannot be included in the statement of financial position.

There has been a marked increase in the volume of narrative reporting as entities look to find a suitable manner in which to inform investors about internally generated intangibles such as trained staff, processes and key customers. These are not recognised in the financial statements but are essential to the future success of the entity and are likely to generate future revenue. This information is therefore needed to help users make informed investment decisions.

Examiner's comments

This question was answered very well. Almost all candidates were able to state the recognition criteria for an asset and the structure of many answers was excellent. The majority of candidates correctly identified why human capital failed the recognition criteria and concluded that it could not be included in the statement of financial position. Other valid points, other than those noted above in the outline marking guide, were well-made and given credit.

---

43   HUMAN CAPITAL (MAR 11 EXAM)

(a)   **Analysis of financial statements of service and knowledge-based industries**

Entities operating in service and knowledge-based industries are often heavily reliant upon intellectual capital for revenue generation. Intellectual capital can be defined as "knowledge which can be used to create value" and includes human resources, intellectual assets and intellectual property. For many entities operating in service and knowledge-based industries the most important element of their intellectual capital will be the collective experience, knowledge and skills of their staff.

Entities that depend on their staff and other intellectual capital to generate revenue will often have a relatively low level of physical assets. This makes the statement of financial position look under-capitalised and it is difficult to see where the value of the entity lies. Common ratios targeting efficiency and financial position, like return on capital employed and return on assets will not provide investors with useful measures as the key assets of the business are not reflected in the financial statements.

For successful entities the gap between market capitalisation and book value of net assets can be considerable and it is therefore important for entities to inform the market of key personnel resource, processes or intellectual capital.

Key members of staff are likely to be the resource that helps the business generate future revenue but without any information on the resource itself it will be difficult for potential investors to estimate the future revenue generating ability of the business.

(b) **Recognition issues**

The recognition of assets requires certain criteria to be met; an asset must be "a resource controlled by an entity as a result of a past event and from which future economic benefit is expected to flow". This asset must then be capable of being reliably measured in order to be recognised in the statement of financial position.

Human resources (staff) are expected to generate future economic benefit for the entity, however the resource is one that cannot be controlled. Staff members are free to leave at any time taking their skills and intellectual capital with them.

Notwithstanding the issue of control, there are also a number of issues concerning the measurement of a staff resource as an asset. The cost of staff is their training costs and remuneration. It could be argued that training costs have an on-going benefit and therefore could be capitalised, however, remuneration relates to a service provided by the staff in that year and therefore should be taken to the income statement as a period cost. It is possible to value assets on a fair value basis, however, for staff this would involve establishing future cash flows and discounting to present value. It is difficult to see how this could be achieved on a reliable basis due to the estimation required.

Staff resource therefore fails the recognition criteria for an asset and cannot be included in the statement of financial position.

44 BNM (MAY 11 EXAM)

(a) **Potential advantages to BNM**

Narrative reporting will enable BNM to provide information about social, economic and environmental policies. Many users are influenced by an entity's policies regarding, for example, fair trade and equal opportunities and the inclusion of a narrative report on BNM progress in these areas could have a positive influence on current and potential investors.

Narrative reporting could help BNM highlight to investors the entity's reliance on the knowledge and skill of its staff. The IFRSs prohibit the recognition of human capital – but this is BNM's main revenue generating resource. Traditional analysis (ratios) of performance and efficiency are not relevant and users will need to rely on other information – information that BNM could provide in narrative reports.

Similarly the specific processes, the key customer relationships and order books are likely to influence the users' assessment of future performance and BNM has the ability to share this information with investors in a narrative report which would otherwise be absent from the financial statements because these "assets" fail the recognition criteria.

The UK's operating and financial review is a recommended addition to the financial statements and the IASB is currently developing its "Management Commentary" which is likely to help formalise the recommended content and structure of narrative reports included in financial statements.

(b)   **Drawbacks of voluntary disclosures**

The absence of formal guidance on the content and structure of voluntary disclosures results in a lack of comparability between entities.

The nature of voluntary disclosures means that entities are free to choose which policies and practices to disclose and this may result in entities using the disclosures as a PR opportunity by reporting on only the positive aspects.

Voluntary information may not be audited and therefore may not be reliable. This may reduce the usefulness of the information to users.

Additional disclosures will incur time and therefore cost and any additional expense reduces the future returns available to shareholders.

Examiner's comments

Part (a) was not answered particularly well with candidates answering this as a question on the recognition issues of human capital. Candidates must attempt to stay relevant to the questions, especially on the narrative questions for syllabus sections C and D. The core subject area tested may be the same but the focus of the question most definitely will not – sometimes from the viewpoint of entities, sometimes from investors, advantages or disadvantages, etc. Candidates must answer the question asked.

Part (b) was more knowledge-based and as a result was well attempted.

---

45   SRT (SEP 11 EXAM)

(a)   Pressures to extend financial reporting to include voluntary disclosures on environmental policies, impacts and practices.

The overall objective of financial statements is to provide information to users that is useful in helping them make economic decisions. This is particularly important for existing and potential investors who need to make decisions about whether or not to invest in the entity. However, financial statements are by their nature backward-looking, based primarily on historical information and are therefore limited in their usefulness for decision-making. This has led to general pressure by the markets and investors for entities to provide additional information to that contained in the financial statements. Disclosures on matters such as human and intellectual capital and environmental issues are increasingly being provided on a voluntary basis.

Many investors nowadays have sophisticated needs when it comes to assessing their investments. Whilst financial returns are very important, many investors want to invest in and support entities that have good social and environmental practices and are considered to be good corporate citizens. Financial statements do not traditionally provide the necessary information for such investors to assess entities' social and environmental policies.

There has also been a marked interest generally over the last 10 to 20 years in the environment, with numerous pressure groups pushing for greater corporate responsibility on environmental issues. The activities of corporate entities often have a direct impact on the environment and investors want to know details of that impact and the policies that entities are adopting to address it if required.

These issues are among the most common that have resulted in increasing pressures for financial reporting to be extended and for voluntary narrative disclosures to be encouraged.

(b) **Advantages and disadvantages to SRT**

If SRT were to provide environmental disclosures, there would clearly be a benefit to investors in terms of the additional information, which ultimately should help to keep the share price stable or indeed improve it. The advantages and disadvantages to SRT of providing such disclosures centre around the impact on investors and the share price.

There is no IAS or detailed guidance giving SRT the freedom to interpret what to include in such a report. The downside of this is that it is likely to be judged by investors by what its competitors are producing – if their reports are more comprehensive there may be pressure on SRT to provide more information or some investors may think by omitting disclosures that SRT has something to hide and hence the share price could fall.

The report could be used to promote any particularly positive policies or practices that SRT has developed or adopted. This may attract new investors to the entity who are particularly interested in good environmental practices. Also if SRT has a good track record on limiting environmental impact then it would be good for its reputation. The potential drawback would be if there was something negative to report in the future as there would be pressure to maintain the level of detail contained in the voluntary disclosures.

The information provided will have a cost of production and once it is produced it will be expected by users in the future, although there will be no additional costs of regulation as these statements are not audited.

Section 4

ANSWERS TO SECTION B-TYPE QUESTIONS

GROUP FINANCIAL STATEMENTS

46   AC, BD AND CF (MAY 09 EXAM)

(a)   The initial investment made by AC in BD should be accounted for as an acquisition of a subsidiary as the 70% stake allows AC to exercise control over the financial and operating policies of BD. In the year ended 31 December 20X8 a further 20% stake was purchased taking AC's ownership to 90% and reducing the NCI's holding to 10%. This is reflected as a transfer between owners (from the NCI to AC's shareholders).

The difference between the cost of the additional investment and the reduction in non-controlling interests is transferred to other equity as a gain or loss.

The 40% investment in CF gives AC significant influence over the operating and financial policies of CF, making it an associate. CF will be included in the group accounts using equity accounting.

The remaining investment is an available for sale investment, as per IAS 39, which will be held at fair value at the statement of financial position date with any gains or losses on valuation being taken to reserves and being shown within other comprehensive income.

(b)   **Consolidated statement of financial position for AC group at 31 December 20X8**

	$000	$000
Assets		
Non-current assets		
Property, plant and equipment (25,700 + 28,000)	53,700 ✓	
Available for sale investments	2,600 ✓	
Goodwill (W3)	1,200 ✓	
Investment in associate (W6)	8,140 ✓	
	―――――	
		65,640
Current assets (17,000 + 14,000)		31,000 ✓
		―――――
		96,640 ✓
		―――――

Equity and liabilities
Equity attributable to the parent

Share capital ($1 ordinary shares)	30,000
Revaluation reserve (W8)	3,400
Other reserves (W9)	140
Retained earnings (W5)	27,100
	60,640
Non-controlling interest (W4)	3,000
	63,640
Total equity	63,640
Non-current liabilities (6,000 + 4,000)	10,000
Current liabilities (15,000 + 8,000)	23,000
	96,640

Workings

(W1) **Group structure**

14m/ 20m =	70%	1.3.X3
	20%	1.7.X8 (6 mths)

AC

40%
1.2.X5

BD   CF

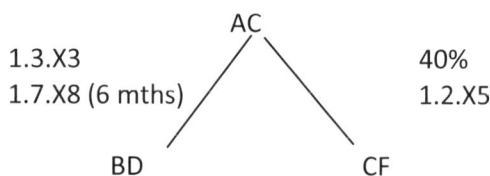

(W2) **Net assets of subsidiary**

In BD	Acquisition 1.3.X3 $000	Acquisition 1.7.X8 $000	Reporting date 31.12.X8 $000
Share capital	20,000	20,000	20,000
Revaluation reserve	1,000	1,000	1,000
Retained earnings	3,000		9,000
9,000 – (6/12 x 1,600)		8,200	
	24,000	29,200	30,000

(W3) **Goodwill in BD**

	$000
Parent's investment	18,000
Value of NCI at acquisition	
30% x 24,000 (W2)	7,200
Net assets at acquisition	(24,000)
Goodwill at acquisition and reporting date	1,200

(W4) **Non-controlling interest**

		$000
Value at acquisition (W3)		7,200
Share of post-acquisition reserves to date of transfer		
30% x (29,200 – 24,000) (W2)		1,560
		8,760
Transferred to AC on 1.7.X8		
20/30 x 8,760		(5,840)
Share of post-acquisition reserves after transfer		
10% x (30,000 – 29,200) (W2)		80
		3,000

(W5) **Retained earnings**

		$000
AC		22,000
PUP (W7)		(40)
Share of post acquisition profits of BD		
70% x (29,200 – 24,000) (W2)		3,640
90% x (30,000 – 29,200) (W2)		720
Share of post acquisition profits of ~~BD~~ *CF*		
40% x (9,000 – 6,000) \ Date of Acq/		1,200
Impairment of investment in CF		(420)
Y/E		
		27,100

(W6) **Investment in associate**

		$000
Cost of investment		7,000
Share of post acquisition reserves		
1,200 (W5) + 400 (W8) ↖ group share of revaluation (post Acq)		1,600
Less: PUP (W7)		(40)
Less: impairment ↖ impairment in CF		(420)
		8,140

(W7) **PUP**

		$000
Inventory at year end	800 x 50%	400
Profit in inventory	400 x 25%	100
Associate share	100 x 40%	40

(W8) Revaluation reserve

	$000
AC	3,000
Share of post acquisition change in revaluation reserve of CF 40% x 1,000	400
	3,400

(W9) Other reserves

	$000
AC	1,000
Gain on available for sale investments 2.6m – 2.3m (W11)	300
Loss on transfer (W10)	(1,160)
	140

(W10) Step acquisition

	$000
Cash paid	(7,000)
Transfer from NCI (W4)	5,840
Loss on transfer	(1,160)

(W11) Cost of available for sale investment

	$000
Total investments	34,300
Less:	
Investment in BD on 1.3.X3	(18,000)
Investment in BD on 1.7.X8	(7,000)
Investment in CF on 1.2.X5	(7,000)
	2,300

47   AT (MAY 07 EXAM)

> **Key answer tips**
>
> Start by drawing up the group structure: a subsidiary (to be consolidated); a joint venture (to be proportionately consolidated) and an associate (to be equity accounted). The acquisition of a further 5% of BU during the year does not change its status (it was a subsidiary throughout the year), but it does affect the non-controlling interest calculation.

Consolidated income statement for the year ended 31 March 20X7

	$000
Revenue (W2)	3,783
Cost of sales (W3)	(2,800)
	———
Gross profit	983
Distribution costs (94 + 22 + (1/3 × 77))	(141.7)
Administrative expenses (280 + 165 + (1/3 × 120) − 12)	(473)
Interest received	2
Loss on investment in financial asset (W4)	(4.2)
Finance costs (26 + 92.2 (W5))	(118.2)
Share of profit of associate (35% × 79 × 3/12)	6.9
	———
Profit before tax	254.8
Income tax expense (40 + 50 + (1/3 × 12))	(94)
	———
Profit for the period	160.8
	———
Attributable to:	
Equity holders of the parent (β)	141.1
Non-controlling interest (11.4 + 8.3) (W6)	19.7
	———
	160.8
	———

Workings

(W1) **Group structure**

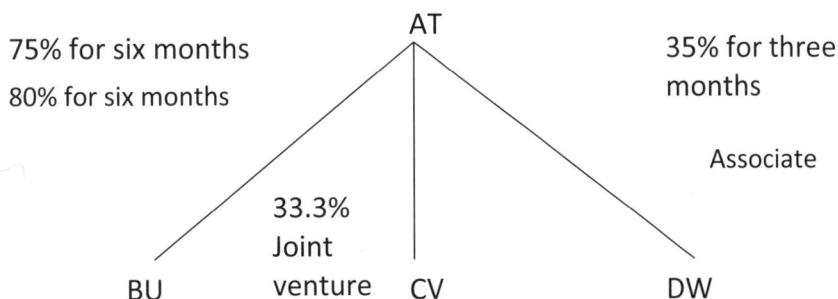

(W2) **Revenue**

	$000
AT	2,450
BU	1,200
CV ($^1/_3 \times 675$)	225
	3,875
Less: Intra-group sales	(80)
Less: Admin services supplied to BU	(12)
	3,783

(W3) **Cost of sales**

	$000
AT	1,862
BU	870
CV ($^1/_3 \times 432$)	144
	2,876
Less: Intra-group sales	(80)
Add: provision for unrealised profit	4
(80k $\times 25\% \times 20\%$)	
	2,800

(W4) **Loss on investment in financial asset**

	$000
Cost of investment (4,000 × 1332c)	53.3
Fair value at 31 March 20X7 (4,000 × 1227c)	(49.1)
	4.2

(W5) **Finance costs**

Y/e 31 March	Opening bal	Effective interest @ 9%	Interest charge 5% x $1m	Closing bal
	$000	$000	$000	$000
2005	950.0	85.5	(50)	985.5
2006	985.5	88.7	(50)	1,024.2
2007	1,024.2	92.2		

(W6) **Non-controlling interest (BU)**

	6 months to 30 September 2006 $000	6 months to 31 March 2007 $000
Adjusted profit for the period (95 – 4)	45.5	45.5
Loss on financial asset		(4.2)
	45.5	41.3
NCI share (25% / 20%)	11.4	8.3

48 PURPLE

Consolidated statement of financial position at 30 September 20X6

		$000
Non-current assets		
Goodwill	(W3) (1,719+1,794)	3,513
Tangible assets	(23,410+6,640+5,900+1,000 (W2))	36,950
Investments	(15,420+10,200+1,000–11,000–10,200–3,000)	2,420
Investment in Associate	(W8)	3,406.5
Current assets		
Inventory	(14,975+7,560+3,870–805 (W7))	25,600
Receivables	(12,680+6,350+3,275–3,950)	18,355
Bank	(6,925+4,465+2,230+300 in transit)	13,920
		104,164.5
Equity		
Share capital		30,000
Retained earnings	(W5)	26,695.5
Equity attributable to parent		56,695.5
NCI	(W4)	11,664
Total equity		68,359.5
Non-current liabilities	(10,000+5,000+1,500)	16,500
Current liabilities		
Payables	(9,640+5,800+2,835–2,150-1,500)	14,625
Taxation	(2,450+1,490+740)	4,680
		104,164.5

Workings

(W1) **Group structure**

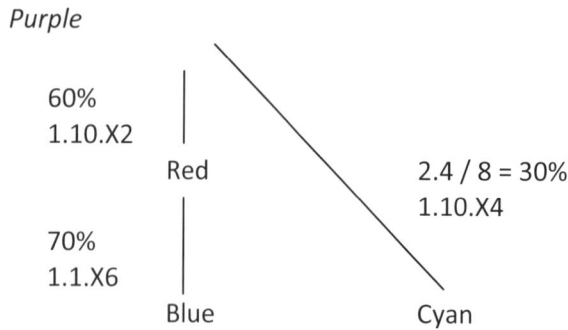

Purple

60%
1.10.X2

Red   2.4 / 8 = 30%
             1.10.X4

70%
1.1.X6

Blue   Cyan

Red will be consolidated as a 60% sub from 1.10.X2

Blue will be consolidated as a 42% (60% x 70%) sub from 1.1.X6 (mid year acquisition).

Cyan is an associate from 1.10.X4.

(W2) **Net assets of subsidiaries**

Red

	Acquisition date	*Reporting date*
Share capital	10,000	10,000
Retained earnings	3,750	12,925
FV – land	1,000	1,000
FV – inventory (2,400–2,000)	400	–
PUP (W7)		(805)
	15,150	23,120

Blue

	Acquisition date		*Reporting date*
Share capital	5,000		5,000
Retained earnings	5,300	(W6)	6,200
	10,300		11,200

(W3) **Goodwill**

	Red $000	Blue $000
Parent's investment	11,000	10,200
Less: IHA (40% x 10,200)		(4,080)
		6,120
Value of NCI at acquisition		
40% x 15,150 (W2)	6,060	
58% x 10,300 (W2)		5,974
Less net assets at acquisition	(15,150)	(10,300)
	1,910	1,794
Impairment (10% x 1,910)	(191)	–
	1,719	1,794

(W4) **Non-controlling interests**

	$000	$000
Red:		
Value at acquisition (W3)	6,060	
Share of post acquisition reserves		
40% x (23,120–15,150) (W2)	3,188	
IHA (W3)	(4,080)	
		5,168
Blue:		
Value at acquisition (W3)	5,974	
Share of post acquisition reserves		
58% x (11,200–10,300) (W2)	522	
		6,496
		11,664

(W5) **Retained earnings**

Purple	21,320
Red (60% x (23,120–15,150))	4,782
Blue (42% x (11,200–10,300))	378
Cyan (30% x (2,465–1,110))	406.5
Impairment (W3)	(191)
	26,695.5

(W6) **Blue's retained earnings at acquisition**

	$000
Retained earnings @ 30.9.X6	6,200
Profit 1.1.X6 to 30.9.X6	
9/12 x $1,200,000	(900)
Retained earnings @ 1.1.X6	5,300

(W7) **PUP**

20/120 x (3,600 + 1,230) = $805k

Reduce inventory and retained earnings of Red in (W2).

(W8) **Investment in associate**

	$000
Cost of investment	3,000
Share of post acquisition reserves	
30% x (2,465 – 1,110)	406.5
	3,406.5

49 AX (NOV 07 EXAM)

Key answer tips

Notice that part (a) asks you to discuss the reasons why the calculation is done in the way that it is; it may help to think about the definition of liabilities and the definition of equity in the *Framework*. In part (b), notice that the disposal takes the ownership percentage from 80% to 60% so control is retained. As such there is no gain or loss on disposal, just a reclassification between parent shareholders' equity and non-controlling interests.

(a) The convertible bond issue is a compound or hybrid financial instrument, according to IAS 32 *Financial Instruments: Presentation*. It is a "hybrid" in the sense that it contains both a liability and an equity element. The liability embodies the issuer's obligation to pay interest and to redeem the bond. The equity element comprises the bond holder's right to claim a share of the issuer's equity. The appropriate accounting treatment is to determine the fair value of the liability element and to recognise this as part of liabilities. The residual difference between the proceeds of the instrument and the fair value of the liability portion should be recognised as part of equity.

The IASB Framework includes "substance over form" as an important characteristic of financial statements. The required treatment of compound financial instruments follows this approach. The form of the convertible bond is that of a liability, but in substance the instrument contains elements of both debt and equity, and both should be recognised. Another important characteristic is "faithful representation" and the IASB argues that the required accounting treatment in IAS 32 of this type of financial instrument is a more faithful representation.

(b) **AX Group Consolidated statement of financial position at 31 October 20X7**

	$000
Assets	
Non-current assets	
Property, plant and equipment	
(20,000 + 8,900 + 5,000 + 500 (W2) − 250 (W2))	34,150
Goodwill (2,250 + 2,500) (W3)	4,750
	38,900
Current assets (34,500 + 9,500 + 4,700)	48,700
	87,600
Equity and liabilities	
Equity	
Called-up share capital	20,000
Other reserves (W7)	1,828
Retained earnings (W5)	21,650
Equity attributable to equity holders of the parent	43,478
Non-controlling interests (W4)	5,150
	48,628
Non-current liabilities (2,400 + 1,000 + 9,472) (W7)	12,872
Current liabilities (18,000 + 5,000 + 2,700 + 400)	26,100
	87,600

Workings

(W1) **Group structure**

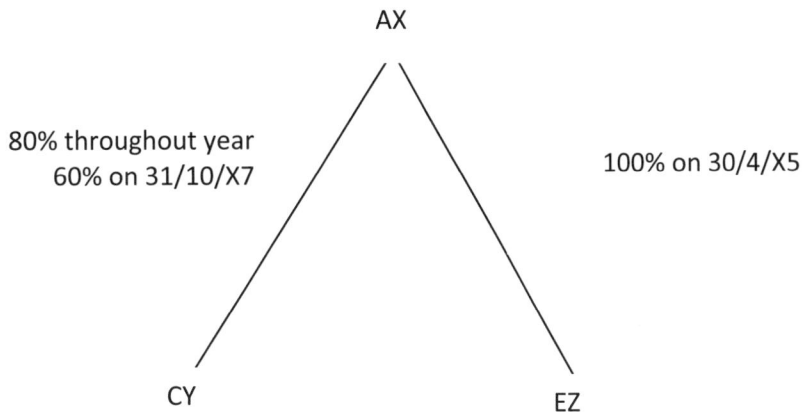

AX

80% throughout year
60% on 31/10/X7

100% on 30/4/X5

CY

EZ

(W2) **Net assets**

	CY		EZ	
	Acquisition	31/10/X7 (transfer)	Acquisition	31/10/X7
	$000	$000	$000	$000
Share capital	4,000	4,000	3,000	3,000
Retained earnings	3,500	7,000	1,500	3,000
Fair value adjustment:				
Plant and equipment			500	500
Additional depreciation (30/60)				(250)
	7,500	11,000	5,000	6,250

(W3) **Goodwill**

	CY $000	EZ $000
Parent's investment	8,000	7,500
Fair value of NCI at acquisition	1,750	–
Fair value of net assets acquired	(7,500)	(5,000)
Goodwill at acquisition and y/e	2,250	2,500

(W4) **Non-controlling interests (CY)**

	$000
Value at acquisition	1,750
Share of post acquisition reserves 20% × (11,000–7,500) (W2)	700
Transfer from parent	
(11,000 (W2) + 2,500 (W3)) x 20%	2,700
	5,150

(W5) **Consolidated retained earnings**

	$000
AX	18,000
Tax on disposal of shares	(400)
	17,600
CY: (80% × (11,000 – 7,500)) (W2)	2,800
EZ: (100% × (6,250 – 5,000)) (W2)	1,250
	21,650

(W6) **Other reserves**

	$000
Convertible bonds – equity element (W7)	528
Proceeds	4,000
Transfer to NCI (W4)	(2,700)
	1,828

(W7) **Convertible bonds**

	$000
Interest:	
Year ended 31/10/20X8 (10m × 5% × 0.935)	467.5
Year ended 31/10/20X9 (10m × 5% × 0.873)	436.5
Year ended 31/10/20Y0 (10m × 5% × 0.816)	408
Principal (10m × 0.816)	8,160
Liability	9,472
Equity (balance)	528
Issue proceeds	10,000

50 AZ (MAY 06 EXAM)

(a) **Profit or loss on disposal after tax**

(i) **In AZ's own financial statements**

	$000
Sale proceeds	1,250
Less: cost of investment (1/3* × 2,730)	(910)
Profit before tax	340
Tax at 30%	(102)
Profit after tax	238

*520/2,600 = 20% holding sold = 1/3 of original 60% holding.

(ii)   **In the group consolidated financial statements**

	$000
Sale proceeds	1,250
Fair value of retained interest	2,000
	3,250
Less: carrying value of subsidiary disposed of:	
Net assets at disposal date (W2)	(4,655)
Unimpaired goodwill (W3)	(730)
NCI at disposal date (W8)	2,202
Gain/ loss to the group	67
Tax on parent gain	(102)
Post tax loss to the group	(35)

(b)   **Consolidated reserves at 31 March 20X6**

	$000
AZ	10,750
Profit on disposal (from part a)	67
Tax on profit	(102)
	10,715
BY 80% × (5,640 – 4,250) (W2)	1,112
CX 60% × (4,655 – 3,900) (W2)	453
CX (Assoc) 40% × (2,140 – 2,055 (W5))	34
	12,314

(c)   **Consolidated statement of financial position at 31 March 20X6**

	$000	$000
Assets		
Non-current assets:		
Property, plant and equipment (10,750 + 5,830)	16,580	
Goodwill (W3)	310	
Investment in associate (W6)	2,034	
Other investments (W7)	860	
		19,784
Current assets:		
Inventories (2,030 + 1,210 – 30) (W2)	3,210	
Trade receivables (2,380 + 1,300)	3,680	
Cash (1,380 + 50)	1,430	
		8,320
		28,104

Equity and liabilities

Equity:

Share capital	8,000	
Reserves (part (b))	12,314	
		20,314
Non-controlling interest (W4)		1,778
		22,092
Current liabilities:		
Trade payables (3,770 + 1,550)	5,320	
Income tax (420 + 170 + 102 (part (a)))	692	
		6,012
		28,104

Workings

(W1) **Group structure**

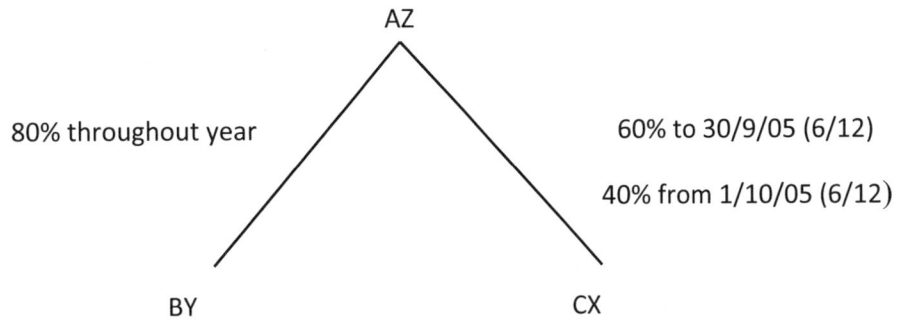

	AZ	
80% throughout year		60% to 30/9/05 (6/12)
		40% from 1/10/05 (6/12)
BY		CX

(W2) **Net assets of subsidiaries**

	BY		CX	
	At Acquisition	*Reporting date*	*At acquisition*	*Disposal date*
	$000	$000	$000	$000
Equity shares	2,300	2,300	2,600	2,600
Reserves	1,950	3,370	1,300	2,055 (W5)
PUP (20/120 × 180)		(30)		
	4,250	5,640	3,900	4,655
Preferred shares	1,000	1,000		

(W3) **Goodwill**

	BY $000	CX $000
Parent's investment	3,660	2,730
Fair value of NCI	900	1,900
Less: net assets at acquisition (W2)	(4,250)	(3,900)
Goodwill at acquisition and y/e / disposal	310	730

No goodwill arises on the preferred shares as they were purchased at par.

(W4) **Non-controlling interest (BY only)**

	$000
Value at acquisition	900
Share of post acquisition reserves 20% x (5,640 – 4,250) (W2)	278
NCI share of preferred shares (60% × 1,000)	600
	1,778

(W5) **Reserves of CX at date of disposal**

	$000
At 1 April 20X5	1,970
Six months to 30 September 20X5 ((2,140 – 1,970) × 6/12)	85
	2,055

(W6) **Investment in associate**

	$000
Fair value of retained interest	2,000
Share of profits since disposal date 40% x (2,140 – 2,055 (W5))	34
	2,034

(W7) **Other investments**

	$000
Per AZ statement of financial position	7,650
BY equity shares	(3,660)
BY preference shares (40% × 1,000)	(400)
CX	(2,730)
	860

(W8) **NCI in CX at disposal date**

	$000
Value at acquisition	1,900
Share of post acquisition reserves 40% x (4,655 – 3,900) (W2)	302
	2,202

51   AJ (MAY 05 EXAM)

(a)   AJ owns 80% of the shares in BK, which points to the existence of a parent/ subsidiary relationship. Provided that AJ controls the activities of BK (and there is nothing to suggest that it does not have control) AJ will account for its investment in BK as a subsidiary and will prepare consolidated financial statements, using the acquisition method.

AJ acquired 40% of the shares in CL. An investment of 40% in another entity would normally indicate that the investor has a significant influence over (but not control of) the entity's activities. The fact that AJ has the power to appoint one director to the board tends to support this conclusion. Also, the fact that three other investors hold most of the remainder of the shares makes it unlikely that another investor in CL would be able to control the entity's activities. AJ will account for CL as an associate using the equity accounting method.

(b)   **AJ Group consolidated statement of financial position at 31 March 20X5**

		$000
Assets		
Non-current assets		
Property, plant and equipment (12,500 + 4,700 + 195 (W2))		17,395
Goodwill (W3)		2,344
Investment in associate (W6)		4,560
Other financial assets (W7)		4,100
		———
		28,399
Current assets	$000	
Inventories (7,200 + 8,000 − 200 (W2))	15,000	
Trade receivables (6,300 + 4,300)	10,600	
Cash	800	
	———	
		26,400
		———
		54,799
		———

Equity and liabilities

Equity

Share capital	10,000	
Reserves (W5)	13,391	

Equity attributable to equity holders of the parent		23,391
Non-controlling interests (W4)		1,608
		24,999
Non-current liabilities: Loan notes (10,000 + 3,000 – 2,000)		11,000

Current liabilities

Trade payables (8,900 + 6,700)	15,600	
Tax liabilities (1,300 + 100)	1,400	
Short term borrowings (600 + 1,200)	1,800	
		18,800
		54,799

Workings

(W1) **Group structure**

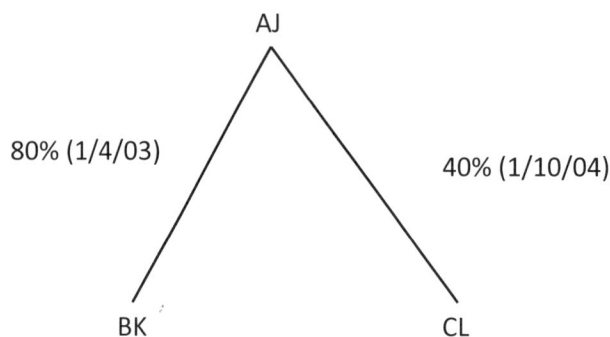

(W2) **Net assets of subsidiary**

	Acquisition	Reporting date
	$000	$000
Share capital	5,000	5,000
Reserves	1,500	1,000
Fair value adjustment (1,115 – 920)	195	195
Provision for unrealised profit (25/125 x 1,000)		(200)
	6,695	5,995

(W3) Goodwill (BK)

	$000
Parent's investment	7,500
Fair value of non-controlling interest	1,800
Less: net assets at acquisition (W2)	(6,695)
	2,605
Impairment loss (10% x 2,605)	(261)
	2,344
... reporting date	

...nterests

	$000
...n	1,800
...isition reserves 20% x (5,995 – 6,695) (W2)	(140)
...irment 20% x 261 (W3)	(52)
	1,608

...es

	$000
	14,000
...695) (W2)	(560)
...900)	160
...ment 80% x 261	(209)
	13,391

... associate

	$000
Cost of investment	4,400
Share of post-acquisition profit (40% × (4,300– 3,900))	160
	4,560

(W7) Other financial assets

	$000
Investments	18,000
Less:	
BK (shares)	(7,500)
BK (loan notes)	(2,000)
CL	(4,400)
	4,100

52   EAG (MAY 08 EXAM)

> **Key answer tips**
>
> The best approach for statements of cash flow is to lay out your proforma with the usual headings and line items. Work your way down the income statement and statement of financial position dealing with items using T accounts where possible. The examiner asks for **full workings** so you can gain marks easily.

EAG Group: Consolidated statement of cash flows for the year ended 30 April 20X8

	$m	$m
Cash flows from operating activities		
Profit before tax	2,604.2	
Adjustments for:		
Depreciation	2,024.7	
Impairment of goodwill (1,865.3 – 1,662.7)	202.6	
Amortisation of intangibles (25% x 372.4)	93.1	
Profit on disposal of associate	(3.4)	
Share of profit of associate	(1.6)	
Finance cost	510.9	
	———	
Operating profit before working capital changes	5,430.5	
Increase in inventories (5,217 – 4,881)	(336.0)	
Decrease in receivables (4,633.6 – 4,670)	36.4	
Increase in trade payables (5,579.3 – 5,356.3)	223.0	
	———	
Cash generated from operations		5,353.9
Interest paid (W5)		(390.0)
Income taxes paid (W3)		(831.0)
		———
Net cash from operating activities		4,132.9
Cash flows from investing activities		
Payments to purchase intangibles (W4)	(27.2)	
Payments to purchase property, plant and equipment (W1)	(4,917.0)	
Proceeds from sale of associate	18.0	
Dividend received from associate (W2)	0.8	
	———	
Net cash used in investing activities		(4,925.4)
Cash flows from financing activities		
Proceeds from issue of share capital (4,300 – 3,600)	700.0	
Dividend paid to non-controlling interests (W6)	(88.0)	
	———	
Net cash from financing activities		612.0
		———
Net decrease in cash and cash equivalents		(180.5)
Cash and cash equivalents at beginning of period (88.3 – 507.7)		(419.4)
		———
Cash and cash equivalents at end of period (62.5 – 662.4)		(599.9)
		———

Workings

(W1)   **Property, plant & equipment**

	$m		$m
Balance b/f	19,332.8		
		Depreciation	2,024.7
Additions (bal. fig.)	**4,917.0**	Balance c/f	22,225.1
	24,249.8		24,249.8

(W2)   **Investment in associate**

	$m		$m
Balance b/f	13.8	Disposal (below)	14.6
Share of profit to disposal	1.6	**Dividend (bal. fig.)**	**0.8**
		Balance c/f	0
	15.4		15.4

	$m
Disposal proceeds	18.0
Investment in associate (β)	(14.6)
Profit on disposal (in I/S)	3.4

(W3)   **Income tax**

	$m		$m
		Balance b/f	884.7
Cash paid (bal. fig.)	**831.0**	Income statement	723.9
Balance c/f	777.6		
	1,608.6		1,608.6

(W4)   **Intangible assets**

	$m		$m
Balance b/f	372.4		
Purchase of patent (Bal. fig.)	**27.2**	Amortisation (25% x 372.4)	93.1
		Balance c/f	306.5
	399.6		399.6

(W5) **Interest paid**

Finance cost in the income statement comprises of interest on both short and long term borrowings.

	$m
Total finance cost	510.9
Less: interest on long-term borrowings – below	(420.9)
Interest on short term borrowings	90.0

Total cash outflow = 90 + 300 (below) = 390

Year ended	Balance b/f	Effective interest at 7%	Interest paid at 5%	Balance c/f
30/4/07	5,900.0	413.0	(300.0)	6,013.0
30/4/08	6,013.0	**420.9**	**(300.0)**	6,133.9

(W6) **Dividends payable to non-controlling interest**

	$m			$m
		Balance b/f		1,870.5
Cash paid (balancing figure)	**88.0**	Income statement		228.0
Balance c/d	2,010.5			
	2,098.5			2,098.5

53 DX AND EY (NOV 08 EXAM)

Key answer tips

Part (a) should be simple to address as it is testing comprehension so you may have more time to tackle the rest of the question. Remember to lay out your workings clearly to enable the marker to give you credit where possible. Make sure you attempt the statement of changes in equity as there are many marks available to pick up, even if you don't finish it.

(a) An entity's functional currency is the currency of the primary economic environment in which it operates. Entities need to consider the following factors in determining their functional currency:

- Which currency primarily influences selling prices for goods and services?
- Which country's competitive forces and regulations principally determine the selling prices of the entity's goods and services?
- In which currency are funds for financial activities (debt and equity instruments) generated?
- In which currency are receipts from operations generally kept?
- Which currency influences labour, material and other costs of providing goods or services?

(b) (i) **Consolidated statement of comprehensive income for the year ended 31 October 20X8**

	DX	EY @ ave rate 2.6	Consol
	$	$	$
Revenue	3,600,000	461,538	4,061,538
Cost of sales, other expenses and income tax	(2,800,000)	(384,615)	(3,184,615)
Net profit	800,000	76,923	876,923
Other comprehensive income			
Forex loss on translation of EY (W2)			(99,467)
Total comprehensive income			777,456
Attributable to:			
Parent shareholders (100% owned)			777,456

(ii) **Consolidated statement of financial position at 31 October 20X8**

	$
PPE (5,000,000 + (1,500,000 @ 2.7))	5,555,556
Current assets (4,400,000 + (2,000,000 @ 2.7))	5,140,741
	10,696,297
Share capital	1,000,000
Group retained earnings (W1)	5,429,630
Current liabilities (3,600,000 + (1,800,000 @ 2.7))	4,266,667
	10,696,297

(c) **Consolidated statement of changes in equity for year ended 31 October 20X8**

	Parent shareholders $
Balance b/f (W3)	5,852,174
Total comprehensive income	777,456
Dividends	(200,000)
Balance c/f	6,429,630

Workings

(W1) **Group reserves**

	$	$
DX		4,825,000
EY (100% x (1,650,000 @ 2.7))		611,111
Exchange difference on parent's investment:		
At closing rate: 25,000 x 2 / 2.7	18,519	
At acquisition rate	(25,000)	
		(6,481)
		5,429,630

(W2) **Calculation of group exchange difference**

			$	$
Opening net assets	Franc 1.5m	@2.70 (closing rate)	555,556	
	Franc 1.5m	@2.30 (opening rate)	652,174	
		Loss		(96,618)
EY's PAT	Franc 200k	@2.70 (closing rate)	74,074	
	Franc 200k	@2.60 (average rate)	76,923	
		loss		(2,849)
Total exchange difference				(99,467)

(W3) **Equity attributable to parent shareholders brought forward**

	$	$
DX equity b/f		5,225,000
Exchange difference on parent's investment		
At opening rate: 25,000 x 2 / 2.3	21,739	
At acquisition rate	(25,000)	
		(3,261)
EY post acq retained earnings b/f		
(Franc 1. 5m equity − 50k share capital) / 2.3		630,435
		5,852,174

54   AD, BE AND CF (NOV 06 EXAM)

(a)   The non-current financial asset falls into the category of loans and receivables, and, according to the Standard, should be accounted for using the amortised cost method. The effective interest rate inherent in the financial instrument is used to calculate the annual amount of interest receivables, which is credited to the income statement. If an annual amount of interest is receivable, this is credited to the financial asset (with the related debit to cash or receivable).

The current financial asset in this case falls into the category of "held-for-trading" and should be accounted for at fair value through profit and loss account. Where securities are actively traded, the statement of financial position amount (at fair value) is likely to differ from the amount at which the asset was originally recognized. Fair value differences are debited or credited to profit or loss, and appear in the income statement.

(b)   **Consolidated statement of financial position at 30 June 20X6**

	$000	$000
Assets		
Non-current assets		
Property, plant and equipment (1,900 + 680)		2,580
Goodwill (W3)		430
Investment in associate (W6)		110.8
Financial assets (W7)		1,062.4
		4,183.2
Current assets		
Inventories (223 + 127)	350	
Trade receivables (204 + 93 – 5)	292	
Other financial asset (W8)	26.8	
Cash (72 + 28 + 5)	105	
		773.8
		4,957
Equity and liabilities		
Equity		
Share capital		1,000
Retained earnings (W5)		2,555.2
		3,555.2
Non-controlling interest (W4)		242.8
Non-current liabilities		600
Current liabilities		
Trade payables (247 + 113)	360	
Income tax (137 + 62)	199	
		559
		4,957

Workings

(W1) **Group structure**

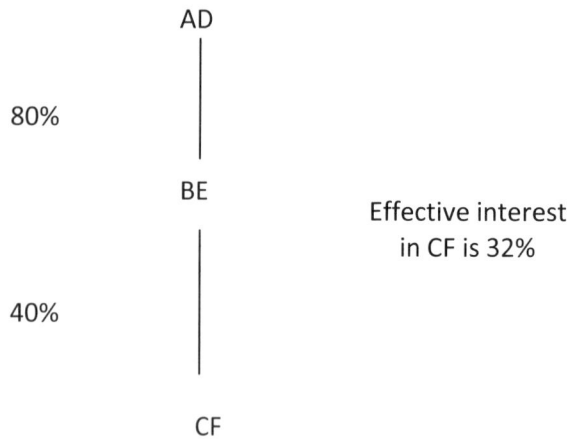

AD

80%

BE

Effective interest
in CF is 32%

40%

CF

(W2) **Net assets of BE**

	Acquisition	Reporting date
	$000	$000
Share capital	300	300
Retained earnings	350	557
PUP (40% x 30% x 10)	–	(1.2)
	650	855.8

(W3) **Goodwill in BE**

	$000
Parent's investment	880
Fair value of NCI	200
Less fair value of net assets at acquisition (W2)	(650)
Goodwill at acquisition and y/e	430

(W4) **Non-controlling interest**

	$000
Value at acquisition	200
Share of post-acquisition reserves 20% x (855.8 – 650) (W2)	41.2
Share of investment in Associate post-acq reserves 20% x 40% x (122 – 102)	1.6
	242.8

(W5) **Retained earnings**

	$000
AD per question	2,300.0
Investment income (debenture) (W7)	82.4
Gain on re-measurement (shares) (W8)	1.8
BE (80% x (855.8 – 650) (W2))	164.6
CF (80% x 40% x (122 – 102))	6.4
	2,555.2

(W6) **Investment in associate**

	$000
Cost of investment	104
Share of post-acquisition reserves	
40% x (122 – 102)	8
Less: PUP (W2)	(1.2)
	110.8

(W7) **Non-current financial asset**

Year ended 30 June	Opening balance	Interest at 8%	Cash received	Closing balance
	$000	$000	$000	$000
20X5	1,000	80	(50)	1,030
20X6	1,030	82.4	(50)	1,062.4

The 82.4 should be added to the asset and to AD's retained earnings figure.

(W8) **Current financial asset**

	$000
FV at acquisition (6.25 x 4,000)	25
FV at year end (6.70 x 4,000)	26.8
Gain on re-measurement	1.8

55 SOT, PB AND UV (MAY 10 EXAM) 👣 *Walk in the footsteps of a top tutor*

Key answer tips

This question tests the disposal of a subsidiary where control is lost. You need to remember to pro-rate the subsidiary's results and consolidate up until the date of disposal. Also learn the profit on disposal calculation.

Tutor's top tips:

The requirement asks for a consolidated statement of comprehensive income so draw up your consolidation schedule on one sheet of paper with the key headings and then start on another piece of paper with your workings. Remember to leave lots of space so you can add in any additional line items, for example in this question you need to leave space for the "share of profit of associate".

When planning the question, read the scenario actively for example annotate the question with details of the adjustment e.g. PUP, FV dep'n. Also try to add notes of where you will need to show this in the SOCI e.g. CoS, Admin. This should help set you up with a clear order to progress through the question.

Consolidated statement of comprehensive income for the SOT group the year ended 30 September 20X9

	$000
Revenue (6,720 + (5/12 x 6,240) + (9/12 x 5,280))	13,280
Cost of Sales (3,600 + (5/12 x 3,360) + (9/12 x 2,880))	(7,160)
	6,120
Admin Expenses (760 + (5/12 x 740) + (9/12 x 650) + 10(W1) + 23(W2) − 40(W5))	(1,549)
Distribution costs (800 + (5/12 x 700) + (9/12 x 550))	(1,505)
Gain on disposal of investment in UV (W3)	163
Finance Costs (360 + (5/12 x 240) + (9/12 x 216))	(622)
Share of profit of associate (35% x 684 x 3/12)	60
Profit before tax	2,667
Income tax expense (400 + (5/12 x 360) + (9/12 x 300))	(775)
Profit for the year	1,892

Other comprehensive income:

Actuarial gains on defined benefit pension plan (110 + (9/12 x 40))	140
Tax effect of other comprehensive income (30 + (9/12 x 15))	(41)
Recognised gains on AFS investments	46
Recycling of previously recognised gains on AFS investment	(40)
Share of other comprehensive income of associates, net of tax (35% x 25 x 3/12)	2
	___
Other comprehensive income for the year, net of tax	107
	___
Total comprehensive income for the year	1,999
	___

Profit for the year attributable to:

Equity holders of the parent (1,892 – 196)	1,696
Non-controlling interest (W6)	196
	___
	1,892
	___

Total comprehensive income attributable to:

Equity holders of the parent (1,999 – 201)	1,798
Non-controlling interest (W6)	201
	___
	1,999
	___

Tutor's top tips:

There is lots to do in this question but don't forget to leave time for the straight forward marks. Adding across the revenue, cost of sales, distribution and tax cost is a straight forward part of the question.

Leave time to make the split of attributable profit. The examiner is looking for you to understand the principals of this so don't worry if you haven't finished other parts of the question – follow through marks will be awarded so long as you use the right method.

Workings

(W1) **Fair value adjustments**

	$000
Increase in value at acquisition date	960
Remaining useful life from acquisition date	40 years
Annual charge	24
Charge from date of acquisition ($24,000 x 5/12) charged to admin expenses	10

(W2) **Goodwill impairment**

	$000	$000
Consideration transferred		2,800
Non-controlling interest at proportionate share (20% x 3,210)		642
Net assets at acquisition:		
Share capital	200	
Reserves	2,050	
Fair value uplift	960	
		(3,210)
Goodwill		232
10% impairment to be charged to administrative expenses		23

(W3) **Gain on disposal of UV**

	$000	$000
Fair value of consideration received		960
Plus fair value of 35,000 shares retained		792
Less share of fair value of consolidated carrying values of the subsidiary at date control is lost:		
Share capital (75% x $100,000)	75	
Reserves (1,300 + (9/12 x 709)) x 75%	1,374	
Unimpaired goodwill (W4)	140	
		(1,589)
Gain on sale		163

Tutor's top tips:

Learn the above pro-forma for profit on disposal of a subsidiary. Remember though that a profit is only recognised where control is lost.

See end of the solution for an alternative way to calculate this gain on disposal, using the standard SFP workings.

(W4) **Goodwill on acquisition of UV**

	$000	$000
Fair value of consideration transferred		980
Non-controlling interest at proportionate share of net assets (25% x 1,120,000)		280
		1,260
Net assets at acquisition:		
Share capital	100	
Reserves	1,020	
		(1,120)
Goodwill		140

(W5) Recycling of previously recognised gains of $40,000 from reserves to administrative expenses, recorded as:

Dr Reserves

Cr Administrative expenses

Examiner's comments (extract)

The other technical area that was covered, other than the consolidation, was the treatment of the disposal of available for sale investment. Many candidates clearly knew there was an issue of recycling of a previous gain but were unsure of how this should be presented in the SOCI. Many took the 50 gain back out of profit for the year and into OCI.

Tutor's top tips:

In recent years it has been common for financial assets (IAS 39) to be tested within the consolidation question. Notice there is no lengthy calculation involved in this adjustment, if you memorise the rules then some easy exam marks can be picked up.

(W6) **Non-controlling interests**

	Profit for the year	Total comprehensive income
	$000	$000
As per PB accounts	840	840
Additional depreciation on FV	(24)	(24)
	816	816
20% NCI x 5/12	68	68
As per UV accounts	684	709
25% NCI x 9/12	128	133
Total NCI in PFY (68 + 128)	**196**	
Total NCI in TCI (68 + 133)		**201**

Examiner's comments (extract)

Some candidates made a good attempt at calculating the NCI share of profit for the year and of total comprehensive income. These candidates were clearly prepared for the format of the allocations in accordance with IAS 1. The most common errors in this section were to take NCI % of the overall group profit and TCI, also preparing an allocation of OCI rather than TCI. There were, however many answers submitted where there was nothing beyond Profit for the year – these candidates lost out on a huge section of the available marks – remember that a core part of group income statements is the split of profits – so this is of course where significant marks were allocated.

Tutor's top tips:

To help with the calculation of the gain on disposal in W3, the standard SFP workings can be used to calculate the consolidated carrying value of the subsidiary at the disposal date as set out below.

Gain on disposal of UV using standard SFP workings

	$000	$000
Fair value of consideration received		960
Plus fair value of 35,000 shares retained		792
Less share of fair value of consolidated carrying values of the subsidiary at date control is lost:		
Net assets (W7)	1,932	
Goodwill (W4)	140	
NCI (W8)	(483)	
	———	(1,589)
		———
Gain on sale		163
		———

(W7) **Net assets of UV**

	Acquisition $000	Disposal $000
Share capital	100	100
Reserves	1,020	
At 1 Oct 20X8		1,300
From 1 Oct 20X8 to 1 July 20X9		
9/12 x 709		532
	———	———
	1,120	1,932
	———	———

(W8) **NCI of UV at disposal**

	$000
Value at acquisition (W4)	280
Share of post acquisition reserves	
25% x (1,932 – 1,120) (W7)	203
	———
	483
	———

56   ROB (NOV 10 EXAM)

(a)   **Treatment of PER**

IFRS 3 Business combinations requires goodwill on acquisition to be calculated at the date control is gained. The second acquisition gives ROB a 75% holding and therefore control over PER. The simple investment of 15% will be derecognised and the 75% holding will be fully consolidated as a subsidiary in the group financial statements. The goodwill will be calculated as the cost of the 60% acquired in the year plus the fair value of the previously held interest of 15%, compared with the fair value of the net assets at the date of acquisition, 1 April 20X2.

(b)   **Consolidated statement of financial position for the ROB Group as at 30 September 20X2**

All workings in $000	ROB
ASSETS	**$000**
Non-current assets	
Property, plant and equipment (22,000 + 5,000)	27,000
Goodwill (W1)	405
	27,405
Current assets	
Inventories (6,200 + 800 – 40 (W2))	6,960
Receivables (6,600 + 1,900)	8,500
Cash and cash equivalents (1,200 + 300)	1,500
	16,960
Total assets	44,365
EQUITY AND LIABILITIES	
Equity	
Share capital ($1 equity shares)	20,000
Retained earnings (W3)	8,629
Other components of equity (W6)	–
	28,629
Non-controlling interest (W4)	1,604
Total equity	30,233
Non-current liabilities	
5% Bonds 20X5 (W5)	4,032
Current liabilities (8,100 + 2,000)	10,100
Total liabilities	14,132
Total equity and liabilities	44,365

Workings:

(W1) **Goodwill**

	$000	$000
Consideration transferred for the 60%		2,900
Fair value of 15% holding at 1 April 20X2		800
Fair value of non-controlling interest		1,250
		4,950
Net assets acquired:		
Share capital	1,000	
Retained earnings (5,000 – 1,500)	3,500	(4,500)
		450
Impaired by 10%		(45)
Net value of goodwill		405

(W2) **Unrealised profit on inventories**

	$000
Sales from PER to ROB	400
50% in inventories	200
Profit margin 20% – adjust inventories and retained earnings of PER	40

(W3) **Retained earnings**

	ROB	PER
	$000	$000
As at 30 September 20X2	7,500	5,000
Pre-acquisition (5,000 – (3,000 x 6/12))		(3,500)
Less unrealised profit of PER (W2)		(40)
		1,460
Group share 75%	1,095	
Group share of impairment (75% x 45)	(34)	
Additional finance costs on bonds (W5)	(132)	
Group profit on derecognition of AFS Investment – gain to date of deemed disposal 1 April 20X2 (800 – 600)	200	
Consolidated retained reserves	8,629	

(W4) **Non-controlling interest**

	$000
Fair value at 1 April 20X2	1,250
Plus 25% adjusted post-acquisition reserves 1,460 (W3)	365
Less NCI share of goodwill impairment (25% x 45)	(11)
NCI at 30 September 20X2	1,604

(W5) **Bonds – amortised cost**

	$000	$000	$000	$000
	Opening value	Effective rate 8.5%	Interest paid 5% x $4m	Value at 30 September
To 30 September 20X2	3,900	332	(200)	4,032

The difference of $132,000 must be added to the value of the bond liability and deducted from ROB's retained earnings.

(W6) **Other reserves and AFS investment**

IFRS 3 requires that the 15% simple investment be derecognised and on derecognition any gain/loss would be considered realised. The gain of $200,000 (FV of $800,000 at date of derecognition less the investment cost of $600,000) represents the group gain and will be included in the consolidated reserves.

The balance on other reserves again relates to the treatment of the investment in the parent's own accounts and the gains on the AFS investment (PER) and not relevant for the group accounts – as the PER has been fully consolidated.

Examiner's comments

It was encouraging to see that a number of candidates scored full marks for goodwill, NCI and the subsequent measurement of bonds. Many candidates lost out on the follow through marks by not adjusting group reserves for the additional finance costs on the bonds and the transfer from other reserves. Most candidates did adjust for the impairment of goodwill and the unrealised profit on inventories but some made the mistake of not adjusting for only the group share. The marks most missed were those relating to the other reserves/derecognition of the AFS investment previously held – but to be fair this is probably the trickiest adjustment in group accounting and credit was given where candidates could display an understanding of the correct principles – e.g. eliminating the balance on other reserves.

---

57 ERT (MAR 11 EXAM)

(a) **Fair value adjustments**

Impact on calculation of goodwill at acquisition:

In this case the calculation of goodwill on the acquisition of BNM should be based on the fair value of the consideration paid plus the fair value of the NCI less the fair value of the net assets acquired. The fair value of the net assets acquired should include any fair value adjustments required to take the book values of individual assets and liabilities up to (or down to) their fair value.

The increase in the values of property, plant and equipment and inventories will increase the value of net assets at acquisition, which in turn will reduce goodwill. The intangible asset will be recognised as an asset at acquisition because it meets the definition of an intangible asset in IAS 38. It will increase the net assets at acquisition and hence reduce goodwill.

The contingent liability is also specifically allowed to be included within the fair value of the net assets at acquisition. However, as a liability this will reduce the fair value of net assets and hence increase goodwill.

Impact on consolidated financial statements for year ending 31 December 20X0:

PPE:

In the consolidated statement of financial position as at 31 December 20X0 the value of PPE will be increased by $800,000 and reduced by the additional depreciation arising for the period. The additional depreciation is calculated as the FV adjustment divided by the estimated remaining life of the assets from the date of acquisition. This additional depreciation will be charged to the consolidated income statement each year.

Inventories:

As the inventories have been sold by 31 December 20X0, no adjustment will be required to the inventories balance in the statement of financial position. However, in the consolidated income statement an additional charge should be made within cost of sales. This will obviously also impact retained earnings for the group.

Intangible Asset:

The intangible asset will be recorded in the consolidated statement of financial position and amortised over its life (which in this case is 20 months). The amortisation charge will go through the consolidated income statement and impact group retained earnings.

Contingent Liability:

The contingent liability will be recorded as a current liability in the consolidated statement of financial position. In the consolidated income statements the reduction in the liability will in effect increase profits.

(b) **Consolidated statement of financial position as at 31 December 20X0 for the ERT Group**

All workings in $000

ASSETS	$000
Non-current assets	
Property, plant and equipment (12,000 + 4,000 + 750 (W1))	16,750
Goodwill (W2)	208
Intangible asset (W1)	90
	17,048
Current assets	
Inventories (2,200 + 800 – 30 (W3))	2,970
Receivables (3,400 + 900)	4,300
Cash and cash equivalents (800 + 300)	1,100
	8,370
Total assets	25,418
EQUITY AND LIABILITIES	
Equity	
Share capital ($1 equity shares)	10,000
Retained earnings (W4)	7,893
Total equity attributable to parent	17,893
Non-controlling interest (W5)	1,741
Total equity	19,634
Non-current liabilities	
Long term borrowings	2,700
Current liabilities (2,000 + 1,000 + 84)	3,084
Total liabilities	5,784
Total equity and liabilities	25,418

Workings:

(W1) **Fair value adjustments**

	At acquisition date $000	Movement $000	31 December 20X0 $000
PPE	800	(50)	750
Inventories	200	(200)	–
Intangible assets	150	(60)	90
Liabilities	(210)	126	(84)
	940	(184)	756

(W2) **Goodwill**

	$000	$000
Consideration transferred		3,800
NCI at fair value		1,600
		5,400
Net assets at fair value:		
Share capital	1,000	
Retained earnings	3,200	
Fair value adjustments	940	(5,140)
Goodwill on acquisition		260
20% impairment		(52)
Goodwill at 31 December 20X0		208

(W3) **Unrealised profit on inventories**

	$000
Sales of $300k x 20% x 50% left in inventories at y/e =	30

(W4) **Retained earnings**

	ERT	BNM
	$000	$000
As per SoFP	7,500	4,000
Pre-acquisition reserves		(3,200)
Adjustments arising from movement in FV adjustments		(184)
		616
Group share 75%	462	
Unrealised profit on inventory transfer	(30)	
Goodwill impairment (75% x 52) (W2)	(39)	
Consolidated reserves	7,893	

(W5) **Non-controlling interests**

	$000
NCI at acquisition (at fair value)	1,600
25% x post acquisition retained earnings $616,000 (W4)	154
Goodwill impairment (25% x 52) (W2)	(13)
	1,741

Tutorial note:

Kaplan's standard SFP workings are useful in this question, as there are a number of fair value adjustments that need to be made to the net assets of the subsidiary. See below for an alternative version of the solution using these workings.

(W1) **Net assets of BNM**

	Acquisition	Reporting date
	$000	$000
Share capital	1,000	1,000
Retained earnings	3,200	4,000
FV adjustments:		
PPE	800	800
Depreciation on PPE 800/16		(50)
Inventories	200	–
Intangible	150	150
Amortisation of intangible 150 x 8/20 months		(60)
Contingent liability	(210)	(84)
	5,140	5,756

(W2) **Goodwill in BNM**

	$000
Parent's investment	3,800
Fair value of NCI	1,600
Less fair value of net assets at acquisition (W1)	(5,140)
Goodwill at acquisition	260
Impairment of 20%	(52)
Goodwill at year end	208

(W3) **Non-controlling interest**

	$000
Value at acquisition	1,600
Share of post-acquisition reserves 25% x (5,756 – 5,140) (W1)	154
Share of impairment 25% x 52 (W2)	(13)
	1,741

(W4) **Retained earnings**

	$000
ERT per question	7,500
Unrealised profit (300k x ½ x 20%)	(30)
Share of post-acquisition reserves in BNM	
75% x (5,756 – 5,140) (W1)	462
Share of impairment	
75% x 52 (W2)	(39)
	7,893

58   A, B AND C (MAY 11 EXAM)

Summarised consolidated statement of comprehensive income for the A Group for the year ended 30 September 20X5

All workings in A$000

	A$000
Revenue (4,600 + 3,385 (W1))	7,985
Costs and expenses (3,700 + 2,462 (W1))	(6,162)
Share of associate's profit (W3)	160
Profit before tax	1,983
Income tax expense (200 + 231 (W1))	(431)
Profit for the year	1,552
Other comprehensive income	
Revaluation gains net of tax (200 + 185 (W1))	385
Share of associate's OCI (W3)	28
FOREX gain in year (W4)	803
Total OCI	1,216
Total comprehensive income	2,768
PFY attributable to:	
Equity holders of the parent	1,414
Non-controlling interest (W5)	138
	1,552
TCI attributable to:	
Equity holders of the parent	2,432
Non-controlling interest (W5)	336
	2,768

Consolidated statement of financial position as at 30 September 20X5 for the A Group

All workings in A$000

ASSETS	A$000
Non-current assets	
Property, plant and equipment (7,000 + 6,349 (W1))	13,349
Goodwill (W2)	635
Investment in associate (W6)	1,220
	15,204
Current assets (3,000 + 3,175 (W1))	6,175
Total assets	21,379
EQUITY AND LIABILITIES	
Equity attributable to the parent	
Share capital	2,000
Retained reserves (W8)	13,522
	15,522
Non-controlling interest (W7)	1,476
Total equity	16,998
Current liabilities (2,000 + 2,381 (W1))	4,381
Total equity and liabilities	21,379

Workings:

(W1) **Translation of B**

	B$000	Rate @ average rate	A$000
Statement of comprehensive income			
Revenue	2,200	A$/B$0.65	3,385
Cost of sales and expenses	(1,600)	A$/B$0.65	(2,462)
Profit before tax	600		923
Income tax	(150)	A$/B$0.65	(231)
Profit for year	450		692
Other comprehensive income:			
Revaluation gains on PPE	120	A$/B$0.65	185
Total OCI	120		185
Total comprehensive income	570		877

Statement of financial position

Non-current assets

Property, plant and equipment	4,000	@CR B$0.63	6,349
Current assets	2,000	@CR B$0.63	3,175
	6,000		9,524

Equity and liabilities

Share capital	1,000	@HR B$0.50	2,000
Pre-acquisition reserves	1,800	@HR B$0.50	3,600
Post-acquisition reserves	1,700	Bal fig	1,543
Total equity	4,500		7,143
Current liabilities	1,500	@CR B$0.63	2,381
	6,000		9,524

(W2) **Goodwill**

	B$000	*Rate*	A$000
Consideration transferred	2,600	A$/B$0.50	5,200
NCI @FV	600	A$/B$0.50	1,200
NA acquired:			
Share capital	(1,000)	A$/B$0.50	(2,000)
Retained earnings	(1,800)	A$/B$0.50	(3,600)
Goodwill at 1 October 20X2	400		800
FOREX loss (balancing figure)			(237)
Goodwill at 30 September 20X4	400	A$/B$0.71	563
FOREX gain (balancing figure)			72
Goodwill at 30 September 20X5	400	A$/B$0.63	635

(W3) **Share of associate's profit/OCI**

	A$000
Share of associate's PFY (40% x A$400,000)	160
Share of associate's other comprehensive income (40% x A$70,000)	28

(W4) FOREX gains/losses in the year

	A$000
Closing net assets @CR (B$4,500,000/0.63) or from W1	7,143
Less opening net assets @OR ((B$4,500,000 less TCI B$570,000)/0.71)	(5,535)
Less TCI for year @ average rate (B$570,000/0.65)	(877)
FOREX gain on translation of subsidiary's net assets	731
Plus FOREX gain on translation of goodwill	72
Total FOREX gains on translation of subsidiary	803

(W5) NCI share of PFY/TCI in year

	PFY A$000	TCI A$000
Subsidiary's PFY/TCI (W1)	692	877
20% share	138	175
FOREX gain on translation of subsidiary (20% x A$803,000)		161
	138	336

(W6) Investment in associate

	A$000
Investment at cost	900
Plus share of post-acquisition reserves 40% x (A$1,500,000 – A$700,000)	320
	1,220

(W7) Non-controlling interest

	A$000
NCI on acquisition (W2)	1,200
NCI share of post-acquisition reserves of subsidiary (20% x A$1,543,000 (W1))	309
NCI share of net FOREX losses on translation of goodwill (20% x A$(237,000-72,000))	(33)
NCI at 30 September 20X5	1,476

(W8) **Reserves**

	A A$000	B A$000
As per SoFP	12,100	5,143
Less pre-acquisition reserves (W1)		(3,600)
		1,543
Group share 80% x A$1,543,000	1,234	
Group share of associate's post-acquisition reserves (W6)	320	
Group share of net FOREX losses on translation of goodwill (80% x A$(237,000-72,000))	(132)	
Group reserves	13,522	

Examiner's comments

This question was probably the worst attempted consolidation question we have seen in the last 4 diets. A huge number of candidates completely ignored the translation of the subsidiary or made no attempt to calculate the gain or loss on translation. This had a significant impact on the marks. The associate was very well dealt with and the preparation of accounts was well done. Having commented previously that the quality and layout of the consolidation workings had improved in the past few exam sessions, that could not be said for this question. Workings were poorly constructed and rarely completed giving the impression that candidates were at a loss as to how to deal with the translation effects of the sub.

There was confusion over whether to divide or multiply on translation but candidates were not penalised for making this error as it was the principles of IAS 21 and the selection of the appropriate rates that was being tested – not the ability to perform arithmetic calculations.

Tutorial note:

There are a number of different approaches that can be taken to producing a consolidated set of financial statements including a foreign subsidiary. An alternative to the examiner's solution above is produced below. The translation of the subsidiary is principally performed on the face of the statements and, in the workings, the subsidiary figures are kept in the foreign currency for as long as possible, translating only when the figures then are taken into the main financial statements. The main thing to remember is that SCI figures should be translated using the average rate and SFP figures translated using the closing rate.

Using this approach does result in a slightly different split of the exchange difference between reserves attributable to the parent and to the NCI (of 16). The examiner has allocated exchange differences relating to goodwill on the basis of the percentage shareholdings, however when the fair value method is used to calculate non-controlling interests the proportion of goodwill allocated to the parent in reality is greater than 80% (as the parent will pay a premium for the controlling interest). Your treatment of this should not affect your overall mark.

Alternative solution:

Summarised consolidated statement of comprehensive income for the A Group for the year ended 30 September 20X5

All workings in A$000

	A$000
Revenue (4,600 + (2,200/0.65))	7,985
Costs and expenses (3,700 + (1,600/0.65))	(6,162)
Share of associate's profit (40% x 400)	160
Profit before tax	1,983
Income tax expense (200 + (150/0.65))	(431)
Profit for the year	1,552
Other comprehensive income	
Revaluation gains net of tax (200 +(120/0.65))	385
Share of associate's OCI (40% x 70)	28
FOREX gain in year (W6)	803
Total OCI	1,216
Total comprehensive income	2,768
PFY attributable to:	
Equity holders of the parent	1,414
Non-controlling interest (W5)	138
	1,552
TCI attributable to:	
Equity holders of the parent	2,432
Non-controlling interest (W5)	336
	2,768

Consolidated statement of financial position as at 30 September 20X5 for the A Group

All workings in A$000

ASSETS	A$000
Non-current assets	
Property, plant and equipment (7,000 +(4,000/0.63))	13,349
Goodwill (400/0.63) (W2)	635
Investment in associate (900 + 40% x (1,500-700))	1,220
	15,204
Current assets (3,000 + (2,000/0.63))	6,175
Total assets	21,379

EQUITY AND LIABILITIES

Equity attributable to the parent

Share capital	2,000
Retained reserves (W4)	13,506
	15,506
Non-controlling interest (940/0.63) (W3)	1,492
Total equity	16,998
Current liabilities (2,000 + (1,500/0.63))	4,381
Total equity and liabilities	21,379

Workings:

(W1) **Net assets of B (in B's currency)**

	Acquisition	Reporting date
	B$000	B$000
Share capital	1,000	1,000
Reserves	1,800	3,500
	2,800	4,500

(W2) **Goodwill in B (in B's currency)**

	B$000
Parent's investment (5,200 x 0.5)	2,600
Fair value of NCI	600
Less fair value of net assets at acquisition (W1)	(2,800)
Goodwill at acquisition and year end	400

(W3) **Non-controlling interest (in B's currency)**

	B$000
Value at acquisition	600
Share of post-acquisition reserves	
20% x (4,500 – 2,800) (W1)	340
	940

(W4) **Retained earnings (in A's functional currency – A$)**

		A$000
A per question		12,100
Share of post-acquisition reserves in B		
80% x (4,500 – 2,800)/0.63 (W1)		2,159
Exchange difference arising on A's investment		
At closing rate: 2,600/0.63	4,127	
At acquisition rate: 2,600/0.5	(5,200)	
		(1,073)
Share of associate post-acquisition reserves		
40% x (1,500 – 700)		320
		13,506

(W5) **NCI share of PFY/TCI in year**

	PFY	TCI
	B$000	B$000
B's PFY/TCI	450	570
Translated at average rate	/0.65	/0.65
Subsidiary's PFY/TCI (W1)	692	877
20% share	138	175
FOREX gain on translation of subsidiary (20% x 803)		161
	138	336

(W6) **Group exchange difference for the year**

			A$000	A$000
Opening net assets	3,930/0.63	(closing rate)	6,238	
(4,500-570)	3,930/0.71	(opening rate)	(5,535)	
		Gain		703
B's TCI	570/0.63	(closing rate)	905	
	570/0.65	(average rate)	(877)	
		Gain		28
Goodwill	400/0.63	(closing rate)	635	
	400/0.71	(opening rate)	(563)	
		Gain		72
Total exchange difference				803

59   AB (SEP 11 EXAM)

Consolidated statement of cash flows for AB Group for the year ended 30 June 20X1

Cash flows from operating activities	$000	$000
Profit before tax	6,290	
Add back non-operating and non-cash items:		
Depreciation	3,100	
Goodwill impairment (W1)	570	
Share of profit of associate	(1,500)	
Investment income	(320)	
Finance costs	1,350	
Changes in working capital:		
Decrease in inventories (W2)	4,800	
Decrease in receivables (W2)	200	
Decrease in payables (W2)	(2,300)	
	———	
Cash inflow from operating activities	12,190	
Less interest paid	(1,350)	
Less tax paid (W3)	(2,650)	
	———	
Net cash inflow from operating activities		8,190
Cash flows from investing activities		
Acquisition of property, plant and equipment (W4)	(5,950)	
Acquisition of subsidiary, net of cash acquired (500–200)	(300)	
Investment income received on HTM asset	120	
Dividend received from associate (W5)	620	
	———	
Cash outflow from investing activities		(5,510)
Cash flows from financing activities		
Proceeds of share issue (W6)	10,450	
Dividend paid to shareholders of parent (W7)	(2,130)	
Dividend paid to non-controlling interest (W8)	(800)	
Repayment of long term borrowings (53,400–41,100)	(12,300)	
	———	
Cash outflow from financing activities		(4,780)
		———
Net outflow of cash and cash equivalents		(2,100)
Cash and cash equivalents at 1 July 20X0		12,300
		———
Cash and cash equivalents at 30 June 20X1		10,200
		———

Workings:

(W1) **Goodwill**

	$000
Opening balance	7,200
Arising on acquisition (see below)	1,370
	8,570
Impairment (balancing figure)	(570)
Closing balance	8,000

Goodwill on acquisition	$000
Consideration transferred (1m x $3.95) + cash $500,000	4,450
Non-controlling interest (30% x $4,400,000)	1,320
Less fair value of net assets acquired	(4,400)
Goodwill arising	1,370

(W2) **Changes in working capital**

	Inventories	Receivables	Payables
	$000	$000	$000
Opening balance	36,000	26,400	30,600
On acquisition	3,600	2,000	3,800
	39,600	28,400	34,400
Movement (balancing figure)	(4,800)	(200)	(2,300)
Closing balance	34,800	28,200	32,100

(W3) **Tax paid**

	$000
Opening balance (2,700 + 600)	3,300
Tax on profit	1,800
Tax on OCI	250
	5,350
Movement (balancing figure)	(2,650)
Closing balance (1,800 + 900)	2,700

(W4) Acquisition of property, plant and equipment

	$000
Opening carrying value	44,400
On acquisition	2,400
	46,800
Revaluation	1,450
Depreciation	(3,100)
	45,150
Additions (balancing figure)	5,950
Closing balance	51,100

(W5) Dividend received from associate

	$000
Opening balance	23,400
Share of associate's profit	1,500
Share of OCI of associate	120
	25,020
Dividends received from associate (balancing figure)	620
Closing balance	24,400

(W6) Proceeds of share issue

	$000
Opening balance	30,000
Issued on acquisition	3,950
	33,950
Issue for cash (balancing figure)	10,450
Closing balance ($36m + $8.4m)	44,400

(W7) Dividend paid to shareholders of the parent

	$000
Opening balance	20,100
Profit for the year attributable to equity holders	3,880
	23,980
Dividend paid (balancing figure)	(2,130)
Closing balance	21,850

(W8) Dividend paid to non-controlling interest

	$000
Opening balance NCI	18,300
On acquisition (see W1)	1,320
NCI share of TCI for year	680
	20,300
Dividend paid to NCI (balancing figure)	(800)
Closing balance NCI	19,500

Tutorial note

Revaluation reserve breakdown	$000
Revaluation in the year	1,450
Less deferred tax arising on revaluation gain	(250)
Share of associate's revaluation gains	120
NCI share of subs OCI	(70)
	1,250

ISSUES IN RECOGNITION AND MEASUREMENT

60   TYD (MAY 07 EXAM)

To: Committee of Lending Officers

From: Accounting Adviser

Subject: TYD's financial statements for the year ended 30 September 20X6

Date: 22 May 20X7

As requested, I have considered the accounting treatment of significant items in TYD's financial statements and analysed the financial statements. I set out my comments and recommendations below.

(i)   **Treatment of significant items in TYD's financial statements**

Sale of inventories to HPS

The key issues here are which party actually owns the assets and whether a sale has actually taken place. The IASB's *Framework for the Preparation and Presentation of Financial Statements* states that transactions and other events should be accounted for and presented in accordance with their substance and economic reality, and not merely their legal form.

The legal form of this transaction is that there has been a sale. However, IAS 18 *Revenue* states that a sale should only be recognised if the risks and rewards of ownership have been transferred to the buyer. There are several indications that this has not occurred.

The inventories continue to be stored on TYD's premises and TYD bears the cost of insuring them. The bank is likely to exercise the option to require TYD to repurchase the inventories, as it will gain $10,000 by doing so. The substance of the transaction is that of a secured long-term loan. The difference between the sum of $85,000 received by TYD on 30 September 20X6 and the sum of $95,000 for which the inventories will be repurchased after two years is effectively interest on the loan. Therefore the transaction should be treated as an interest bearing loan, rather than as a sale and the financial statements of TYD should be adjusted to reflect this.

Inventories sold on a sale and return basis

The key issue here is similar i.e. whether the goods actually been sold. IAS 18 *Revenue* sets out a number of conditions that must be met before a sale can be recognised. As before, the risks and rewards of owning the inventories must have been transferred to the buyer and the seller must no longer have any effective control over them.

In practice it appears that a significant proportion of buyers do exercise their right to return the goods. Therefore neither of the conditions has been met. The sales cannot be recognised as long as it remains possible that the goods will be returned. The inventories must continue to be recognised as assets of TYD. Again, the financial statements should be adjusted.

(ii)   **Adjustment of TYD's financial statements**

Key answer tips

Here the income statement and the statement of financial position have been completely redrafted to help you to understand the impact of the adjustments. However, the Examiner has said that other types of working, such as journal entries, would be acceptable, provided that they demonstrated correct understanding of the adjustments that were required.

Income statement for the year ended 30 September 20X6

	$000	Transaction 1 $000	Transaction 2 $000	Adjusted $000
Revenue	600	(85)	(40)	475
Cost of sales	(450)	85	32	(333)
Gross profit	150			142
Operating expenses	(63)			(63)
Finance costs	(17)			(17)
Profit before tax	70			62
Income tax expense	(25)			(25)
Profit for the period	45	–	(8)	37

Statement of financial position at 30 September 20X6

	$000	$000	Transaction 1 $000	Transaction 2 $000	Adjusted $000
Assets					
Non-current assets:					
Property, plant and equipment		527			527
Current assets:					
Inventories	95		85	32	212
Trade receivables	72			(40)	32
Cash	6				6
		173			250
		700			777
Equity and liabilities					
Equity:					
Share capital	100				100
Retained earnings	245			(8)	237
		345			337
Non-current liabilities:					
Long-term borrowings		180	85		265
Current liabilities:					
Trade and other payables	95				95
Bank overdraft	80				80
		175			175
		700			777

Alternative answer: journal adjustments

		$000	$000
1	Sale and repurchase agreement		
	Debit Revenue	85,000	
	Credit Cost of sales		85,000
	Debit Inventories	85,000	
	Credit: Long-term loan		85,000
2	Sale or return items		
	Debit Revenue (40% × 100,000)	40,000	
	Credit Cost of sales (40% × 100,000 × 80%)		32,000
	Debit Inventories	32,000	
	Credit: Trade receivables		40,000

(iii) **Analysis of the financial statements**

The key ratio calculations are shown below. They have been calculated before and after the adjustments to the financial statements described above.

	Before adjustment		*After adjustment*
Gearing			
$\dfrac{180 + 80}{(180 + 80 + 345)} \times 100$	43.0%	$\dfrac{265 + 80}{(265 + 80 + 337)} \times 100$	50.6%
Current ratio			
$\dfrac{173}{175}$	0.99 : 1	$\dfrac{(212 + 32 + 6)}{175}$	1.43 : 1
Quick ratio			
$\dfrac{(72 + 6)}{175}$	0.45 : 1	$\dfrac{(32 + 6)}{175}$	0.22 : 1
Profit margin			
$\dfrac{70}{600} \times 100$	11.7%	$\dfrac{62}{475} \times 100$	13.1%

TYD is highly geared. Even before the financial statements are adjusted the gearing ratio is 43%. When the sale and repurchase agreement is treated as a loan, gearing increases to 50.6%, which is well above the 45% threshold that normally causes an application to be rejected.

Because the adjustments increase inventories and decrease receivables, they improve the current ratio significantly, to an apparently healthy 1.43. However, the quick ratio, which is already low, falls still further to a very low 0.22. The quick ratio is probably a more useful guide to the solvency of the business than the current ratio. After the adjustments, inventories form approximately 85% of current assets. The company would probably find it difficult to convert these inventories into cash quickly. In the absence of further information about the nature of TYR's business, its quick ratio suggests possible liquidity problems, meaning that the company might be unable to repay its borrowings.

Although revenue is decreased, profitability improves when the financial statements are adjusted. However, the profit margin will be reduced in future periods as a result of interest on the secured loan from HPS.

On the basis of the key ratios and the other information available, TYR's application for loan finance should be rejected.

61   NED AND ABC (NOV 08 EXAM)   *Walk in the footsteps of a top tutor*

Key answer tips

The three scenarios requiring correction are standard situations that you could be tested upon. Make sure you're happy preparing journal entries to make corrections. If you struggle with this, it may be simpler to consider what ABC has done, what they *should* have done and therefore what is needed to correct the errors. The 7 marks in part (b) follow on directly from (a) so work these parts together to save time.

(a)   **Accounting treatment and adjustments**

Tutorial note:

This style of question enables the examiner to test substance within the "issues in recognition and measurement" part of the syllabus. As it has a 20% weighting you cannot afford to ignore any elements of this section of the syllabus.

*For each transaction, discuss what the indicators are for arriving at your decision for how the transaction **should** have been accounted for.*

Remember to put down your thought process to gain marks rather than just writing out the answer in one sentence.

1   **Sale and repurchase**

Per IAS 1 *Presentation of financial statements* the substance and economic reality of a transaction must be reflected in the financial statements, not merely its legal form.

The legal view of the transfer of plant by ABC to XB is that of a sale. However, the substance of the transaction is that ABC has taken out a loan from XB secured on the item of plant. This is because in essence the risks and rewards of holding the plant have not been transferred over to XB. ABC still insures it and holds the plant on its premises. A

BC will repurchase the plant either on 1 October 20X8 or 1 October 20X9 which will be the repayment of the loan, including interest as the repurchase price is greater than the original selling price.

The journal entries to record the secured loan should have been:

Dr Cash	$1,000,000
Cr Long term liabilities	$1,000,000

The interest ABC has to pay on the loan i.e. $100k to 1 October 20X8 and another $110k to 1 October 20X9 if applicable, should be recognised over the period of the loan.

The journal entries required to correct the error and deal with the interest for the year ended 30 September 20X8 are:

To reinstate the asset and record the loan:

Dr Non-current asset	$1,000,000
Cr Long term liabilities	$1,000,000

To eliminate the revenue recorded:

Dr Revenue	$1,000,000
Cr Cost of sales	$1,000,000

To record the interest for the year ended 30 September 20X8:

Dr Finance cost	$100,000
Cr Long term liability	$100,000

2 **Debt factoring**

As above, IAS 1 must be adhered to so ABC must consider the substance of the debt factoring transaction. ABC has derecognised the receivables balance because the cash has been received from the factor. ABC must consider whether the risks and benefits of holding the receivables have been transferred to LM. It appears that they have not, because ABC must pay LM for any receivables that are uncollectible, so bear this risk. Also, ABC's finance cost payable is dependent upon cash received from customers.

Therefore instead of crediting receivables, ABC should have credited current liabilities. Journal entries to correct the error are:

Dr Receivables	$1,500,000
Cr Current liabilities	$1,500,000

As the factoring agreement was entered into a few days before the reporting date there will be no interest to record in the year ended 30 September 20X8.

3 **Redeemable preference shares**

Tutorial note:

The key word that the examiner is looking for here is "obligation". If an obligation to deliver cash exists then the shares should be accounted for as a liability and the servicing of the shares i.e. dividends should be deducted in profit or loss as financial cost.

IAS 32 *Financial instruments: presentation* provides guidance on whether a financial instrument should be classified as either equity or liability. The classification is based on substance, not legal form and is founded upon whether there is an obligation for the issuer to deliver cash.

As the preference shares are to be redeemed in 20Y5 and there is an obligation for ABC to pay the dividend, the shares should be classified as a liability rather than equity. Consequently the servicing of the shares i.e. the dividend, should be recorded as a finance cost in the income statement rather than dividends in the statement of changes in equity.

Journal entries required to correct the error:

Dr Equity	$2,000,000
Cr Long term liabilities	$2,000,000
Dr Finance cost	$160,000 (8% x $2,000,000)
Cr Retained earnings	$160,000

(b)   **Adjustment to ratios**

Tutorial note:

The easiest way to answer part (b) is to set up workings to enable you to put through the adjustments necessary and then rework the calculations. You can then make the adjustments to the workings as you work through part (a)

Return on capital employed $= \dfrac{\text{Profit before interest}}{\text{Debt +Equity}} = \dfrac{2,972,000}{22,853,500(\text{W3}) + 20,350,800(\text{W2})}$

$= 6.9\%$

Net profit margin $= \dfrac{\text{Profit before tax}}{\text{Revenue}} = \dfrac{2,972,000 - 1,501,000(\text{W1})}{31,850,000 - 1,000,000}$

$= 4.8\%$

Gearing $= \dfrac{\text{Debt}}{\text{Debt + Equity}} = \dfrac{22,853,500(\text{W3})}{22,853,500(\text{W3}) + 20,350,800(\text{W2})}$

$= 52.9\%$

Workings

(W1) **Interest**

	$
Interest per question	1,241,000
Adjustments:	
1 Sale and repurchase	100,000
3 Preference shares	160,000
	——————
	1,501,000
	——————

(W2) **Equity**

Equity per question	22,450,800
Adjustments:	
Interest from W1	(100,000)
3 Preference shares	(2,000,000)
	——————
	20,350,800
	——————

(W3) **Debt**

Debt per question	18,253,500
Adjustments:	
1 Sale and repurchase	1,100,000
2 Debt factoring	1,500,000
3 Preference shares	2,000,000
	22,853,500

Tutorial note:

Remember that any adjustments to profit for the year must also be made to equity.

The interest on the preference shares does not affect equity as the cost was previously deducted from retained earnings and is now deducted from profit for the period.

Current liabilities owed to the factor, LM, are interest bearing and so are included in the calculations.

(c) **Implications for non-executive director**

Tutorial note:

Use common sense to answer this part briefly for 3 marks. How do the adjustments change the results? Does ABC still hit its targets? What would a non-executive director be concerned about?

It appears that ABC's results have been prepared with some bias to ensure that the financial targets are met. Taking into account the adjustments required to correct the errors, all of the measures now fall outside target.

Ned needs to speak to the Board about the targets and the pressure being applied from the three institutional shareholders. It is directors' responsibility to ensure that the financial statements are prepared in accordance with IFRS, which is currently not the case.

Ned may like to consider independent legal advice to be clear about his own position.

FINANCIAL STATEMENT ANALYSIS

62 TEX (NOV 08 EXAM) *Walk in the footsteps of a top tutor*

Key answer tips

The question tells you there are 8 marks available for calculating ratios. Make sure your calculations will help you discuss TEX in the context of SWW considering lending it money. It is useful to attempt part (b) at the same time so when you are considering an explanation for a movement, you can think about whether further information would enable easier analysis.

Tutor's top tips:

This is a standard analysis style question. The important thing to do first is to get an idea of what the company you are looking to analyse actually does and to get an overview of its results and position.

Do this by reading the background information thoroughly and highlighting/ underlining/ adding comments in the margin of your question paper.

Before you start thinking about ratios, just look at the financial statements you've been given. Has the entity made a profit or loss? Has the revenue/ gross profit/ net profit increased on last year. With the statement of financial position assess non-current asset movements, whether there are cash balances, movements in current and non-current liabilities and inventory holdings etc.

*Then you can start to calculate **appropriate** ratios to better understand the big picture you have identified.*

REPORT

To: CFO, SWW

From: Chief Financial Officer's Assistant

Subject: Analysis of financial information relating to TEX

Date: 18 November 20X8

As requested, I have analysed the financial information provided for TEX for the two years ended 30 September 20X8 and I set out my comments below. As part of my analysis I have calculated a number of key ratios and these are included in the attached Appendix.

I have also addressed some areas of uncertainty and provided a list of additional information that would be useful in arriving at a decision whether to lend to TEX.

(a)   **Analysis of information**

Tutor's top tips:

It is imperative to use headings and short paragraphs to make as many succinct but well explained points as possible given the information and your time allocation to the question.

As well as stating what has happened, think about why it has happened and what the effect of this will be.

*The examiner has said that students using the word **"because"** in their answer frequently will tend to score good marks on this style of question.*

Profitability

The first and important thing to note is that TEX has made a loss before tax of $4.9m in the current year. The prior year reported a pre tax profit of $1.1m so the fall is significant. Revenue has fallen by 9% and gross profit by 13%. Therefore not only are the number of sales or the selling price falling, TEX's control on its costs may also be worsening as the gross profit percentage has fallen.

Given that the incentive for SWW making a loan to TEX is that they will enjoy lower future prices, this does not appear to be possible whilst maintaining a reasonable gross profit percentage and indeed a profit making business.

Despite the fact that revenue has fallen, selling and distribution costs has increased marginally. Due to their nature you would expect these costs to have fallen together with revenue so this may indicate a fall in prices rather than sales volume.

Administrative expenses have increased by almost 20% to 7% of revenue compared to 5.5% in 20X7. TEX may have enforced some redundancies to try to control future costs or again it may be a sign of operating inefficiencies.

The key measure of return on capital employed has fallen from 3.25% to 0.22%. This is critical to TEX. The business is not using its resources efficiently to generate profit. This appears to be entirely due to the selling price or volumes and cost control as net asset turnover is high. Consequently assets are being used intensively to generate a very small margin per product.

Solvency

Gearing is already relatively high at 61% in 20X8. It has increased from 20X7 and this is because short term borrowings have more than doubled. Long term borrowings have actually fallen by 15%.

The increase in short term borrowings is concerning as long term borrowings are likely to be a cheaper and more stable source of finance than short term borrowings, which may be called at any time.

Due to a repayment of long term borrowings, one would expect finance costs to fall but this has not been the case fully as interest has only fallen by 13%. This is likely to be caused by more expensive short term borrowing.

Interest cover was 1.18 in 20X7 so TEX was only just making sufficient profit to meet its interest payments, with very little margin for profits to fall. Unfortunately in 20X8 there was insufficient profit to cover interest. This resulted in the loss and interest cover was 0.09.

As a potential lender to TEX, interest cover is of paramount importance and unless TEX can show how profits will increase over the short term as a result of the loan potentially offered by SWW, it looks unlikely that they can pay higher interest charges for any length of time before becoming insolvent.

Liquidity

Current assets just about cover current liabilities as shown by the current ratio of 1.03 but the majority of the current assets are inventories. Because inventories are realised into cash much more slowly, I have excluded them in calculating the quick ratio which is only 0.29 compared to 0.36 in 20X7.

This shows that if cash is needed to repay current liabilities TEX has insufficient funds available in the short term.

Efficiency

Inventory turnover is relatively low at 1.71 compared to 1.94 last year. As a producer of cotton clothing you would expect inventories to turnaround quickly as fashions change. If inventories are held for a long period of time, over 6 months, there may be a risk of obsolescence if customers' tastes have moved on. This would in turn require potential inventory write downs and further losses.

(b)   **Additional information required**

Tutor's top tips:

Use a separate piece of paper for part (b) and add points as you think of them whilst attempting part (a). For example, if you are struggling to explain the movement in borrowings, extra information would be needed o short and long term debt i.e. terms, interest rates, security and who the lenders are.

It is unclear why TEX's gross profit percentage has fallen. SWW needs information to ascertain whether it is due to cut prices to encourage sales or whether cost control needs tightening up.

A breakdown of administrative costs would be useful to understand cost control.

Efficiency improvements are mentioned as a use for the loan. SWW will need a summary of the improvements to be made and forecasts of the financial effect.

TEX has an investment in an associate company, which has been making a loss for the prior two years. SWW needs to discuss this matter with TEX to determine the strategy of the associate to become profit making. TEX cannot sustain a loss making investment in the medium term.

SWW requires information about TEX's customers and details of any contractual arrangements for future sales. This may be sensitive data to obtain as SWW is also a customer of TEX.

The accounts are not yet audited so we need to be aware that there is a possibility of changes to the figures.

In conclusion, further information is required to understand the negative changes that TEX has seen over the previous year. Based on the current information it does not seem prudent to lend TEX the money as it is likely to encounter problems paying back interest and capital.

APPENDIX

Financial ratio calculations (figures in $m)

>
> *Tutor's top tips:*
>
> *Calculate your ratios in a separate appendix to make it clearer for the marker. Refer to your appendix when writing your report.*

	$ m	20X8	$ m	20X7
Return on capital employed		0.22%		3.25%
Profit from operations	0.5		7.3	
Capital employed	227.8		224.6	
Net profit margin		0.20%		2.60%
Profit from operations	0.5		7.3	
Revenue	256.3		281.7	
Net asset turnover		112.51%		125.42%
Revenue	256.3		281.7	
Capital employed	227.8		224.6	
Gearing		60.54%		54.79%
Debt	57.2 + 28.7		67.1 + 12.4	
Equity	141.9		145.1	
Interest cover		0.09		1.18
Profit from operations	0.5		7.3	
Finance cost	5.4		6.2	
Current ratio		1.03		1.09
Current assets	184.1		188.6	
Current liabilities	178.8		173.6	
Quick ratio		0.29		0.36
Trade rec. + cash	51.7		63.0	
Current liabilities	178.8		173.6	
Inventory turnover		1.71		1.94
Cost of sales	226.6		243.1	
Inventory	132.4		125.6	

(W1) **Profit from operations**

= Gross profit − Selling and distribution costs − Admin expenses + share of profit of associate

20X8: 29.7 − 9.2 − 18.7 − 1.3 = 0.5

20X7: 38.6 − 8.9 − 15.6 − 6.8 = 7.3

(W2) **Capital employed**

= Equity + long term debt + short term borrowings

20X8: 141.9 + 57.2 + 28.7 = 227.8

20X7: 145.1 + 67.1 + 12.4 = 224.6

63   ELB (MAY 09 EXAM)

(a)   Refer to appendix

(b)   Report

To:	Board of Directors
From:	Assistant to Chief Financial Officer
Date:	May 20X9
Subject:	Financial performance and position of ELB

Financial performance

Revenue has increased by 18% on the prior year due to the aggressive expansion policy ELB directors have followed. The gross profit margin has stayed largely the same so the new products that are being offered do not have a lower margin attached to them which is positive for future prospects.

As there has been an increase in market share ELB may be tempted to increase their profit margin by increasing prices but there is no evidence of this to date.

Distribution costs and administrative expenses have risen by 55% which exceeds the growth of revenue. This could be due to heavy advertising and marketing costs due to new product launches. The distribution method of the new product lines may have changed and this may increase transport costs for example, if goods are being shipped directly to customers. The increase is borne out by the falling operating profit margin from 18.5% to 14.9%.

Finance costs have increased by 15% on the prior year despite borrowing staying almost static. This may reflect increasing interest rates or increased charges by the bank if ELB are deemed to be less able to repay debts. This is discussed further below. The covenant requires interest cover of at least 9.5 times so the fall from 11.9 is significant.

Return on capital employed has fallen from 19.5% to 14.6% i.e. by a quarter. This is explained by the fall in operating profit described above and an increase in capital employed. The main reason for the increase in capital employed is the revaluation of non-current assets and there was also a smaller gain on available for sale investments.

Financial position

The target for gearing is 50% so ELB has been successful in reducing its gearing to below this level in 20X8. Gearing was relatively high in 20X7 at 68.7% which would cause concern to lenders.

The reduction in gearing has been achieved by the revaluation of property and retention of retained earnings rather than any reduction in levels of debt. Stripping out the effect of the revaluation gearing would be 56%.

The current ratio has fallen from 1.9 to 1.45. As a manufacturing company ELB would be expected to have significant inventories and receivables. However, the cash balance has moved into an overdraft and trade payables have increased by 23%. Some of this increase is expected due to higher production levels to support higher sales but the increase exceeds revenue growth suggesting a policy to retain funds within the company.

Both the current and quick ratios have fallen below the target ratios for the banking covenant.

The quick ratio has fallen below 1 which signals a lack of short term resources to pay short term debts. This is mainly due to the cash balance moving into overdraft. The quick ratio was only just within the banking covenant in 20X7 so this is an area of concern.

Given the failure of ELB to meet two of the banking covenants and the proximity of the remaining two ratios to the target, liquidity and solvency are a significant problem for ELB to address. This, coupled with a lack of cash and the aggressive expansion, points to overtrading and a need to restructure financing.

(c) Additional points

- ELB needs to identify its sources of working capital. There needs to be a plan in place to increase working capital sources to avoid relying on the bank overdraft and pressing customers to pay more quickly as evidenced in reduced receivables days.

- The available for sale investments have generated an unrealised gain in the previous year so it may be a good time to realise this cash and sell the investments.

- Working capital control must be maintained. For example, to keep inventory days as low as possible with potentially a just in time inventory management system. Trade receivables days cannot continue to be reduced and care must be taken to maintain customer relationships. Similarly supplier relationships may be worsened if payables days remain around 3 months.

- The bank overdraft terms and interest need reviewing. This may have arisen as a short term solution but the increased finance costs may signal that restructuring is necessary to secure cheaper financing.

- The bonds are due for repayment in 2010 which is one to two years away. There must be a plan to source the cash to repay the bonds and to secure alternative future financing.

Appendix

	20X8		20X7	
Gearing – debt/ equity	11,400/23,460	48.6%	11,200/16,300	68.7%
Interest cover	(10,200–5,120)/ 520	9.8	(8,650–3,300)/ 450	11.9
Current ratio	8,800/6,070	1.45:1	8,920/4,700	1.90:1
Quick ratio	4,300/6,070	0.71:1	5,320/4,700	1.13:1
Gross profit margin	10,200/34,200	29.8%	8,650/28,900	29.9%
Operating profit margin	(10,200–5,120)/ 34,200	14.9%	(8,650–3,300)/ 28,900	18.5%
Return on capital employed	(10,200–5,120)/ 23,400+11,400	14.6%	(8,650–3,300)/ 16,300+11,200	19.5%
Asset utilisation	34,200/(23,400+11,400)	0.98	28,900/(16,300+11,200)	1.05
Inventory holding period	4,500/24,000 x 365	68 days	3,600/20,250 x 365	65 days
Receivables collection period	4,300/34,200 x 365	46 days	5,200/28,900 x 365	66 days
Payables collection period	5,800/24,000 x 365	88 days	4,700/20,250 x 365	85 days

64 BHG (MAY 08 EXAM)

Key answer tips

The first part of the requirement asks for discussion of five accounting ratios for 5 marks in total. You are therefore looking for three good points per ratio, don't try to go into too much detail for any given one.

(a) **Earnings per share**

Earnings per share (EPS) is calculated by dividing the earnings attributable to ordinary shareholders by the weighted average number of shares in issue during the period. Its disclosure is required by IFRS for listed businesses and is an important ratio for assessing performance, as the assistant states.

It is of limited use however, when comparing different entities for potential investment as, the number of shares in issue will vary. Also, even for ongoing appraisal over time, it is of most use to an investor holding a relatively small number of shares and BHG's aim is to obtain control or significant influence at the least.

EPS forms part of the calculation of the price earnings ratio (P/E ratio) and as such could be useful in comparing listed businesses for whom the market price is readily available. However, once control or significant influence had been obtained it would be of little use.

Dividend yield

This ratio is calculated as the dividend as a percentage of current market price. It measures dividend policy rather than performance and as such has limited value in appraising companies. Once again it is only useful for listed entities. Once BHG has control over its investment, it can control the dividend policy so there is no use for dividend yield in ongoing appraisal.

A high dividend yield is a product of a high dividend compared to low market price but this is based on historical dividends and the share price may reflect market opinion that the entity is overvalued and will have to sustain a future dividend cut. Conversely a low dividend yield may be caused by a high share price in anticipation of future growth.

The assistant is right in saying it enables comparison with other investments but only when the investor can realise their cash and invest in an instrument with a higher yield at short notice.

Gearing

Gearing is calculated as debt as a percentage or equity or total debt plus equity. It measures the level of interest bearing debt used as a source of finance in the business. It is a useful measure to judge the riskiness of an investment as the higher the level of debt, the higher the levels of fixed interest payments which are not within the control of the business. Therefore the assistant is correct in her views.

BHG would review gearing in initial appraisal of targets and it may serve as a disincentive to invest in entities where their gearing level is deemed by BHG to be too high. Once acquired BHG would wish to reduce the debt which could be expensive.

Once BHG has invested, gearing policy would be under their control, or at least BHG would be able to influence it greatly, so the ratio diminishes in importance.

Gross profit margin

The gross profit margin tells investors how well the business controls cost of sales and generates its revenue. As such it is a very important ratio for use in initial and ongoing appraisal.

Care needs to be taken when comparing the margin between entities as the basis for calculation must be comparable. Revenue recognition policies will affect when revenue hits the income statement and this may vary, particularly in BHG's software industry. Also, the classification of costs between cost of sales and administrative costs must be comparable.

If a potential target makes the cost breakdowns and revenue policy available, this would greatly increase the usefulness of the ratio in initial appraisal. On an ongoing basis, BHG would clearly have this information and it would remain to be a useful ratio in analysis.

Asset turnover ratio

This ratio is calculated by dividing revenue by capital employed or net assets. It does reflect how well the business uses its assets to generate revenue, as the assistant states. It is a useful ratio that is often used multiplied by net profit margin to calculate return on capital employed, which is a key performance measure.

Asset turnover itself can also be broken down into non-current asset turnover, reflecting how well the business uses its non-current assets.

The ratio can be used to compare businesses and over time, but the basis of the calculation must be consistent. For example, asset revaluations would distort comparison as would differing revenue recognition policies. Also, modern business which does not always rely heavily on tangible assets may well look favourable. For example, a software business relies heavily on staff expertise and intellectual capital that is not recorded in the statement of financial position.

Once a business is acquired, consistency in the ratios can be ensured and therefore asset turnover would be useful on an ongoing basis.

(b) **Use of common accounting standards**

BHG's potential acquisition targets may or may not be listed entities. In many countries listed entities are required to comply with IFRS but unlisted entities and entities in jurisdictions not adopting IFRS are entitled to prepare their financial statements under local GAAP which may differ significantly from IFRS. The figures underlying the ratio calculations must therefore be consistent with BHG's understanding.

Judgement in choice of accounting policies

Even where financial statements are prepared using a common set of accounting standards, there may still be significant variations in accounting policies. IFRS, for example, permits the adoption of either the cost or revaluation models for property, plant and equipment. Depreciation charges are likely to vary significantly, depending upon which model is adopted, and so the policy difference affects not only the statement of financial position but also the income statement.

Incomparability of companies due to their size

If BHG compares the ratios of a much smaller entity with its own financial statements, the comparison may not be truly valid because of the effects of, for example, economies of scale.

Local economic situation

It is often the case that national economies experience cycles of economic growth and decline that differ from the patterns experienced in other economies. An entity that appears to be performing badly in a particular national context may, compared to others, be performing relatively well.

Comparability of activities

Other software companies may appear to be operating very similar businesses to BHG but this may only be at a very superficial level. An awareness of the businesses particular market is necessary to be able to draw any useful comparisons. For example, different margins will be obtained when selling wholesale or retail and different labour markets will determine salary policies.

65   DAS (NOV 07 EXAM)

Key answer tips

Be careful which ratios you calculate. The nature of the business means that many of the standard ratios are irrelevant because they would produce meaningless results. For example, the current ratio would be distorted by the very high level of inventories; these inventories are unusual and are not capable of being converted directly to cash. As always, use the additional information you are given.

REPORT

To: A business associate

From: A management accountant

Subject: Analysis of financial information relating to DAS

Date: 22 November 20X7

As requested, I have analysed the financial information provided for the two years ended 31 August 20X7 and I set out my comments below. As part of my analysis I have calculated a number of key ratios and these are included in the attached Appendix.

Profitability

The financial statements and the other information do not support the description of a rapidly expanding business given in the job advertisement. Revenue and gross profits fell by 35% and 38% respectively between 20X6 and 20X7. Despite this, the gross profit margin fell only very slightly, from 20.7% to 19.9%.

Only two years' figures are available, but the accompanying information suggests that revenue and profits may fluctuate from year to year, depending on the stage of completion of building projects. During the year ended 31 August 20X7, only 675 houses were sold compared with 1,080 in 20X6. A further development of 225 houses was nearing completion at the year end, but none of these was sold during the year. Sales revenue from this project will presumably be recognised in 20X7/20X8.

DAS appears to be attempting to break into a different sector of the market and possibly to move away from the type of project that it has previously undertaken. The houses that will be sold in the early part of 20X7/20X8 are a large development and are considerably more expensive than the houses that the company has sold to date. The new houses are expected to sell for between $425,000 and $600,000 each compared with an average sales value of $234,000 in 20X7 and $225,000 in 20X6. The project is expected to generate total revenue of between $95 million and $135 million. This means that even at the most optimistic estimate, the total revenue generated by the hospital development will fall considerably short of even total revenue in 20X7. The company will need to undertake other projects within the next few months if it is to generate enough additional revenue to make up the shortfall.

To date, the company's operations have been profitable, with what appears to be a steady increase (of approximately 4% per annum) in the price of houses sold. There are some worrying indications that the hospital development may not be as successful as the directors believe. Included in inventories at 31 August 20X7 is an amount of $140.5 million relating to properties under construction. It is likely that all or most of this amount relates to the new development. If so, it will be released to cost of sales when the properties are sold. On this basis, at best the project will barely break even. A more prudent estimate suggests a loss of around $25 million (the average sales price of each house is estimated at $512,500, therefore total revenue will be approximately $115 million).

Finance costs fell slightly in the year, but other expenses increased. This appears to be the main reason for the sharp fall in the net profit margin, from 11.6% to 6.3%. Other expenses are probably mainly administrative expenses. The increase may be a result of the move into a different type of development or, more probably, lack of management control, possibly as a result of over-optimism. Return on capital employed has fallen sharply from 21.8% to 11.0%. As the overall make-up of net assets has remained approximately the same, this is also a reflection of the fall in both profits and revenues.

Liquidity and gearing

Although the company has had significant short term borrowings throughout the period, it also had a positive cash balance of $2.8 million at 31 August 20X6. However, during the year ended 31 August 20X7 this cash balance was reduced to zero. Loans seem to have been renegotiated during the year. Short term borrowings have fallen from $75.4 million to $52.6 million while long term borrowings remain roughly the same. However, the amount of loans and borrowings included in current liabilities remains worryingly high. A low acid test ratio may be a normal aspect of this type of business (which has almost no trade receivables). Even so, the high level of short term loans means that the ratio is alarmingly low (0.04:1 in 20X7; 0.06:1 in 20X6).

Provided that all the houses in the hospital development are sold, the company will eventually receive cash of approximately $110 million ($512,500 × 225 – deposits received of approximately $5 million). In itself this will be more than sufficient to repay the short term loans. However, the nature of the business means that there is a considerable time lag between cash outflows to pay sub-contractors and others and the resulting cash inflows from the sale of houses. At present the company is heavily dependent on both short and long term borrowings to finance its ongoing activities. It would almost certainly find it difficult to continue to operate if the loans were called in.

Gearing fell from 70.3% to 65.9% in 20X7, but still remains high. Finance costs fell slightly, but the fall in profits has meant that interest cover has fallen from just over 3 times in 20X6 to 1.82 times in 20X7. The company's loans appear to bear average interest of just over 7%; as interest rates on low risk lending have been running at between 5% and 6% this suggests that banks and other lenders view DAS as a riskier than average prospect. If loans have been renegotiated towards the year end, the current rate of interest could be higher than 7%.

Future prospects

You have said that you are looking for a 'stable and prosperous employer'. DAS operates in a sector of the market where economic conditions are buoyant. It is not prosperous yet, but could become prosperous in future, provided that it engages in sufficient projects to generate a steady stream of revenue and profits. However, on the basis of the information available, it is far from clear that this will happen.

At present, the business is certainly not stable. Its revenues and profits are volatile and depend on the number of projects currently in progress and their stage of completion at the year end. Another reason why the business lacks stability is its high gearing and its poor liquidity. High gearing tends to exaggerate the effect of fluctuating profits, because loan interest has to be paid regardless of the level of profits. This reduces the amount available for dividends or reinvestment. It also increases the risk that the company will experience severe cash flow problems or go into liquidation.

The company will need to find sufficient funds, not only to pay its immediate liabilities, but to finance future projects. It currently holds land for redevelopment, but the amount fell from $210 million in 20X6 to $130 in 20X7. At some stage it will need to purchase more land to redevelop. The company is listed, so presumably at some stage the directors intend to offer more shares to the public, but the company has not paid a dividend for two years (probably due to lack of cash). This, together with the fluctuating profits and high gearing, means that potential investors may not be willing to take the risk. Further borrowing will almost certainly incur higher rates of interest and make the company even less attractive to investors. The company will need to convince potential investors and lenders that it is, or can become, highly profitable.

In conclusion, if you accepted a job with DAS there is a significant chance that you would risk being made redundant again at some point in the future. If, as you say, stability is one of your main criteria for choosing an employer I do not recommend that you apply for this post.

I hope that my comments have been helpful. If you have any further questions, please do not hesitate to contact me.

Appendix: Ratios

	20X7	*20X6*
Gross profit margin	$\dfrac{31.4}{157.9} \times 100\% = 19.9\%$	$\dfrac{50.3}{243} \times 100\% = 20.7\%$
Average revenue per house sold	$\dfrac{157.9}{675} = \$234{,}000$	$\dfrac{243}{1{,}080} = \$225{,}000$
Pre-tax profit margin	$\dfrac{10.0}{157.9} \times 100\% = 6.3\%$	$\dfrac{28.3}{243} \times 100\% = 11.6\%$
Return on capital employed	$\dfrac{22.2}{86.4+114.7} \times 100\% = 11.0\%$	$\dfrac{41.7}{79.2+112} \times 100\% = 21.8\%$
Acid test ratio	$\dfrac{3.2}{81.9} = 0.04{:}1$	$\dfrac{6.5}{100.1} = 0.06{:}1$
Gearing	$\dfrac{114.7+52.6}{86.4+114.7+52.6} \times 100\% = 65.9\%$	$\dfrac{112+75.4}{79.2+112+75.4} \times 100\% = 70.3\%$
Interest cover	$\dfrac{22.2}{12.2} = 1.82 \text{ times}$	$\dfrac{41.7}{13.4} = 3.11 \text{ times}$
Average interest rate	$\dfrac{12.2}{114.7+52.6} = 7.3\%$	$\dfrac{13.4}{112+75.4} = 7.1\%$

66 PJ GAMEWRITERS (NOV 05 EXAM)

REPORT

To:	The Finance Director of OPQ
From:	Assistant
Subject:	Financial Performance and position of PJ Gamewriters
Date:	22 November 20X5

As requested, I have analysed the information provided from the financial statements of PJ Gamewriters. Calculations of key performance measures are set out in the attached Appendix.

(a) **Profitability**

PJ Gamewriters is clearly a profitable operation. The income statement for the year ended 31 July 20X5 shows that revenue has risen by 26% and profit from operations has risen by 29% compared with the previous year. Gross profit margin is 55% and operating profit margin is 40%. Both these margins have risen slightly in the year. All costs except directors' remuneration have risen approximately in line with sales.

Return on capital employed (ROCE) is extremely high at 112%, although it has fallen from 122% in 20X4. One reason why ROCE is so high is that the assets of the business are understated. Non-current assets consist mainly of freehold property, which is stated at historic cost. Measuring the property at market value would reduce ROCE to approximately 83%. In addition, the assets actually used to generate revenues and profits are all intangible and have not been recognised. These assets consist of copyrights to the games and the technical skills of the two directors and the employees. The value of these intangibles is unknown and it is impossible to calculate a meaningful figure for ROCE without it.

Dividend payments in 20X5 are almost 50% higher than in 2004. Because profits have risen, dividend cover is not significantly reduced. As most of the equity shares are owned by the two directors and their parents, the dividend can be seen partly as additional directors' remuneration and partly as a repayment of capital.

Financial position

The business does not appear to have any liquidity problems. The current ratio has risen from 1.25 in 20X4 to just over 2 in 20X5. Inventories and trade payables appear low when compared to revenue and cost of sales; as production is outsourced trade payables probably relate only to administrative overheads. The collection period for trade receivables has risen from 54 days to 60 days; this is fairly high but does not give any real cause for concern.

Despite the substantial dividend payment, there has been a cash inflow of $196,000 in the year. No additional finance has been raised and no assets appear to have been sold, so the additional cash must have been generated from operations. There is no long-term debt and the main liability is for income tax for the current year.

Conclusion

The extracts from the financial statements show that PJ Gamewriters is highly profitable and that revenue and profits are increasing. There are no apparent liquidity or gearing problems and the business had a healthy cash surplus at 31 July 20X5.

However, this analysis has been based on extremely limited information. The business has intangible assets which have not been recognised on the statement of financial position and which are used to generate sales. Therefore it is impossible to calculate any meaningful figure for return on capital employed or to make any judgement as to how efficiently the business is using its assets. As you will be aware, much more information is needed before any investment decision can be made.

Signed: Assistant

Appendix: Ratio calculations

	20X5	20X4
Gross profit margin	$\frac{1,523}{2,793} = 55\%$	$\frac{1,168}{2,208} = 53\%$
Operating profit margin	$\frac{1,108}{2,793} = 40\%$	$\frac{858}{2,208} = 39\%$
Employment costs/Sales	$\frac{700}{2,793} = 25\%$	$\frac{550}{2,208} = 25\%$
Production costs/Sales	$\frac{215}{2,793} = 8\%$	$\frac{160}{2,208} = 7\%$
Operating expenses/Sales	$\frac{415}{2,793} = 15\%$	$\frac{310}{2,208} = 14\%$
Return on capital employed (ROCE)	$\frac{1,108}{987} \times 100 = 112\%$	$\frac{858}{703} \times 100 = 122\%$
Return on capital employed (ROCE) based on market value	$\frac{1,108}{987+350} \times 100 = 83\%$	
Dividend cover	$\frac{784}{500} = 1.6$ times	$\frac{570}{350} = 1.6$ times
Current ratio	$\frac{744}{367} = 2:1$	$\frac{403}{320} = 1.25:1$
Receivables collection period	$\frac{460}{2,793} \times 365 = 60$ days	$\frac{324}{2,208} \times 365 = 54$ days

(b)   **Limitations of the analysis**

The nature of the business and the way in which it operates mean that the financial statements alone cannot provide enough relevant information on which to assess the financial performance and position of the company.

- The business owns the copyrights to its existing computer games. These are a very significant intangible asset (one of its original games brings in a significant proportion of its revenue), but they have not been recognised on the statement of financial position. It will be necessary to value the copyrights, not only to assist in assessing PJ's financial performance but also in order to arrive at the purchase price should OPQ acquire the business.

- The business has another important intangible asset: the technical expertise of its directors and its games writers. However, this cannot be recognised on the statement of financial position because the business does not control its employees and cannot prevent them from leaving to work elsewhere. This type of business cannot operate without suitably qualified and talented staff. Any investment decision must take into account the fact that the business will lose the skills of the two directors (who wish to pursue other interests). It is also possible that some of the staff will leave. It will be necessary to assess the likelihood of staff moves and the possible long-term impact on revenue and the development of new products if key employees cannot be easily replaced.

- It is possible that the amounts included for employee costs are unrealistic. Directors' remuneration has remained constant, but the directors appear to have taken some of their remuneration in the form of dividends. Some of the games writers hold shares in the business; as a result they may have accepted salaries below the market rate. Information about staff salaries and directors' remuneration paid by competitors would be useful, given the importance of retaining or replacing key employees.

- There is no information about accounting policies. Information about revenue recognition would be particularly useful. Many software companies have adopted 'aggressive' policies that recognise revenue at the earliest possible stage, before it has been properly earned. It is possible that revenue is overstated.

- The business outsources the manufacture and distribution of the software. Information is needed about these operations and of their impact on the financial statements. It is possible that the distributor holds inventory on sale or return or consignment inventory or that there are other complex transactions. If so, the way in which these are treated may have affected reported revenue, production costs, operating expenses, receivables and inventories. It would be useful to compare PJ's financial statements with those of other small companies in the same sector to gain an idea of what is 'normal' for this type of business.

67   BZJ (MAY 06 EXAM)

> **Key answer tips**
>
> The main difficulty here is not getting carried away with the calculations; practically every ratio you could calculate provides useful information and supports the overall picture: declining performance; and an attempt to expand the business which may or may not have succeeded. There are probably more calculations here than you would need to produce a good answer in the exam, but notice that some of them are particularly relevant to a private investor (e.g. dividend cover, dividend payout rate, return on shareholders' equity).

(a)   **Earnings per share for the year ended 31 December 20X4**

$$\frac{3,676,000}{2,800,000} = 131.3c$$

Earnings per share for the year ended 31 December 20X5

$$\frac{2,460,000}{2,850,000} = 86.3c$$

Working: Weighted average number of shares in issue

$2,800,000 \times 10/12$	2,333,333
$3,100,000 \times 2/12$	516,667
	2,850,000

(b)   **REPORT**

To:	Investor in BZJ Group
From:	Investment advisor
Subject:	Performance and position of BZJ Group **Date:** May 20X6

As requested, I set out my comments on the performance and position of the BZJ Group as shown by its financial statements for the year ended 31 December 20X5. I have calculated a number of key ratios based on the financial statements and these are included in the attached Appendix.

Financial performance

The general impression is one of declining performance. Revenue has fallen by 0.8% between 20X4 and 20X5. This is surprising, given the effort that has apparently been made to increase market share and to develop new products. Gross profit margin and operating profit margin have both fallen. Some of this fall in profitability may have been caused by additional depreciation on the new non-current assets and there may have been additional costs connected with developing the new product line (this would be borne out by the slight increase in cost of sales). The comments in the Chairman's statement suggest that the group has gone through major changes in personnel and overall strategy during the year and the decline in profitability may be temporary. On the other hand, sales of new products and sales to new markets may mean that profit margins will continue to be lower than they were previously. This need not result in a permanent fall in overall earnings provided that sales increase in future periods.

Return on capital employed (ROCE) and return on shareholders' equity have both fallen very sharply. ROCE has fallen from 15.3% to 8.5% and return on shareholders' equity has fallen from 21.5% to 12%; a fall of nearly 50% in both cases. Some of this decrease will have been caused by the purchase of non-current assets during the year; these are included in capital employed, but have probably not yet begun to generate significant increases in sales and profits. Non-current asset turnover shows that in 20X4 the non-current assets generated sales of nearly five times their value, while in 20X5 they generated only 2.76 times their value; another fall of almost 50%.

It is noticeable that interest payable has increased by 62%, which reduces the profit available for dividends. Interest cover has fallen from 7.3 times to 3.7 times but, on that basis, the company should still be able to meet interest payments reasonably easily. However, interest payable for 20X5 is only 4.8% of total borrowings at the year-end and total borrowings have almost doubled during the year. This suggests that the interest charge for 20X6 and subsequent years may be significantly higher. Unless sales or profit margins improve considerably, overall earnings may fall dramatically in future periods. Earnings are likely to be volatile in any case because the group is highly geared.

Financial position

As the Chairman's statement explains, the group has invested in new non-current assets during the year. Actual new assets appear to have cost approximately $17.3 million (there was also a revaluation during the year) and this investment was financed partly by a share issue that raised $1.5 million and partly by an increase of $10 million in long-term borrowings. This means that gearing (as measured by the debt/equity ratio) has increased from just under 63% to almost 82%. This is quite a high level of gearing and means that many people would consider equity shares in the group to be a risky investment. It may be difficult for the group to obtain further long-term finance if this is required in future periods.

In addition, the group has moved from having a small positive cash balance in 20X4 to having short-term borrowings of $3.7 million in 20X5. Presumably these have also been used to finance the additional capital investment and to meet other costs connected with the planned expansion. The current ratio has fallen from 1.73 to 1.44 and the acid test ratio has fallen from 0.68 to a worryingly low 0.41.

All the elements of working capital except receivables have increased during the year. Inventory turnover has risen from 97 days to 131 days. This may be because inventory levels are being deliberately built up in anticipation of orders but it may also be a sign that that the group is finding it difficult to sell its new product range. This seems to be borne out by the decrease in receivables days and the decrease in receivables. Both of these could have resulted from improved credit control during the year, but the fall in overall sales suggests that the more likely explanation is that sales fell towards the end of the year. Trade payables days have increased from 87 days to 111 days; a worrying increase which suggests that the group may be using suppliers as a source of finance.

The Chairman's comments

The Chairman's comments can be read as an attempt to put a positive 'spin' on the group's disappointing performance and to justify the reduction in dividends. Earnings per share, dividend per share and dividend payout rate (the proportion of profit for the year paid out as dividend) have all fallen and the dividend per share is less than half that of the previous year.

The increase in non-current assets and working capital shows that the group is actually attempting to expand its operations. The additional investment has not yet resulted in increased sales and profits.

According to the Chairman's statement, the replacement of directors took place in March 20X5 and the new storage systems went into production in September 20X5, only four months before the year end. Given these timings it is quite possible that the new product range was only just starting to be sold at the year-end. It is difficult to predict future results, but it is not impossible that performance will improve in 20X6 and subsequent periods. There are some positive signs: a successful share issue two months before the year-end suggests that investors are reasonably confident of the group's future.

However, in the meantime the group has potential liquidity problems and a high level of gearing. If the directors' new policies do not lead to improved profits within the next two or three years, the group will probably face severe financial difficulties.

Appendix: Ratio calculations

	20X5	*20X4*
Gross profit margin	$\frac{17,342}{120,366} \times 100\% = 14.4\%$	$\frac{19,065}{121,351} \times 100\% = 15.7\%$
Operating profit margin	$\frac{5,377}{120,366} \times 100\% = 4.5\%$	$\frac{6,617}{121,351} \times 100\% = 5.5\%$
Return on shareholders' equity	$\frac{3,908}{30,428 + 2,270} \times 100\% = 12.0\%$	$\frac{5,711}{24,623 + 1,947} \times 100\% = 21.5\%$
Return on capital employed	$\frac{5,377}{30,428 + 2,270 + 26,700 + 3,662} \times 100\% = 8.5\%$	
		$\frac{6,617}{24,623 + 1,947 + 16,700} \times 100\% = 15.3\%$
Non-current asset turnover	$\frac{120,366}{43,575} = 2.76$	$\frac{121,351}{24,320} = 4.99$
Interest cover	$\frac{5,377}{1,469} = 3.7$	$\frac{6,617}{906} = 7.3$
Debt/equity	$\frac{26,700}{30,428 + 2,270} \times 100\% = 81.7\%$	$\frac{16,700}{24,623 + 1,947} \times 100\% = 62.9\%$
Current ratio	$\frac{52,030}{36,207} = 1.44:1$	$\frac{44,951}{26,001} = 1.73:1$
Acid test ratio	$\frac{14,922}{36,207} = 0.41:1$	$\frac{17,691}{26,001} = 0.68:1$

Inventory turnover	$\dfrac{37,108}{103,024} \times 365 = 131.5$ days	$\dfrac{27,260}{102,286} \times 365 = 97.3$ days
Receivables turnover	$\dfrac{14,922}{120,366} \times 365 = 45.2$ days	$\dfrac{17,521}{121,351} \times 365 = 52.7$ days
Trade payables turnover	$\dfrac{31,420}{103,024} \times 365 = 111.3$ days	$\dfrac{24,407}{102,286} \times 365 = 87.1$ days
Dividend per share	$\dfrac{155}{3,100} = 5c$	$\dfrac{364}{2,800} = 13c$
Dividend payout rate	$\dfrac{155}{2,460} \times 100\% = 6.3\%$	$\dfrac{364}{3,676} \times 100\% = 9.9\%$

68 BSP (MAY 07 EXAM)

Key answer tips

The requirement 'leads' you by saying what you should cover in the report and gives you a structure to use. As always when answering this type of question, make sure that you use all the additional information in the scenario. All of it is relevant.

Also, notice how few ratios have been calculated. Much of the analysis can be carried out just by looking carefully at the statement of cash flows.

To: Marketing Director of BSP

From: Assistant to Finance Director

Subject: Draft statement of cash flows for the year ended 31 March 20X7

Date: 22 May 20X7

As requested, I have analysed the draft statement of cash flows. Relevant calculations are set out in the attached Appendix.

The difference between cash and profit

There are several reasons why profit or loss for a period may be significantly different from cash inflow or outflow for the same period. The profit for the period is calculated on an accruals basis and may also depend on the accounting policies adopted by the business. Cash flow information is often believed to be more reliable than information about profits and losses, because it is harder to manipulate. However, a statement of cash flows should always be interpreted with caution. Businesses cannot survive without cash, but a high cash balance by itself is not always a good sign.

BSP's cash has increased by $1,091,000 during the year. However, the statement of cash flows shows that most of the cash has been generated by investing and financing activities, rather than from business operations. BSP received cash of $3,170,000 for the year. Of this amount, $2,320,000 came from the sale of the subsidiaries and $850,000 from the issue of share capital. These are exceptional cash flows and cannot be repeated in future periods. Although the company has a high positive cash balance at 31 March 20X7, most of its cash inflows have been absorbed by the purchase of property, plant and equipment and, more worryingly, by an outflow of $1,441,000 from operations.

Profitability

The company's profit before tax has fallen dramatically between 20X6 and 20X7, even before unusual items are taken into account. Profit before tax for the year ended 31 March 20X6 was reduced by exceptional training and marketing costs and would have been $756,000 if these costs had not been incurred. In the year ended 31 March 20X7 the company made a substantial profit by disposing of the two foreign subsidiaries, which reduced the company's loss before tax by $667,000. The 'true' loss before tax is approximately $1,120,000. Based on the adjusted figures, loss before tax was 9.1% of revenue in 2007, compared with a positive profit margin of 6.2% in 20X6.

Working capital

In 20X7 the company made an operating loss of $937,000 and cash generated by operations was reduced still further by increases in working capital. There were significant increases in both inventories and receivables during the year. Inventories increased by 11% in 20X6 and by 34.6% in 20X7. Receivables increased by 15% between 20X6 and 20X7 (compared with an increase of 2.3% in 2006). In contrast, payables only increased by a small amount in 20X6 and 20X7, although this did offset some of the total cash outflow from movements in working capital.

The increase in inventories may be a result of the company's decision to sell additional products. However, even under these circumstances, an increase in inventories of over one third appears unusually high. It suggests that cash is being tied up unnecessarily.

The increase in receivables is worrying, as revenue has only increased by a very small amount. The receivables days ratio shows that it takes approximately 61 days to collect amounts due from customers at the 20X7 year-end, compared with approximately 49 days in 20X6. (Note that receivables days for 20X6 and 20X7 are not strictly comparable because the 20X6 revenue and receivables figures include amounts relating to the two subsidiaries sold during the year. The figures for 20X7 have been adjusted to exclude amounts relating to the subsidiaries.) The increase in receivables days is probably a result of the extended credit and discounts offered to customers. This policy appears to have generated some additional sales, but it has also absorbed a considerable amount of cash.

Future prospects

The company almost achieved its sales targets in 20X7 in both burglar alarms and fire alarms. Therefore you may be correct to say that the lack of profitability is caused by poor cost control. Revenue increased very slightly in 20X7, but this appears to have been achieved at the expense of profit margins and cash flow. Unless revenues increase further in the near future, it is unlikely that the company's policy of attracting customers by offering discounts and extended credit terms can be continued in the long term. The company almost certainly needs to control its costs more carefully in future, but it is also possible that margins are falling within the industry as a whole. Unfortunately the decline in profitability may not necessarily be a short-term problem.

Sales of burglar alarms have fallen by almost 10% in the year. They now account for just under 90% of total revenue , with the remainder coming from fire alarm and sprinkler systems. This suggests that the change in business strategy may be justified. However, it is not yet clear whether sales of fire alarms will increase sufficiently to make up the shortfall in revenue from the sale of burglar alarms, particularly if these sales continue to fall.

Interest charges increased in 20X7, which suggests either that rates increased or that the company had short-term borrowings at some point during the year. The sale of the two foreign subsidiaries has generated a substantial cash inflow. As a result, the company should not need to borrow cash or incur interest charges in the short term. This should improve profits to some extent.

However, the subsidiaries were profitable and accounted for approximately 10% of group sales in the year ended 31 March 20X7. They were sold in March and therefore the group revenue for 20X7 will include almost a full year's sales. Without these sales, revenues and profits will fall even further in 2008, unless the performance of the remaining business improves.

Dividends paid were $200,000 in the year ended 31 March 20X6, but no dividend was paid in 20X7. The fact that the company was able to issue shares during the year suggests shareholder confidence, but sooner or later the shareholders will want a return on their investment. They may be prepared to wait for a short time while the change in business strategy takes effect, but failure to pay a substantial dividend in 20X8 will probably affect the share price and make it difficult to raise further finance if this is needed.

Conclusion

The statement of cash flows shows a healthy cash balance, but it also reveals a number of problems. There have been substantial cash inflows during the year, but these have probably been achieved at the expense of profits in the longer term. The company urgently needs to improve its working capital management and probably also its cost control. However, there are more fundamental issues. Unless BSP can generate increased sales and become profitable within a reasonably short time, losses and other cash outflows will quickly absorb its remaining cash resources.

Appendix: Ratio calculations and other relevant calculations

	20X7	20X6

(Loss)/profit before tax as a percentage of revenue

Based on the draft financial statements $\frac{(453)}{12,320} \times 100 = (3.7\%)$ $\frac{306}{12,110} \times 100 = 2.5\%$

After adjustment for unusual items $\frac{(1,120)}{12,320} \times 100 = (9.1\%)$ $\frac{756}{12,110} \times 100 = 6.2\%$

Tutorial note:

20X6: unusual marketing and advertising costs are added back (306 + 200 + 250).

20X7: profit on disposal of subsidiaries is deducted ((453) – 667).

Receivables days

Based on year-end figures $\frac{1,856}{12,320 \times 90\%} \times 365 = 61.1$ days $\frac{1,614}{12,110} \times 365 = 48.6$ days

Tutorial note:

Receivables at 31 March 20X7 do not include any amounts relating to the two foreign subsidiaries sold in March 20X7. Therefore revenue for 20X7 has been reduced to exclude the 10% of group sales made by the subsidiaries during the year.

Movements in working capital

	20X5	20X6	20X7
Inventories	$591,000	$656,000	$883,000
		+$65,000	+$227,000
% increase year on year		11.0%	34.6%
Receivables	$1,578,000	$1,614,000	$1,856,000
		+$36,000	+$242,000
% increase year on year		2.3%	15%

69   FJK (MAY 08 EXAM)

Key answer tips

The requirement asks for comments on financial performance and position so try to split your time between the income statement and statement of financial position. The analysis was leading you in a particular direction with regards to FJK's lack of cash and increased borrowing. Try to pick up on the big picture rather than focusing on individual and distinct ratios.

REPORT

To: Kay

From: Financial Advisor

Subject: Analysis of financial information relating to FJK

Date: 20 May 20X8

As requested, I have analysed the financial information provided for FJK for the two years ended 31 March 20X8 and I set out my comments below. As part of my analysis I have calculated a number of key ratios and these are included in the attached Appendix.

I have also addressed possible risks and problem areas raised from the financial statement review and suggested actions that the directors could undertake.

Financial performance

Profit before tax and revenue have increased in 20X8 by 44% and 54% respectively and gross profit margin has also increased marginally. This is almost certainly due to the international sales which were incorporated into 20X7's results for only a few months of the year but really started to take off in the year ended March 20X8. The better margin may be explained by higher achievable selling price or by better control of manufacturing costs.

Distribution costs have risen from only 2.7% of revenue to 4.5% but this is inevitable given the international expansion and necessary distribution channels. Administrative costs have remained stable as a percentage of revenue but have increased by 59% year on year. One would expect administrative expenses to be largely fixed in nature so this may suggest a lack of control in this area.

Return on capital employed has actually fallen as, despite the increased profit before tax, there have been increases in the funding to the business which have not yet borne out in the results. Long term loans have increased by 68% and short term debt by 317%. These additional funds appear to have been used to invest in non-current assets which is discussed below.

Interest cover has fallen from 18 to 11 times. This is still a relatively high figure i.e. the profit before interest could pay the finance cost eleven times over. Finance costs have more than doubled due to the increases in borrowing. It seems likely that dividends would be safe as the profit can cover finance costs so there would be surplus profits for distributions to the owners.

Financial position

Return on capital employed (ROCE) can be broken down into its constituent parts of operating profit margin and net asset turnover. Net asset turnover has fallen from 2.03 to 1.83 showing that FJK is not utilising its assets to generate revenue. The key element in this is the increase in non-current assets.

Non-current assets have more than doubled in value in 20X8, even after removing the effect of the revaluation. This reflects considerable investment in assets for long-term use in the business. There may have been branches set up in neighbouring countries which demand infrastructure. In 2006/07 the expansion was made by establishing a sales force in additional countries but the financial statements suggest more significant investment. This investment may well bear fruit in the next financial year 08/09 so the trend in ROCE may reverse.

Inventory turnover has increased in 20X8. FJK are manufacturing and selling items of furniture approximately every two months and are turning the stock over more quickly than in 20X7. There is less risk of obsolescence and write downs. There is also less working capital tied up in raw materials, work in progress and unsold finished goods, which is particularly important for a growing business. FJK need to make sure however, that there is still sufficient stock available to meet orders.

Receivables days have reduced from 52 to 44 days. There may have been a concerted effort to manage credit better. Again, this reduces working capital necessary to operate the business and provides extra free funding. Conversely, potential customers may be put off by a short credit period or excessive chasing so care needs to be taken.

Payables days have increased from 74 to 104 days. FJK are squeezing their suppliers to offer long credit terms to reduce working capital but they need to be careful as they risk reducing supplier goodwill. A reliable source of good quality raw materials must be maintained.

FJK's current ratio has reduced to below one meaning there are no longer sufficient current assets to cover current liabilities as they fall due. There are indications of more serious problems as the quick ratio, excluding inventories, has fallen from 0.67 to only 0.42. FJK does not have enough current assets to turn into cash quickly to, for example, pay suppliers if they demand it.

Gearing has increased from 41% to 50% because of the increase in long and short term borrowings. Even though interest cover is not a problem at the minute, care needs to be taken to ensure that interest payments can be maintained with the growing levels of borrowing.

Risks and problem areas

The interest tax expense for 20X8 is understated and this would have an effect on the figures. Using the effective rate for 20X7 as a guide the tax payable in 20X8 could rise by $72,000 having the knock on effect of further worsening the liquidity ratios discussed above.

The current and quick ratios are of concern and FJK could find themselves in difficulty if the relationships with suppliers worsen and they demand faster payment. The short term loans and borrowings probably consist of bank overdrafts and these could also be called at any time.

A concern for a growing business such as this is overtrading whereby the business is profitable but does not have sufficient cash in the short term to meet payments as they fall due. The capital injection of $250,000 would help with this situation if the funds are invested in working capital. However, caution should be exercised when considering the funding. The request from Fay and Jay may suggest that alternative sources of finance have been exhausted and there needs to be some explanation of where the extra funds would be invested and how much difference they would make.

FJK must produce forecasts and sensitivity analysis for the next three financial years to determine what the funding requirements are in total. The business may need to consider different sources of finance which may mean losing some control over the business. For example, venture capital or a listing.

Appendix

		20X8	20X7
Gross profit margin	$\dfrac{\text{Gross profit}}{\text{Revenue}}$	$\dfrac{1{,}655}{5{,}973} = 27.7\%$	$\dfrac{1{,}018}{3{,}886} = 26.2\%$
Return on capital employed	$\dfrac{\text{Profit before interest}}{\text{Debt} + \text{equity} *}$	$\dfrac{968 + 97}{2{,}167 + 763 + 327} = 32.7\%$	$\dfrac{671 + 40}{1{,}363 + 453 + 103} = 37.1\%$
Operating profit margin	$\dfrac{\text{Profit before interest}}{\text{Revenue}}$	$\dfrac{968 + 97}{5{,}973} = 17.8\%$	$\dfrac{671 + 40}{3{,}886} = 18.3\%$
Net asset turnover	$\dfrac{\text{Revenue}}{\text{Debt} + \text{equity}}$	$\dfrac{5{,}973}{2{,}167 + 763 + 327} = 1.83$	$\dfrac{3{,}886}{1{,}363 + 453 + 103} = 2.03$
Distribution costs	$\dfrac{\text{Distribution costs}}{\text{Revenue}}$	$\dfrac{270}{5{,}973} = 4.5\%$	$\dfrac{106}{3{,}886} = 2.7\%$
Interest cover	$\dfrac{\text{Profit before interest}}{\text{Finance cost}}$	$\dfrac{968 + 97}{97} = 11$	$\dfrac{671 + 40}{40} = 18$
Inventory turnover	$\dfrac{\text{Cost of sales}}{\text{Inventory}}$	$\dfrac{4{,}318}{677} = 6.4$	$\dfrac{2{,}868}{510} = 5.6$

Receivables days	$\dfrac{\text{Receivables}}{\text{Revenue}} \times 365$	$\dfrac{725}{5,973} x365$ = 44.3 days	$\dfrac{553}{3,886} x365$ = 51.9 days
Payables days	$\dfrac{\text{Payables}}{\text{Cost of sales}**} \times 365$	$\dfrac{1,227}{4,318} x365$ = 103.7 days	$\dfrac{578}{2,868} x365$ = 73.6 days
Current ratio	$\dfrac{\text{Current assets}}{\text{Current liabilities}}$	$\dfrac{1,402}{1,718}$ = 0.82	$\dfrac{1,075}{845}$ = 1.27
Quick ratio	$\dfrac{\text{Receivables} + \text{cash}}{\text{Current liabilities}}$	$\dfrac{725}{1,718}$ = 0.42	$\dfrac{553+12}{845}$ = 0.67
Gearing	$\dfrac{\text{Debt}}{\text{Equity}*}$	$\dfrac{763+327}{2,167}$ = 50.3%	$\dfrac{453+103}{1,363}$ = 40.8%

*   Equity excludes the revaluation reserve in 20X8 for comparability purposes.

**   Cost of sales used as an approximation for purchases.

70   RG (NOV 09 EXAM)

(a)   **REPORT**

To: Close friend

From: An Accountant

Subject: RG Group financials yr end June 20X9

Date: Nov 20X9

Profitability

Revenue has shown little growth (just $3m which is 0.5%) over the last 12 months however distribution costs and admin expenses have increased significantly. As a result the profit before tax has fallen from $75m to just $60m.

The reason for the distribution cost increase appears to be the cost incurred in setting up the new distribution network and the employment and training of the new sales team. This expenditure was undertaken in order to increase market share (sale revenues), as yet the results of this have not been seen. However, this may be as activity has just recently started in these areas – this can be seen by the fact that June 2009 orders are higher than expected.

There is a slight increase in gross profit margin from 25.3% to 26.7%, it will be important that this is maintained in new market sales.

Administrative expenses as a percentage of sales have increased from 3.9% in 20X8 to 6.4% in 20X9. This increase is masked slightly by the gain on the sale of the available for sale investment of $4m which has been netted off the expenses. Removing this would result in administrative expense % increasing to 7.1% in 20X9. Some of these costs might also be related to the setting up of new sales channels. The increase is quite significant and may also indicate a lack of management control over costs.

Finally, the 20X9 profit before tax includes the share of profit of associate of $5m, without the associate the profit would have fallen by $20m and the net profit percentage for 20X9 falls to just 6.9%. It is imperative that the management now turn their attention to the control of costs to ensure that the expansion in markets brings appropriate net returns.

On a more positive note the management appear to be making good investment decisions in respect of both the financial assets that they have sold and those that they have retained (with gains taken to other comprehensive income in the period of $6m). The investment in the associate has also brought $5m which has helped the bottom line profit. We do not know when during the year the associate was acquired therefore it is possible that the associate's return could be even greater next year.

Efficiency and liquidity

The return on capital employed has fallen and is generally at quite a low level. This may be due to the fact that significant investment was made in 20X8 and the revenues of this investment have not yet been earned. This return would be expected to increase in the next period.

Payables days have remained relatively constant, however the receivables days have increased from 48 days to 69 days. This is another indication that management need to tighten up control. It may be that during the expansion period management attention has necessarily been elsewhere and that next period improvements may be seen as costs etc are brought back under control.

The cash balance has dropped significantly (by $125m). This is the result of the dividend payment ($50m) and the repayment of the loan ($51m). To the extent that the loan has been reduced, this has helped reduce financial (gearing) risk. However it is essential that receivables days are reduced to boost the cash balance and prevent the company having to go into overdraft.

In addition, with the new markets being targeted, RG may have to offer incentives to new customers and so tight control of existing accounts and control of all new receivables should be a priority going forward.

Inventory days have increased from 70 days to 115 days. This could be a result of the increased orders in June. This would be expected to return to a steady level once the level of regular orders is established.

The current ratio has decreased slightly but it still provides adequate cover for current liabilities, however since inventories have increased the quick ratio will provide a more accurate picture. The quick ratio has fallen from 2.1 to 1.14. This is due to the fall in the cash balance.

Capital Structure

The gearing ratio is low and has in fact fallen from 43% to 30% due to the repayment of part of the loan and the share issue in the period. On the whole financial risk seems low and as a result finance costs have been kept to a minimum and interest cover is more than adequate at this time.

Conclusion

It appears that the low returns are temporary and that the investments made in an effort to increase market share are likely to bring future benefits. Although RG needs to regain tighter control of receivables and expenses, the management appear to have made good decisions on investments and have shown good management of working capital up to now.

The finance providers clearly believe RG to be low risk as the long term borrowings carry an interest rate of less than 4%. The shareholders have continued to support the entity via the share issue in the period and appear to have been compensated for the lack of growth by the receipt of a dividend, even though it is not covered by the earnings.

It looks like prospects are good for RG.

(b) **Segmental information**

Segmental disclosures would allow us to analyse the performance of each identifiable part of the business. This is especially useful if one particular segment is underperforming, as this would not be evident from the consolidated financial statements.

In the case of RG this could be the motivation for chasing new market share through the new distribution lines – maybe the new channels will prove more profitable. A segmental analysis would illustrate this as we could separately analyse the profit margins.

Further breakdown of results would also help to monitor how successful the expansion is for the segment in the next period.

Segmental analysis is more useful for assessing performance but less so for the analysis of capital structure and the utilisation of cash which tend to be affected by entity wide decisions (central treasury functions) rather than those taken by individual segments.

Appendix

	20X9	20X8
Gross Profit margin	$154m/$576m = 26.7%	%145m/$573m = 25.3%
Distribution cost percentage	$56m/$576m = 9.7%	$40m/$573m = 7.0%
Admin cost percentage	$37m/$576m = 6.4%	$22m/$573m =3.8%
Admin cost adjusted for profit on disposal	($37m+$4m)/$576m = 7.1%	
Net profit margin	$45m/$576m = 7.8%	$61m/$573m =10.6%
Net profit margin without associate	($45m–$5m)/$576m = 6.9%	
ROCE PBIT* / CE**	$61m/$669m = 9.1%	$83m/$680m = 12.2%
Inventory days	$133m/$422m x 365 = 115 days	$82m/$428m x 365 = 70 days
Receivable days	$109m/$576m x 365 = 69 days	$76m/$573m x 365 = 48 days

Payable days	$91m/$422m x 365	$87m/$428m x 365
	= 79 days	= 74 days
Current ratio	$254m/$106m	$295m/$101m
	= $2.40:$1	= $2.92:$1
Quick ratio	($254m–$133m)/$106m	($295–$82)/$101
	= $1.14:$1	= $2.11:$1
Gearing (D/D+E)	$514m/$669m**	$205m/$680m**
	= 23.0%	= 30.1%
Interest cover	$61m*/$6m	$83m*/$8m
	= 10.2 times	= 10.4 times
*PBIT	$60m – $5m + $6m	$75m + $8m
	=$61m	= $83m
**CE	$515m + $154m	$475m + $205m
	= $669m	= $680m

71   KER (MAY 10 EXAM)

Key answer tips

This question is a fairly general analysis question. Calculation of the ratios should be straight forward. The real test is to be able to use the scenario to make some comments on either why the ratio has changed or the implication (so what) of the change.

The specific theme of this question was to scrutinise the chairman's comments using some professional scepticism. Although his comments on increased revenues and overall profits are valid, when you take a look at the margins some worrying declines in profitability are notable. It would also be worth commenting on the increased financial risk denoted by the increase to loan finance and corresponding fall in interest cover.

(a)   **Briefing note on KER**

The expansion to new markets has resulted in a 40% increase in revenue. This appears to have been achieved, however, at the expense of the profit margins. Gross profit margin has fallen from 31% to 26% in the last year, and with the same product base it is likely then that this is caused by selling at reduced prices to break into new markets.

The distribution costs have increased by 58% from 20X8 and although an increase would be expected with the expansion, it is considerably higher than the increase in revenue. It is possible that the new markets are a significant distance away geographically.

The profit for the year appears to have increased slightly, but this is in fact due to the inclusion of the associate's profit. Without the associate's profit in 20X9, the profit margin is 2.8% compared with 9% in 20X8. This is a significant decrease and is likely to be caused by a combination of reduced gross margins, high distribution costs and finance costs which have doubled in the year.

Interest cover has fallen from 5.2 in 20X8 to 3.7 as a result of diminished profits, increased long-term borrowings and the introduction of an overdraft facility. Although there is still adequate cover, it increases KER's vulnerability to increases in interest rates. The gearing ratio has also increased significantly despite the increases in equity from the revaluation of property, plant and equipment and investments. The increased loans have resulted in an increase in gearing from 43% to 60% and this together with falling interest cover may affect KER's ability to raise further finance in the future.

The return on capital employed has been maintained, however a significant part of the increase in capital employed has come from revaluation and so will not necessarily bring increased future revenues. The increased revenues have however resulted in an increase in non-current asset turnover from 2.5 to 3.0.

The expansion has clearly put pressure on working capital. In addition to moving from a positive cash balance to an overdraft, the receivables days have increased from 48 days to 63 days, and yet payables days have remained static. Inventory days have increased from 34 days to 50 days which although may be as a result of increased orders about to be met, is nonetheless tying up cash. This is a common result of expanding too quickly, however KER must improve its debt collection if it is to avoid a cash crisis.

The Chairman's summary is biased towards the increases in revenue, but the expansion has reduced profitability and compromised cash flow as a result of increase in receivables. In addition, the increases in non-current assets appear to come from revaluation rather than investment in assets for the future generation of trading revenue and so future revenue increases may not be sustainable. The profit share from the associate masks the falling margins resulting in KER being sensitive to interest rate changes in the future.

Examiner's comments

The quality of the analysis was generally good with many candidates appreciating the impact of the expansion on profitability and the impact of the additional finance on gearing, finance costs and interest cover. Most correctly highlighted working capital to be a major problem. There was once again problems with the calculation of certain key ratios, namely operating profit margin, interest cover, return on capital employed and asset turnover – again the dangers of rote learning are evident when candidates compare revenue with total non-current assets – when the associate and available for sale investments contribute nothing to revenue.

(b)   **Affect of accounting policies on entity comparison**

Although many of the alternative treatments within IFRS have been removed, there are still some accounting standards that allow for choice. The most obvious being IAS 16 Property, plant and equipment, which permits assets to be held under the cost or valuation method. Where entities being compared adopt different policies then the totals for non-current assets, depreciation (and therefore profit for the year) and equity will all be affected. This affects performance ratios such as profit margin, financial structure ratios such as gearing and interest cover and efficiency ratios, such as ROCE.

In addition the estimates used to determine the value of inventories, the recoverability of receivables and the useful lives of non-current assets are highly subjective. Reduced comparability may result from directors taking a more or less conservative view than the directors of another entity. This could affect efficiency ratios such as inventory and receivables turnover and ROCE.

There is a great deal of flexibility in how entities report the various expenses incurred. Some entities may choose to include, e.g. depreciation in cost of sales rather that in administration or distribution costs, and so even where entities operate in the same segment they could have notably different gross profit margins.

Examiner's comments

Part (b) was misunderstood by many – the question asked about the impact of accounting policies and estimates and the impact that has on comparability. Many issues raised by candidates were more about business policy rather than accounting policies – whether to trade in luxury or basic goods, the size of the entity, etc.

Appendix – relevant ratios that could be selected (up to a maximum of 8 marks)

	20X9	20X8
Gross profit margin GP/ Revenue	372/1,430 x 100 = 26%	317/1,022 x 100 = 31%
Profit for the year Profit/revenue	120/1,430 x 100 = 8.4%	92/1,022 x 100 = 9%
Profit for the year, excluding the share of associate	(120 – 80)/1,430 x 100 = 2.8%	
Interest cover Profit before interest/interest	220/60 = 3.7 times	155/30 = 5.2 times
Gearing Debt/equity	400/663 x 100 = 60%	210/487 x 100 = 43%
ROCE Profit before finance costs/ capital employed	(160 + 60)/(663 + 400) x 100 = 21%	(125 + 30)/(487 + 210) x 100 = 22%
Non-current asset turnover Revenue/ non-current assets	1,430/480 = 3.0 times	1,022/404 = 2.5 times
Receivables days Receivables/revenue x 365 days	(247/1,430) x 365 days = 63 days	(134/1,022) x 365 days = 48 days
Inventory days Inventory/ CoS x 365 days	(145/1058) x 365 days = 50 days	(65/705) x 365 days = 34 days
Gearing Debt/Debt +Equity	400/(400 + 663) x 100 = 37.6%	210/(210 + 487) x 100 = 30.1%
Gearing could be stated including overdraft	437/(437 + 663) =39.7%	
Payable days Payables/CoS x 365 days	(99/1,058) x 365 days = 34 days	(68/705) x 365 days = 35 days

Operating profit (GP less admin less distrib)/rev	(372 – 74 – 158) = 140/1,430 9.8%	(317 – 62 – 100)/1,022 15.2%
Current ratio CA/CL	392/136 2.9	221/68 3.25
Quick ratio CA less inventories	247/136 1.8	156/68 2.3
Profit before tax/revenue	160/1,430 11.2%	125/1,022 12.2%

Changes in the year

Increase in revenue (1,430 – 1,022) / 1,022 = 40%
Increase in distribution costs (158 – 100) / 100 = 58%

72   GD (NOV 10 EXAM)

(a)   **Financial performance**

The financial performance of GD has clearly been affected by the pressure resulting from the new competitor entering the market with revenue falling by 14% from 20X0. Gross profit margin has fallen by 4% since 2009 and this could be due to GD being forced to drop prices to compete with the new competitor.

The net profit margin has fallen from 15% to 11%, however administrative expenses includes the offset of a gain on held for trading investments of $9 million. Without this gain the net profit would have fallen to 10%. The finance costs are still relatively high considering the loan liability has been halved in the year, although it is possible that the loan was actually repaid part way through the year. It should also be noted that GD now has an overdraft which will be relatively expensive to service.

The return on capital employed has dropped 24% since 20X0. Capital employed has reduced in the year, despite a revaluation, mainly due to the loan being repaid. The ROCE, however has fallen, showing the impact that reduced profits has had on the business.

Non-current asset turnover has fallen from 2.9 to 2.1. This is due to reduced revenue, and increases in NCA including the revaluation. There has also been an acquisition in the year and this could have increased NCA from last year. It looks like the investment in PPE has not yet paid off in revenue streams as revenue is down from 20X0.

Financial position

The gearing has fallen from 50% to 18% in the year due to the repayment of the loan. The repayment amounted to a significant cash outflow in the year, however the lender must have been assured that GD could afford to service and repay the loan. The interest cover is more than enough, however the issue will be whether or not GD will have enough cash to actually pay the interest. In addition, the remaining loan is to be repaid by 20X2 and the entity appears to be short of liquid funds.

The current and quick ratios have fallen mainly due to the increased payables and the introduction of the overdraft. The quick ratio has fallen from 0.74 to 0.52 and indicates cash crisis and the fall in current ratio is to 1.03 and so GD is dangerously close to insolvency.

Receivables are still being collected within 35 days which shows good credit control, or loyal customers. This however is not sufficient to generate adequate liquid funds and payables are being stretched as a result, from 63 days to 80 days. This is not a good policy at a time when there is a new market member as suppliers may choose to switch supplies to them. In addition, GD needs to negotiate with its suppliers to reduce costs in order to recover the margins and therefore a good relationship is vital.

The increase in inventories days is consistent with the falling revenue, but GD should test for obsolescence on inventories from the packaging business.

Conclusion and recommendation

GD has liquidity issues, however the management structure appears to be well organised. Credit control appears to be a priority and the management have made some good investments, with upward valuations in both non-current assets and held for trading investments.

The minutes of the Board meetings indicate that management are responsive to change and have reacted positively by applying for long term funding prior to the existing loan being repaid and organising a meeting with suppliers to negotiate better terms. GD is likely to fare better in these meetings if payables have been settled and to this end the funding would assist.

The recommendation is to put the application forward for further consideration.

Appendix I

Ratios

	20X1	20X0
	$m	$m
Gross profit GP/revenue x 100%	360/1,200 x 100% = 30%	470/1,400 x 100% = 34%
Operating profit Profit before finance costs/revenue	(179+11)/1,200 x 100% = 16%	(290+15)/1,400 x 100% = 22%
Net profit PFY/revenue x 100%	129/1,200 x 100% = 11%	205/1,400 x 100% = 15%
Gearing Debt/total equity	90/496 x 100% = 18%	180/364 x 100% = 50%
Current ratio Current assets/current liabilities	292/283 = 1.03 : 1	304/249 = 1.22 : 1
Quick ratio CA – inventories/current liabilities	(292 – 146) /283 = 0.52 : 1	(304 – 120) /249 = 0.74 : 1
Receivables days Receivables/revenue x 365 days	115/1,200 x 365 = 35 days	125/1,400 x 365 = 33 days
Payables days Payables/cost of sales x 365 days	185/840 x 365 = 80 days	160/930 x 365 = 63 days

Inventories days Inventories/cost of sales x 365 days	146/840 x 365 = 63 days	120/930 x 365 = 47 days
Return on capital employed Profit before finance costs/capital employed x 100%	(179 + 11)/(496 + 90) = 190/586 x 100% = 32%	(290 + 15)/(364 + 180) = 305/544 x 100% = 56%
Non-current asset turnover Revenue/non-current assets	1,200/577 = 2.1	1,400/489 = 2.9
Interest cover Profit before finance costs/finance costs	190/11 = 17.3 times	305/15 = 20.3 times

It would be helpful to see some segmental analysis for GD, to establish how much of an impact the segments' results have on the entity as a whole. It would also help to assess the risk of potential write-down of inventories and non-current assets, should the strategy not be successful. Segmental analysis would also help in identifying whether the fall in margins is solely due to the packaging segment or whether any other areas are being affected.

Forecasts with the new strategy being implemented would be helpful to estimate the future profitability and cash flows to gain comfort that GD is setting realistic targets and can afford to service the finance.

Examiner's comments

I am delighted to find that the quality of the financial analysis continues to improve with most candidates having moved away from the dreaded – this is up and this is down. Many were able to appreciate the scenario and consider this together with the results of the ratio calculation. The calculation of the ratios still did cause candidates problems.

---

73 DFG (MAR 11 EXAM)

(a) **To friend**

Report on financial performance and position

The revenue has only marginally increased in the year by 1.6%, however, profit margins have all increased significantly. In particular the gross profit margin has increased from 10% to 19%, which is likely to be as a result of reduced purchase prices from the new supplier contract that was secured in the year. Whilst this is a very positive and important step for DFG (given its low margin in the previous year) it will be important to establish whether this reduced cost also means a reduced level of quality. If quality is being compromised then this increase in margin maybe short-lived as customers may be driven away in the longer term.

In addition, the switch in supplier may be responsible for the lawsuit. It is a risky strategy to pursue aggressive revenue and margin targets at the expense of supplying good quality products. Although a contingent liability of $30 million is included in the notes, the lawyer's assessment is that DFG is likely to lose the court case and the payout may be more. There is already serious pressure on the entity's finances and the entity may not survive if the payout is any more or if other customers decide to sue. There is a potential issue of going concern that would need clarification before you arrive at a final decision concerning employment.

Both administration and distribution costs have increased significantly when compared to a 1.6% increase in revenue. Whilst these costs are not that large in relation to revenues, it will be important to establish that management have good control over expenses for the long term.

The increase in TCI is largely due to the revaluation gain reported within other comprehensive income. The valuation was performed by an internal member of staff, which is perhaps not as ideal as someone external, however you noted that these financial statements were finalised and so I assume they have been audited and that the valuations are fair. One note of caution though is why the directors have chosen this year to change the policy - could it be an attempt to boost income and reduce gearing to make further borrowing easier, especially as the long term borrowings will need to be repaid or re-negotiated relatively soon. However, it maybe shows good commercial sense to ensure that assets that are to be used as security for finance are at the most up-to-date valuation.

The overall liquidity of DFG is on the low side at 1.3:1 and has fallen significantly from 20X0. One contributing factor to the worsening liquidity is the significant increase in inventories in the year. This could be as a result of bad publicity about below standard goods and customer orders being cancelled. There is then an increased risk of obsolete inventories. This is reinforced by the inventories days which have increased from 146 days to 191 days. Receivables days have also increased from 71 days to 104 days, and this be could be as a result of disputed invoices. DFG may then have a problem with slow/non-payment of these debts. Payables days have increased from 108 days to 171 days and this could be resulting from a deliberate attempt by DFG to improve the cash flow by delaying payment or extended credit terms given by the new supplier to attract DFG's business.

The cash position of DFG is clearly a concern as the cash has moved from a positive balance to an overdraft and the long term borrowings are soon to be repaid or re-negotiated. This coupled with the poor working capital management would indicate that DFG must raise some additional funding if it is to survive. The gearing ratio shows deterioration on the previous year, despite an increase in equity from the revaluation. However, it is likely to be the lack of interest cover that would put lenders off. It is unlikely that DFG could afford to pay interest on any additional funding.

I would recommend investigating DFG in more detail before making your decision. Losing the court case and having a large settlement to pay could result in the entity collapsing and despite the fact that details of this are only in the notes, the seriousness of this should not be overlooked. The entity may struggle to survive anyway as there is a lack of cash and funding options (and it should be noted that DFG did not pay a dividend in 20X1). The increases in profitability are not enough of an indicator of a stable/growing entity – especially an entity involved in the building trade which is known for its sensitivity to the economy around it.

(b) **Limitations of ratio analysis**

The financial statement provide only historic information and reflect a point in time (i.e.: the year-end). However, the situation of the entity in question could have progressed significantly by the time you are analysing the information. For example, with the contingent liability for the court case, it could have progressed or be settled and the financial statements will not have reflected that.

The ratio analysis conducted on DFG showed an improvement in profitability margins, in cost of sales particularly, however it looks likely that quality has been compromised in favour of better margins and the result of that has been the filing of a law suit against DFG. This is something that threatens the future of the business but is not reflected in the ratios calculated.

Changes in accounting policies can impact ratio calculations. DFG has changed the accounting policy for subsequent measurement of PPE from depreciated historic cost to revaluated amount. The revaluation in the year then improves the gearing ratio and reduces non-current asset turnover but is due only to a change of policy rather than changes to the underlying environment.

Appendix A

Relevant ratios that could be selected and calculated:

	20X1	*20X0*
(Workings in $m)		
Gross profit GP/revenue x 100%	49/252 x 100 = 19.4%	25/248 x 100 = 10.1%
Operating profit Profit before finance costs/revenue	(49–18–16)/252 x 100 = 6.0%	(25–13–11)/248 x 100 = 0.4%
Net profit PFY/revenue x 100%	7/252 x 100 = 2.8%	(5)/248 x 100 = (2.0)%
Gearing Debt/total equity	(91+39)/231 x 100 = 56.3%	91/184 x 100 = 49.5%
Current ratio Current assets/current liabilities	178/134 = 1.3 : 1	143/66 = 2.2 : 1
Quick ratio CA – inventories/current liabilities	(178–106)/134 = 0.5 : 1	(143–89)/66 = 0.8 : 1
Receivables days Receivables/revenue x 365 days	72/252 x 365 days = 104 days	48/248 x 365 days = 71 days
Payables days Payables/cost of sales x 365 days	95/203 x 365 days = 171 days	66/223 x 365 days = 108 days
Inventories days Inventories/cost of sales x 365 days	106/203 x365 days =191 days	89/223 x 365 days =146 days
Return on capital employed Profit before finance costs/capital employed x 100%	(49–18–16)/(231+91) = 15/322 x 100 = 4.7%	(25–13–11)/(184+91) = 1/275 x 100 = 0.4%
Non-current asset turnover Revenue/non-current assets	252/254 = 0.99	248/198 = 1.3
Interest cover Profit before finance costs/finance costs	(10+12)/12 = 1.8	((7)+8)/8 = 0.1

74   CVB (MAY 11 EXAM)

Report to Friend

Analysis of financial statements of CVB

(a)   **Financial performance**

Turnover has increased 10% since 20X0 although this is at the expense of a drop in the gross margin earned which has fallen from 35.0% to 32.7% which has resulted in only a marginal increase in the absolute value of gross profit. The decline in gross margin could be due to a changing sales mix or to a higher cost of sales for fair-trade clothing. In addition the cost of clothing is largely dependent upon cotton prices which have been increasing rapidly in recent times. CVB has managed to control administrative expenses which have actually fallen. Sales and marketing costs have increased by 10%, which is in line with revenue.

The profit for the year margin has dropped from 3.2% to 1.8%. This is mainly as a result of the decrease in the gross margin but is also affected by the increase in finance costs and the losses generated by the associate. CVB has taken on short term borrowings and this has increased finance costs. The average rate of lending has also increased from 8.6% to 11.0%. This could be the result of the short term borrowings being more costly than the term loan or it could be that the short term borrowings were significantly higher during the year – which is potentially more concerning. Either way, the entity has low gearing and should look to secure more long term funding rather than relying on a short term facility.

The return on capital employed has fallen from 6.7% to 6.0% due to falling returns and the revaluation and investment in PPE. The increase in PPE may not yet have generated returns, however the revaluation has improved total comprehensive income which otherwise would have been significantly lower than 20X0. I don't think we should rule out this being a deliberate attempt to boost the TCI as on the face of it the business seems to be hitting a downturn.

Financial position

The main issue for CVB is management of working capital. Inventories days have increased from 118 to 168 days. Given that CVB operates in the retail sector, having inventories in stock for another 50 days is likely to be problematic and lead to obsolescence of out of trend items. If this movement was in isolation it could indicate that CVB were stock piling the new fair-trade items to meet expected future demand, however given that there are other signs of overtrading this is more likely to be an unfavourable movement.

The increase in payables indicates that CVB are using trade payables as a means of funding working capital. It is collecting receivable amounts at the same rate, which is what would be expected for an entity in the retail sector, but payables are being settled 43 days later than in 20X0. This policy will not be well received by the market especially now that CVB is being supplied by fair-trade operators.

The current ratio, although reduced from 20X0 is at 1.3, however the removal of the inventories highlights the cash crisis that CVB is facing. The quick ratio has fallen to 0.5 and CVB must seek additional funding immediately.

The gearing of CVB indicates a relatively low risk entity with gearing of 26.7%, however the fall in the interest cover from 4.0 to 2.5 would be a concern for any lender. CVB is potentially paying more for the short-term borrowings and there is the added risk that these amounts are likely to be repayable on demand. It would be essential for the entity to secure long-term finance to ensure it can trade for the foreseeable future. If higher returns were expected from trading activities this would help the interest cover. In addition, possibly selling the associate investment could generate some cash, although this may not be lucrative given it is currently loss-making.

Position in the market

Based on the latest share price, the P/E ratio of CVB is 5.4, a slight reduction from the P/E of twelve months ago which was 5.7. The share price has fallen by 40% over the same period which indicates that the stock market has reacted to the decline in profitability, resulting in overall stability in the P/E.

Recommendation

Based on the financial information presented I would recommend not investing until further investigation is conducted. The business has a cash and working capital crisis which the directors must commit to resolving immediately to ensure the business can continue as a going concern.

Examiner's comments

The quality of the analysis in this question was not up to the usual good standard, with few candidates appreciating the timescale and immediate action that is required to be taken. Many commented on all aspects of working capital but fewer were able to provide suggestions as to how the numbers all tied together and possible reasons for the movements.

The calculation of certain ratios still poses problems for most candidates, in particular interest cover, return on capital employed and operating profit margin. Candidates were not able to calculate the ratios ensuring that numerator and denominator were consistent especially relating to the associate. Few candidates knew to include NCI in equity when calculating gearing and ROCE.

(b) **Further financial information that may be useful**

The financial statements used in the analysis are already out of date as the year end was 9 months ago. Therefore it will be important to obtain and consider any information that CVB has published since then, such as quarterly reviews, half year accounts, profit warnings etc.

Details of the held for sale assets and details of the items being sold to determine if this is the result of a change in trading focus or an attempt to raise cash.

The details of the long-term financing and the state of relationships with current lenders may help assess the likelihood of securing additional funding in a short timescale.

Details of the dividend policy and history of dividend payout to assess future expected returns.

Details of the associate company to establish if the associate has had a one-off expense creating a loss or is in a downturn and likely to continue loss-making.

The forecasts for future trading would help assess the directors' expectations for the forthcoming period and for the fair-trade business.

Appendix – Ratio Calculations

All workings in $m	20X1	20X0
Gross profit margin (GP/Revenue x 100)	148/453 x 100 = 32.7%	144/412 x 100 = 35.0%
Operating profit (Profit before associate and finance costs/revenue x 100)	20/453 x 100 = 4.4%	20/412 x 100 = 4.9%
Profit margin PFY/revenue x 100	8/453 x 100 = 1.8%	13/412 = 3.2%
Interest cover Operating profit/finance cost	20/8 = 2.5 times	20/5 = 4 times
ROCE % Operating profit/capital employed	20/(273+55+18–14) x 100 = 6.0%	20/(256+58–16) x 100 = 6.7%
Inventories Inventories / cost of sales x 365	140/305 x 365 = 168 days	87/268 x 365 = 118 days
Payables Payables/cost of sales x 365	144/305 x 365 = 172 days	95/268 x 365 = 129 days
Receivables Receivables /revenue x 365	75/453 x 365 = 60 days	63/412 x 365 = 56 days
Current ratio Current asset/current liabilities	215/162 = 1.3	159/95 = 1.7
Quick CA – inventories/current liabilities	75/162 = 0.5	72/95 = 0.8
Gearing Debt/Equity	55 + 18/273 = 26.7%	58/256 = 22.7%
Average cost of borrowing Finance costs/interest bearing borrowings	8/(55+18) x 100 = 11.0%	5/58 = 8.6%
P/E ratio Price/EPS	1.25/(7/30) = 5.4	2.08/(11/30) = 5.7

75 LKJ (SEP 11 EXAM)

Report to supervisor

Re LKJ for year ended 30 April 20X1

Financial performance

We are aware the LKJ has expanded recently which has had a positive impact on revenue with an increase of 30% since last year. We know that as a result of the expansion a new range of products were launched on 1 October, hence we have not as yet seen a full year's impact. However, it would appear that this significant improvement in revenues has been at the expense of profitability as gross margins have actually fallen from 25.6% to 21.7%. The strategic move to cheaper products targeting the lower-priced market is likely to be one of the main reasons for this decline in margin. Another reason may be that LKJ has reduced the sales prices of the new products in order to undercut competitors and gain market share.

The directors have, however been pro-active in addressing overheads and as a result the operating profit margin has reduced by 1% to 6.5%. Within this, there has been a significant reduction in administrative expenses from the outsourcing of payroll. Administrative expenses have fallen from 8.0% to 4.3% of revenue which is a significant improvement. There has been an increase in distribution costs, but this is likely to be from supplying new customers as a result of the expansion. The control of overheads and the pro-active nature of the directors in this respect suggest good management.

The investment in associate has generated a good return for LKJ and as a result the net profit margin has increased from 4.1% to 6.1%.

The interest cover has fallen from 25.2 to 12.5 as a result of a significant increase in finance costs from $6 million to $20 million. The additional finance costs have arisen because of the change in the entity's financial structure. LKJ has moved from having a positive cash balance of $144 million to an overdraft of $58 million plus an increase of $140 million in long-term borrowings.

ROCE has suffered a significant decrease from 13.6% to 12.0% due mainly to the increased borrowings and the revaluation of non-current assets. The profit has increased slightly but perhaps the returns from the investments in PPE and inventories are still to come. It appears from the statement of financial position as if the cash has been utilised for the expansion. There has been an increase in property, plant and equipment, albeit some of this increase is likely to be from the revaluation in the year. It is likely that cash has also been used to invest in inventories which have more than doubled in the period. The increase in inventories could be in line with the expansion strategy by holding greater amounts of the new products to meet increased future demand. However the inventories days have increased from 32 days to 51 days and hence, LKJ is tying up valuable working capital resources. LKJ must ensure that the more expensive original products are not held at an overstated value as a new cheaper alternative may render them obsolete.

The directors of LKJ appear to have made a sound investment in the associate as it has generated good returns in the period. It is unusual that they have chosen to make such a large investment in the same period as implementing an expansion strategy, unless the associated entity is involved in the supply chain of the new product and LKJ wanted to be able to exercise influence over it.

The receivables days have increased from 47 to 65 days. This would normally suggest poor working capital management, however given that the directors have actively sought to control costs (outsourcing the payroll requirement) it is less likely that they have failed to control receivables while being short of cash. It could be that the new customer base has been offered more advantageous credit terms in order to increase customers and market share. It would still be a recommendation to review these terms to ensure that LKJ are offering something that it can actually afford to offer.

The current and quick ratios have both been affected by the reduction in cash but the increase in inventories has softened the impact on the current ratio. Both ratios still indicate adequate cover, but the fact remains that LKJ are in need of immediate funds.

The increased borrowings have resulted in gearing more than doubling, however a gearing ratio of less than 20% would not normally be a concern and since there is still reasonable interest cover, the entity should still be able to afford to repay the interest on any new finance. One point to note is that the revaluation of PPE is a continuation of an existing policy rather than a deliberate attempt to boost capital employed and improve gearing.

A positive sign is that LKJ has approached us for long-term funding rather than compromising its position with suppliers by increasing payment period, which again indicates that the directors understand that an expansion will need to be funded by longer term borrowings. The payable days has increased only slightly from 31 to 35 days. In addition, the bonus issue in lieu of paying a dividend is a smart move. The entity cannot afford to pay a dividend but has significant retained earnings. The issue will still show shareholders that the directors are continuing to focus on meeting shareholder expectations.

LKJ appears to be a well-managed organisation in the process of expansion and I would recommend that the borrowing is considered further.

Appendix A

All workings in $m	20X1	20X0
Gross profit margin (GP/Revenue x 100)	572/2,630 x 100% = 21.7%	517/2,022 x 100% = 25.6%
Operating profit (Profit before associate and finance costs/revenue x 100)	(572 – 114 – 288)/2,630 x 100% = 6.5%	(517 – 163 – 203)/2,022 x 100% = 7.5%
Profit margin PFY/revenue x 100	160/2,630 x 100% 6.1%	82/2,022 x 100% 4.1%
Interest cover Operating profit/finance cost	(230 + 20)/20 = 12.5 times	(145 + 6)/6 = 25.2 times
ROCE % Operating profit/capital employed	170/(1,295 + 200 + 58 – 140) x 100% = 12.0%	151/(1,047 + 60) x 100% = 13.6%
Inventories Inventories / cost of sales x 365	290/2,058 x 365 days = 51 days	130/1,505 x 365 days = 32 days

Payables Payables/cost of sales x 365	199/2,058 x 365 days = 35 days	128/1,505 x 365 days = 31 days
Receivables Receivables /revenue x 365	468/2,630 x 365 days = 65 days	263/2,022 x 365 days = 47 days
Current ratio Current asset/current liabilities	758/257 = 2.9	537/128 = 4.2
Quick CA – inventories/current liabilities	468/257 = 1.8	407/128 = 3.2
NCA turnover Revenue /PPE	2,630/554 = 4.7	2,022/418 = 4.8
Total asset turnover Revenue / Total assets	2,630/(1,752 – 140 – 300) = 2.0	2,022/(1,235 – 280) = 2.1
Gearing Debt/Equity	(58 + 200)/1,295 = 19.9%	60/1,047 = 5.7%

DEVELOPMENTS IN EXTERNAL REPORTING

76   FW (MAY 05 EXAM)   *Walk in the footsteps of a top tutor*

Key answer tips

This is an interesting question combining environmental reporting with analysis and interpretation of financial statements.   In both parts (a) and (b) you should try to make a positive case for 'doing the right thing', as well as pointing out the disadvantages.

Tutor's top tips:

Part (a) of this question involves adjusting the figures you have been given (best done in a working), recalculating key ratios and then commenting on the effects. As long as you make reasonable comments based on your recalculated figures, you will gain credit. Do not only attempt the calculations and make few comments because you think your calculations are incorrect.

(a) **Briefing Paper**

From: Assistant to the CFO

Subject: Effect of making an environmental provision on FW's key ratios

As requested, I have analysed the effects of making a provision of $500 million for environmental costs on our key financial ratios. The ratios themselves are set out in the Appendix.

Without the provision, all our ratios show an improvement in our performance during the year ended 28 February 20X5. Return on equity and earnings per share show a particularly strong improvement. However, with the provision, the key ratios will all show that our performance has deteriorated. Return on equity and return on net assets will be only slightly lower than in 20X4 and gearing only slightly higher, so these may not have a particularly adverse effect on our share price. Unfortunately operating profit margin will fall to 7.7%; well below the 20X4 figure and earnings per share will fall by almost 4c to 8.4c, a reduction of over 30%.

This means that public perception of the company's performance is likely to be negative, particularly in the short term as the market digests the fall in earnings per share. However, the income statement will still show a healthy profit for the period of $502 million. In the medium term analysts may view the company in a more positive light. By recognising the provision the company shows that it takes its responsibilities towards the environment seriously. There are also advantages in getting the bad news over quickly. It may be possible to mitigate the adverse effects on the market by briefing analysts in a positive way, explaining what has happened.

Appendix: Ratio calculations

	20X5 before provision	*20X5 after provision*	*20X4*
Return on equity	$\dfrac{1{,}670}{4{,}964+5{,}656/2} \times 100\% = 31.5\%$	$\dfrac{1{,}170}{4{,}954+5{,}156/2} \times 100\% = 23.1\%$	24.7%
Return on net assets	$\dfrac{2{,}080}{9{,}016+10{,}066/2} \times 100\% = 21.8\%$	$\dfrac{1{,}580}{9{,}016+9{,}566/2} \times 100\% = 17.0\%$	17.7%
Gearing	$\dfrac{4{,}410}{5{,}656} \times 100\% = 78.0\%$	$\dfrac{4{,}410}{5{,}156} \times 100\% = 85.5\%$	82.0%
Operating profit margin	$\dfrac{2{,}080}{20{,}392} \times 100\% = 10.2\%$	$\dfrac{1{,}580}{20{,}392} \times 100\% = 7.7\%$	10.1%
Earnings per share	$\dfrac{1{,}002}{6{,}000} = 16.7c$	$\dfrac{502}{6{,}000} = 8.4c$	12.2c

Workings

Adjustment to financial statements for the provision

	Draft $m	Provision $m	Adjusted $m
Net assets at 28 February 20X5	10,066	(500)	9,566
Share capital and reserves at 28 February 20X5	5,656	(500)	5,156
Operating profit	2,080	(500)	1,580
Profit before tax	1,670	(500)	1,170
Profit for the period	1,002	(500)	502

(b) **Advantages and disadvantages of publishing an environmental and social report**

Tutor's top tips:

Non-financial reporting is an important part of the syllabus and one which the examiner can add to Section B questions to make up the 10% weighting. Use common sense to identify advantage and disadvantages and remember your role as assistant to FW's chief financial officer.

There are significant advantages of producing an environmental and social report. Increasingly, listed entities are positively expected to provide the public with information about the ways in which they interact with the natural environment and the wider community. By doing this, the company would demonstrate that it was aware of its 'corporate social responsibilities'.

However, there are possible disadvantages of publishing an environmental report and these should not be underestimated. Producing a high quality environmental report will have a cost in time and money. If we simply 'pull something together' or if we produce a report that is very obviously a public relations exercise, we risk harming our reputation, rather than enhancing it. The report may be seen as an attempt to divert attention from 'bad news' elsewhere. We will need to look at what is produced by our competitors and to produce something which is at least as good, if not better.

At present, there is no accounting standard that specifies the content of an environmental report, so in theory we are free to publish as much or as little information as we choose. In practice, guidelines such as those provided by the GRI are very detailed and rigorous. We will need to be consistent in the performance measures that we publish from year to year, even when these have worsened.

Lastly, publishing our environmental policies may lead the public to expect that we will act in particular ways to protect the environment and this may have consequences for the financial statements. If, for example, we say that we will always rectify any damage that we cause, we will have a constructive obligation to do so, even where there is no legal requirement. In this situation, IAS 37 *Provisions, Contingent Liabilities and Contingent Assets* would require us to recognise a provision for the cost of cleaning up damage.

On balance, we should seriously consider publishing an annual environmental and social report, particularly if the company really does have positive achievements to communicate to the public, such as the actions that it takes to reduce pollution and its equal opportunities policies. Environmental reporting is likely to enhance the company's reputation and may even have a positive effect on its share price.

(c)   **Sustainability dimensions**

Tutor's top tips:

The Global Reporting Initiative is on syllabus and should be reviewed at a medium to high level as part of your revision. There are six marks available so part (c) must be attempted.

The three principal sustainability dimensions covered by the GRI's framework of performance indicators are:

- Economic: this includes performance ratios relating to the direct economic impacts of the entity on employees, customers, suppliers and the taxation authorities.

- Environmental: this includes performance ratios relating to the environmental impacts of products and services in areas such as energy, material and water use; greenhouse gas and other emissions; effluents and waste generation; impacts on biodiversity; and fines and penalties for non-compliance.

- Social: this includes performance ratios relating to labour practices; human rights; and broader social issues affecting consumers, communities and other stakeholders.

Signed: Assistant to CFO

77   BCA (NOV 09 EXAM)

Key answer tips

This question really highlights the need to read carefully the requirement – it often directs you as to what to write about in order to score marks. Part (a) the report part specifically asks you to discuss the key challenges that CAD faces and how the acquisition by BCA could change these. Notice the model answer separates this part of the question out under its own heading. This is good exam technique as it should ensure you attempt this part of the question. In (b-ii) you are asked specifically why an OFR could be helpful to investors in CAD. Generic pros and cons of an OFR will not score highly here, you need to use the scenario.

(a)   **REPORT**

To: The Board of BCA

From: An Accountant

Subject: Potential takeover of CAD

Date: Nov 20X9

Profitability

The gross margin achieved by CAD has dropped significantly from 21% last year to 14.5%. This is likely to be due to the cost of the new technology and the bonus paid to the Chief Scientific Officer (CSO).

Sales are up 22% and indications are that future periods will see further revenue increases due to the development of the new technology. The main challenge for CAD will be staying in business long enough to take advantage of these further revenues, as discussed later there are some cash flow issues that they need to address.

If BCA acquire CAD we would have to consider if these future contracts might be compromised – some of them may be with our competitors for example.

Operating costs appear to have been controlled in 20X9. As a percentage of revenue they have fallen to 10.7% (20X8: 16.3%). It is unclear the reason for this but it has helped reduce the impact of the GPM fall on the net profit margin.

Efficiency

The receivables days are very high at 92 days (20X8: 60 days). This has lead to a significant cash outflow this year. CAD's main challenge is dealing with large customers with a significant outstanding balance and may not have the credit control resources to manage these accounts or are not in a position to successfully negotiate because of size and relative dependency. If, however, BCA was to takeover CAD and implemented stricter credit control procedures then this could be eradicated.

Cutting this back to 60 days would release more than $300,000 (see appendix) and so remove the need to rely on expensive short term funding.

The interest paid in 2009 is at approximately 10%, which is quite high. This is likely to be because CAD cannot offer the bank substantial amounts of tangible non-current assets on which security can be taken. This is likely to be less of an issue for BCA as we are an established multinational and would be able to secure funding at more competitive rates if required.

In addition, it is likely that CAD is unable to successfully negotiate with its customers for early payment as the contracts are all with large established companies, however again that may not be an issue if contracts were negotiated by BCA.

Payables looks high (68 days), however the payables days was at a similar level in 20X8 and suppliers have continued to supply as inventories have increased so the delay in settlement seems not to be a problem. BCA may choose to reduce the payables level to avoid any negative impact on its credit rating.

Potential target entity

CAD appears to be a sound investment provided the future services of the CSO can be secured. CAD shareholders are willing to surrender control if the company's future and their own is secure. The business is profitable and future prospects look positive.

Contracts that CAD has are with established companies and there appears to be an order book to provide future services for the next couple of years at least. A key question will be whether these contracts will be retained if there is a takeover.

The issues of funding and debt collection are likely to be able to be solved by BCA. The key personnel member appears to have been well tied into the business and so the current management team clearly know what is vital to the survival of their business.

(b) (i) **Increase in narrative reporting**

Financial statements report historical events and transactions and are generally backward looking. They are therefore often of limited use to users that are focussed on the entity's future prospects and potential results.

The relevance of financial information would be improved if some information about the entity's future objectives and challenges and the strategies in place to overcome those challenges was included. However there might be a compromise on reliability as this information by its nature will be uncertain.

Information on the dynamics and risks of the entity would also be useful – e.g. reliance on key personnel or development of technology. Again this information would be subjective by its nature.

This need for additional information, not supplied in the financial statements has led to the growth in narrative reporting in corporate reports. The entity should give a balanced report on the activities and performance of the period and expected performance for the immediate future and in turn shareholders must recognise that this information does not have the added comfort of an audit opinion.

(ii) **Usefulness of management commentary**

An OFR type report (management commentary) would be helpful to potential investors in CAD as the financial statements do not provide the information that is key to this type of high-tech industry. The low levels of tangible non-current asset make it pointless to calculate traditional ratios like return on capital employed and so comparisons with other potential investments are restricted. It also makes it hard for these entities to raise external finance as there are few assets available as security.

This is an example of where the value of the business lies in the intellectual property (intangible assets) within the entity through the patents and the know-how and technical expertise of the staff. However the key elements in the future viability of the entity lie in the patents and key personnel and the contracts – much of which is absent from the historical financial statements. A management commentary on these areas would be invaluable to investors and other lenders as it would help them understand the underlying business.

The relationships with the CSO would also be discussed under the risks and relationships section as losing the technical developer would have a significant effect on the long term prospects of the entity. The high receivables would also be explained and would enable the entity to explain the details of arrangements as some readers would assume, in the absence of any information to the contrary, that it is as a result of poor credit control.

A narrative report would give the management the opportunity to explain the dynamics of the business and the investment in future technological improvements that are not evident from the numerical information presented in the financial statements.

	20X9	20X8
Gross Profit margin	$628k/$4,330k = 14.5%	$752k/$3,562k = 21.1%
Operating cost percentage	$465k/$4,330k = 10.7%	$580k/$3,562k = 16.3%
Net profit margin	$108k/$4,330k = 2.5%	$125k/$3,562k = 3.5%
Inventory days	$125k/$3,702 x 365 = 12.3 days	$72k/$2,810k x 365 = 9.4days
Receivable days	$1,091k/$4,330k x 365 = 92.0 days	$587k/$3,562k x 365 = 60.2 days
Payable days	$687k/$3,702k x 365 = 67.7 days	$485k/$$2,810k x 365 = 63.0 days
Finance cost – appx %	$13k/$123k = 10.6%	n/a

Note: the absence of "typical" ratios such as ROCE and gearing. This is because these were not relevant to CAD. As mentioned in (b-ii) CAD trades from its intellectual assets which are not recognised in the financial statements. ROCE does not therefore provide a useful indicator of efficiency. Gearing is not relevant as the company has no long term debt. This highlights the importance of thinking before you calculate your ratios, work out what you want to say about a number before you plug it into your calculator.

Affect of receivable days on cash:

Receivables/Revenue x 365 = receivable days

Thus given revenue of $4,330k, if receivable days were reduced to 60 in 20X9, the receivable balance would fall to $712k:

60 days/365 x $4,330k = $712k

This is $379k less than currently outstanding and hence the company has lost over $300k cash in waiting for its customers to pay.

Section 5

SPECIMEN PAPER QUESTIONS

1 AB, CD AND EF

The statements of comprehensive income for AB, CD and EF for the year ended 31 May 20X9 are shown below:

	AB	CD	EF
	$000	$000	$000
Revenue	6,000	3,000	1,000
Cost of sales	(4,800)	(2,400)	(800)
Gross Profit	1,200	600	200
Distribution costs	(64)	(32)	(10)
Administrative expenses	(336)	(168)	(52)
Finance costs	(30)	(15)	(5)
Profit before tax	770	385	133
Income tax expense	(204)	(102)	(33)
PROFIT FOR THE YEAR	566	283	100
Other comprehensive income			
Revaluation of property	200	100	30
Tax effect of revaluation	(42)	(21)	(6)
Other comprehensive income for the year, net of tax	158	79	24
TOTAL COMPREHENSIVE INCOME FOR THE YEAR	724	362	124

Notes:

1   AB operates a defined benefit pension plan for its employees. At the year end, there is an actuarial loss of $52,000 on the pension plan liabilities and an actuarial gain of $40,000 on pension plan assets. These amounts are not reflected in the above statements. In accordance with the amendment to IAS 19 Employee Benefits, AB recognises actuarial gains and losses from the defined benefit plan in other comprehensive income in the period that they occur.

2   AB holds a 15% investment in XY which is designated as available for sale. The fair value of this investment at 31 May 20X9 was $106,000. The investment is currently recorded in the financial statements at $92,000.

3   AB owns 80% of the ordinary share capital of CD and exercises control over its operating and financial policies. AB owns 30% of the ordinary share capital of EF and exerts significant influence over its operating and financial policies.

Required:

Prepare the consolidated statement of comprehensive income for the AB Group, taking account of the information provided in the notes above. Ignore any further taxation effects of notes 1 and 2.   **(Total: 10 marks)**

2   VOLUNTARY DISCLOSURES

Shareholders are becoming increasingly interested in the environmental policies, impacts and practices of business entities, however financial statements have not traditionally provided this information. As a result, there has been significant growth in entities providing narrative environmental information on a voluntary basis.

Required:

Identify and explain the principal arguments against voluntary disclosures by business entities of their environmental policies, impacts and practices.   **(Total: 10 marks)**

3   RP

Convertible bonds

RP issued $4 million 5% convertible bonds on 1 October 20X8 for $3.9 million. The bonds have a four year term and are redeemable at par. At the time the bonds were issued the prevailing market rate for similar debt without conversion rights was 7%. The effective interest rate associated with the bonds is 7% and the liability is measured, in accordance with IAS 39 Financial Instruments: recognition and measurement, at amortised cost. The interest due was paid and recorded within finance costs during the year.

Share options

RP granted share options to its 300 employees on 1 October 20X7. Each employee will receive 1,000 share options provided they continue to work for RP for the following three years from the grant date. The fair value of the options at the grant date was $1.10 each. In the year ended 30 September 20X8, 10 employees left and another 30 were expected to leave over the next two years. For the year ended 30 September 20X9, 20 employees left and another 15 are expected to leave in the year to 30 September 20Y0.

Required:

(a)   **Prepare the accounting entries to record the issue of the convertible bonds and to record the adjustment required in respect of the interest expense on the bonds for the year ended 30 September 20X9.**   **(5 marks)**

(b)   **Discuss the accounting treatment to be adopted for the share options and calculate the amount to be recognised in the income statement in respect of these options for the year ended 30 September 20X9. Prepare appropriate accounting entries.**

    (5 marks)

    (Total: 10 marks)

4   JKA AND CBX

JKA acquired 50% of the issued ordinary share capital of CBX, an entity set up under a contractual agreement as a joint venture between JKA and one of its customers. JKA adopts a policy of proportionate consolidation in accounting for joint ventures.

The statements of financial position for JKA and CBX as at 31 May 20X9 are provided below:

	JKA	CBX
ASSETS	$000	$000
Non current assets		
Property plant and equipment	11,000	7,500
Investment in CBX	2,000	–
	13,000	7,500
Current assets		
Inventories	3,100	1,200
Receivables	3,300	1,400
Cash and cash equivalents	600	400
	7,000	3,000
Total assets	20,000	10,500
EQUITY AND LIABILITIES		
Equity		
Share capital ($1 ordinary shares)	10,000	4,000
Revaluation reserve	1,500	500
Other reserves	500	–
Retained earnings	2,000	4,500
Total equity	14,000	9,000
Non current liabilities	2,000	–
Current liabilities	4,000	1,500
Total liabilities	6,000	1,500
Total equity and liabilities	20,000	10,500

Additional information:

1   **Intra-group trading**

During the year to 31 May 20X9 CBX sold goods to JKA with a sales value of $200,000. 25% of the goods remain in JKA's inventories at the year end. CBX makes 20% margin on all sales. The final invoice amount of $34,000 remains unpaid at the year end.

2   **Sale of land**

On 31 May 20X9 JKA sold a piece of land to DEX Finance for $500,000 when the carrying value of the land was $520,000 (the original cost of the asset). Under the terms of the sale agreement JKA has the option to repurchase the land within the next three years for between $560,000 and $600,000 depending on the date of repurchase. The land must be repurchased for $600,000 at the end of the three year period if the option is not exercised before that time.

JKA has derecognised the land and recorded the subsequent loss within profit for the year ended 31 May 20X9.

Required:

(a)   **Explain how the sale of the land should be accounted for in accordance with the principles of IAS 18 Revenue and the Framework for Preparation and Presentation of Financial Statements.**   **(4 marks)**

(b)   **Prepare the consolidated statement of financial position for JKA as at 31 May 20X9.**
                                                                    (6 marks)

                                                            (Total: 10 marks)

5   **BG AND DG**

BG is an entity with several overseas operations. One of its subsidiaries, DG operates in a country which experiences relatively high rates of inflation in its currency, the Dez. Most entities operating in that country voluntarily present two versions of their financial statements: one at historic cost, and the other incorporating current cost adjustments. DG complies with this accepted practice.

Extracts from the income statement of DG, including adjustments for current costs for the year ended 30 June 20X9 are shown below:

	Dez '000
Historical cost profit from operations	926
Current cost adjustments:	
Cost of sales adjustment	(82)
Depreciation adjustment	(37)
Monetary working capital adjustment	(9)
Current cost profit from operations	798

Required:

(a)   **Discuss the defects of historical cost accounting in times of increasing prices.**
                                                                    (4 marks)

(b)   **Explain how EACH of the three current cost accounting adjustments shown above contributes to the maintenance of capital.**   **(6 marks)**

                                                            (Total: 10 marks)

6   MIC

The consolidated statement of financial position for MIC as at 31 March 20X9 and its comparative for 20X8 is shown below:

	20X9		20X8	
	$000	$000	$000	$000
Assets				
Non-current assets				
Property, plant and equipment		16,800		15,600
Goodwill		2,900		2,400
Investment in associate		8,000		7,800
		27,700		25,800
Current assets				
Inventories	11,600		12,000	
Trade receivables	9,400		8,200	
Held for trading investment	2,200		1,800	
Cash and cash equivalents	1,400		4,100	
		24,600		26,100
Total assets		52,300		51,900
Equity and liabilities				
Equity attributable to owners of the parent				
Share capital ($1 ordinary shares)		12,000		10,000
Share premium		2,800		–
Other reserves		400		400
Retained earnings		7,300		6,300
		22,500		16,700
Non controlling interest		6,500		6,100
Total equity		29,000		22,800
Non-current liabilities				
Long term loans		14,000		18,000
Current liabilities				
Trade payables	8,700		10,200	
Income tax	600		900	
		9,300		11,100
Total liabilities		23,300		29,100
Total equity and liabilities		52,300		51,900

The consolidated income statement for MIC for the year ended 31 March 20X9 is shown below:

	$000
Revenue	12,000
Cost of sales	(8,400)
Gross Profit	3,600
Distribution costs	(400)
Administrative expenses	(1,260)
Finance costs	(450)
Share of profit of associate	500
Profit before tax	1,990
Income tax	(600)
PROFIT FOR THE YEAR	1,390
Attributable to:	
Owners of parent	1,200
Non-controlling interest	190
	1,390

Additional information

1   There were no disposals of property, plant and equipment in the year. Depreciation charged in arriving at profit totalled $1,800,000.

2   MIC acquired 90% of the ordinary share capital of GH on 1 December 20X8 for a cash consideration of $460,000 plus the issue of 1 million $1 ordinary shares in MIC, which had a deemed value of $3.60 per share at the date of acquisition. The fair values of the net assets acquired were as follows:

	$000
Property plant and equipment	800
Inventories	2,200
Receivables	700
Cash and cash equivalents	200
Payables	(500)
	3,400

MIC made no other purchases or sales of investments in the year. The group policy is to value the non-controlling interest at acquisition at the proportionate share of the fair value of the net assets.

3   Finance costs include interest on loans and any gains or losses on held for trading investments. All interest due was paid in the year.

Required:

Prepare the consolidated statement of cash flows for MIC for the year ended 31 March 20X9.

(Total: 25 marks)

7 **XYZ**

XYZ has a strategy of growth by acquisition. Two entities, A and B, have been identified and will be considered at the next board meeting. The target entities are of a similar size and operate within similar economic parameters. Neither entity is listed. The entities are subject to different tax regimes. Takeover is unlikely to be resisted by either entity, provided a reasonable price is offered for the shares.

XYZ can afford to fund only one acquisition and the board are asking for a review of the financial statements of both entities together with a recommendation on which of the entities looks a more promising prospect. In previous acquisitions, the board focussed mainly on key benchmarks of profitability, efficiency and risk and to that end it is expecting any report to include analysis of the following key financial ratios:

- Gross profit percentage

- Profit before tax as a percentage of revenue

- Return on capital employed

- Non-current asset turnover

- Gearing (debt/equity)

The most recent income statements for both A and B are presented below, together with extracts from their statements of financial position.

	A	B
	$000	$000
Revenue	3,800	4,400
Cost of sales	(2,700)	(2,820)
	———	———
Gross profit	1,100	1,580
Distribution costs	(375)	(420)
Administrative expenses	(168)	(644)
Finance costs	(25)	(32)
	———	———
Profit before tax	532	484
Income tax expense	(148)	(170)
	———	———
Profit for the period	384	314
	———	———

Extracts from statement of financial position

	$000	$000
Total equity	950	1,500
Non-current liabilities (loans)	500	650
Non-current assets	1,700	1,500

Notes:

1   A's administrative expenses include a gain of $350,000 on the disposal of non-current assets, following a major restructuring of the entity. The refocusing of the business activities also resulted in some capital investment which was undertaken near the end of its financial period.

2   A has a Held for Trading investment on the statement of financial position. Entity A made a gain on this investment of $20,000 in the period and this has been deducted from finance costs.

Required:

(a)   **Prepare a report for presentation to the board of XYZ, which analyses the financial information provided and recommends the most suitable takeover target.**

(8 marks are available for the calculation of ratios)

(18 marks)

(b)   **Explain the limitations of analysis when comparing two entities, using A and B as examples.** **(7 marks)**

(Total: 25 marks)

Section 6

ANSWERS TO SPECIMEN PAPER

1 AB, CD AND EF

> **Key answer tips**
>
> Start by reading through the additional notes to work out what adjustments you have been given and where in the statement of comprehensive income (SOCI) you need to adjust. In this question the consolidation should be straight forward. You need to consolidate the subsidiary for the year and equity account for the associate.
>
> The notes deal with two items of other comprehensive income (OCI). Few calculations were needed so the main test is of you knowledge of where these items go.

Consolidated statement of comprehensive income for the AB group for the year ended 31 May 20X9

	$000
Revenue (6,000 + 3,000)	9,000
Cost of sales (4,800 + 2,400)	(7,200)
	———
Gross Profit	1,800
Distribution costs (64 + 32)	(96)
Administrative expenses (336 + 168)	(504)
Finance costs (30 + 15)	(45)
Share of profit of associate (30% x $100k)	30
	———
Profit before tax	1,185
Income tax expense (204 + 102)	(306)
	———
PROFIT FOR THE YEAR	879
	———

Other comprehensive income:

Revaluation of PPE (200 + 100)	300
Actuarial gain on pension plan assets	40
Actuarial loss on pension plan liabilities	(52)
Gain on AFS investment (106 – 92)	14
Tax effect of other comprehensive income (42 + 21)	(63)
Share of OCI of associate (net of tax) (30% x 24)	7
Other comprehensive income for the year, net of tax	246
TOTAL COMPREHENSIVE INCOME FOR THE YEAR	**1,125**

	$000
Profit for the period attributable to:	
Owners of the parent entity	822.4
Non-controlling interests (20% x 283)	56.6
	879
Total comprehensive income attributable to:	
Owners of the parent entity	1,052.6
Non-controlling interests (20% x 362)	72.4
	1,125

Note:

CD is a subsidiary and therefore is fully consolidated. EF is an associate and therefore equity accounting is applied.

2 VOLUNTARY DISCLOSURES

Key answer tips

Environmental reporting is increasingly forming part of companies annual reports. This style question is reguarly set by the examiner so you should make sure that you could reproduce a similar answer.

One tip to help when justifyinf a reporting treatment is to think about the framework for preparetion of accounts. Here the qualitiative characteristics of relevance, reliability, comparability and understandability provide a useful reference for discussing the usefulness of environmental disclosures.

Voluntary disclosures of any type are of limited usefulness as they are not readily comparable with other reporting entities. In terms of environmental reporting there is no IAS or detailed guidance giving entities freedom to interpret what to include in such a report. This compromises comparability.

For those entities that choose to disclose their policies and practices, they may well be treated as public relations opportunities, focussing mainly on the positive aspects and less on any negative features. This then affects the relevance of the information provided as the report is not neutral.

Voluntary information may not be audited and therefore the reliability of the information is questionable, and information that fails any of the key qualitative characteristics set out in the Framework is less useful to decision makers.

The information provided will have a cost of production. However, the lack of comparability may mean that the cost of producing the information outweighs the potential benefits to shareholders.

Furthermore any costs incurred will reduce profits and subsequent potential returns to shareholders and since the maximisation of shareholder returns is the priority of the directors, it may be seen as detracting from their main objective.

Where extensive voluntary disclosures are part of the annual report there is a risk of information overload and where this occurs, again the relevance and usefulness of the information is reduced.

3   RP

(a)   **Convertible bonds**

The convertible bonds on issue will be recorded as:

Dr Bank $3,900,000

Cr Liability	$3,729,400
Cr Equity	$170,600

Workings:

	$
Present value of principal ($4,000,000 x 0.763) (i)	3,052,000
Present value of the interest annuity (5% x $4m x 3.387) (ii)	677,400
Total value attributable to the liability	3,729,400
Value attributable to the equity (balance)	170,600
Total value of bonds	3,900,000

(i)   Discounted at 7% for 4 years

(ii)   Discounted as an annuity at 7% for 4 years

The liability will then be accounted for in accordance with IAS 39, i.e. at amortised cost using the effective interest rate of 7%.

	Opening carrying value	Effective interest 7%	Interest paid	Closing carrying value
	$	$	$	$
Y/e 30/9/X9	3,729,400	261,058	(200,000)	3,790,458

The interest paid of $200,000 has already been posted, so the additional $61,058 is recorded as:

Dr	Finance costs	$61,058
Cr	Liability	$61,058

(b)   **Share options**

This is an equity-settled share-based transaction and in accordance with IFRS 2 the fair value of the share options is used to estimate the fair value of the services provided by the employees. The total fair value is allocated over the three year vesting period and is based on the fair value at the grant date.

20X8

1,000 options x $1.10 x (300 – 10 – 30) = $286,000

Amount to be recognised as an expense is $286,000 over the vesting period of 3 years = $95,333

20X9

1,000 options x $1.10 x (300 – 10 – 20 – 15) =	$280,500
Amount to be recognised to date = 280,500 x 2/3 =	$187,000
Less amount recognised in 20X8 =	($95,333)
Amount to be recognised in 20X9 =	$91,667

This will be recorded as:

Dr Staff costs $91,667

     Cr Equity (other reserves) $91,667

4 JKA AND CBX

Key answer tips

Use the question structure to help break down this question into managable chunks. Part a is testing the principal of substance over form on a sale and re-purchase agreement. Attempt this first and stick to the time allocation. Part b then asks for the preparation of the consolidated SFP, and this should include your adjustment from part a. However it is better that you show the examiner that you can apply the normal rules for consolidating a joint venture than worrying about how to get the correction in part a into the accounts.

In part b, as JKA's interest is from the date the joint venture is set up then there will be no goodwill and all of the reserves are post-acquisition. Therefore there is no need for the normal SFP workings.

(a) **Sale of land**

The substance of the transaction is financing and liabilities should be increased by the amount received of $500,000. The risks and rewards of the asset have not been transferred – JKA are open to the main risk associated with the land, being the fall in value of the land below the ultimate repurchase price; JKA are also able to gain the rewards, if land value increases above the already agreed repurchase price. In addition, the sale is to a finance company, indicating that in substance it is a financing arrangement. The land, therefore, should not be derecognised and the sale should be reversed. No adjustments for finance costs need be recorded as the sale occurred at the year end. PPE is increased by $520,000, liabilities are increased by $500,000 and retained earnings are increased by $20,000.

(b) **Consolidated statement of financial position for JKA as at 31 May 20X9**

	$000
ASSETS	
Non-current assets	
Property, plant and equipment (11,000 + (7,500/2) + 520 (part a))	15,270
Current assets	
Inventories (3,100 + (1,200/2) – 5 (W1))	3,695
Receivables (3,300 + (1,400/2) – (34/2))	3,983
Cash (600 + (400/2))	800
	————
Total assets	23,748
	————
EQUITY AND LIABILITIES	
Equity	
Share capital ($1 ordinary shares)	10,000
Revaluation reserve (1,500 + (500/2))	1,750
Other reserves	500
Retained earnings (2,000 + (4,500/2) –5 (W1) + 20 (part a))	4,265
	————
Total equity	16,515
	————
Non-current liabilities (2,000 + 500 (part a))	2,500
Current liabilities (4,000 + (1,500/2) – (34/2))	4,733
	————
Total equity and liabilities	23,748
	————

Workings:

(W1) **Calculation of unrealised profit in inventories**

$50,000 remains in inventories x 20% margin = $10,000

Intra-group share of unrealised profits = 50% x $10,000 = $5,000

Adjustment made to inventories and cost of sales (through retained earnings).

5   BG AND DG

Key answer tips

The answer to part (a) should be relatively easy. Part (b) is a little trickier the key is to use the clues in the question – think through the adjustment examples they have given and try and think of a reason for each.

(a)   **Defects of historic cost accounting**

In times of increasing prices, historical cost accounting shows the following defects:

- Revenues are stated at current values but are matched with costs incurred at an earlier date and therefore a reduced price. As a result, reported profits are overstated.

- Current values of property, plant and equipment may be significantly higher than the carrying value (depreciated historic cost, if the cost model of IAS 16 is adopted). This will not only affect the statement of financial position but will impact profits via the depreciation charge. The depreciation charge based on the historic cost may be an unrealistic estimate of the consumption of the asset and again being artificially low will result in overstated profits.

- The value of monetary assets and liabilities can also be affected by rising prices as the amount of the inflow or outflow can have changed by the date of recovery/settlement. Gains and losses can be made by holding these monetary items, which are not recognised under historical cost accounting.

- Overstatement or understatement of profit can affect performance ratios calculated in financial analysis, including return on capital employed, profitability ratios, etc.

(b)   **How current cost accounting adjustments contribute to the maintenance of capital**

The cost of sales adjustment comprises the additional amount of value, over and above historic cost value, that is consumed at current cost. This extra amount is charged against profits (and therefore retained earnings) and ensures that capital is maintained to ensure the entity can continue to operate at current levels.

The depreciation adjustment is the additional charge resulting from the difference between the current cost and historical cost depreciation. In times of rising prices, this higher charge gives a more realistic estimate of the consumption of the asset. Profit is again reduced and capital is maintained for business at current cost levels.

DG appears to have made a loss on its net monetary position. In times of rising prices, gains can be made by holding liabilities and losses from holding monetary assets. Adjusting for this loss reduces profits in the year and therefore distributable profits, which contributes to capital maintenance again ensuring that the business has set aside sufficient resources to trade in times of rising prices.

6   MIC

(a)   **Consolidated statement of cash flows for MIC Group for the year ended 31 March 20X9**

	$000	$000
Cash flows from operating activities		
Profit before tax	1,990	
Add back non-operating and non-cash items:		
Depreciation	1,800	
Goodwill impairment (W1)	500	
Share of profit of associate	(500)	
Gain on held for trading investment (2,200–1,800)	(400)	
Changes in working capital:		
Decrease in inventories (W2)	2,600	
Increase in receivables (W2)	(500)	
Decrease in payables (W2)	(2,000)	
	―――	
Cash generated from operations	3,490	
Less tax paid (900 + 600 - 600)	(900)	
	―――	
Net cash inflow from operating activities		2,590
Cash flows from investing activities		
Acquisition of property, plant and equipment (W3)	(2,200)	
Acquisition of subsidiary, net of cash acquired (460–200)	(260)	
Dividend received from associate (W4)	300	
	―――	
Cash outflow from investing activities		(2,160)

Cash flows from financing activities

Proceeds of share issue (W5)	1,200
Dividend paid to shareholders of parent (W6)	(200)
Dividend paid to non-controlling interest (W7)	(130)
Repayment of loan (18,000–14,000)	(4,000)

Cash outflow from financing activities	(3,130)

Net outflow of cash and cash equivalents	(2,700)
Cash and cash equivalents at 1 April 20X8	4,100

Cash and cash equivalents at 31 March 20X9	1,400

Workings:

(W1) **Goodwill**

	$000
Opening balance	2,400
Arising on acquisition (see below)	1,000
	3,400
Impairment (bal fig)	(500)
Closing balance	2,900

	$000
Goodwill on acquisition	
Consideration transferred (1m shares x $3.60) + $460,000	4,060
Non-controlling interest (10% x $3,400,000)	340
Less fair value of net assets acquired	(3,400)
	1,000

(W2) **Changes in working capital**

	Inventories	Receivables	Payables
	$000	$000	$000
Opening balance	12,000	8,200	10,200
On acquisition	2,200	700	500
	14,200	8,900	10,700
Movement (balancing figure)	(2,600)	500	(2,000)
Closing balance	11,600	9,400	8,700

(W3) **Acquisition of property, plant and equipment**

	$000
Opening carrying value	15,600
On acquisition	800
	16,400
Depreciation	(1,800)
	14,600
Additions (balancing figure)	2,200
Closing balance	16,800

(W4) **Dividend received from associate**

	$000
Opening balance	7,800
Share of profit of associate	500
	8,300
Dividend received from associate (balancing figure)	(300)
Closing balance	8,000

(W5) **Proceeds of share issue**

	$000
Opening balance	10,000
Issued on acquisition	3,600
	13,600
Issue for cash (balancing figure)	1,200
Closing balance	14,800

(W6) **Dividend paid to shareholders of the parent**

	$000
Opening balance	6,300
Profit for the year	1,200
	7,500
Dividend paid (balancing figure)	(200)
Closing balance	7,300

(W7) **Dividend paid to non-controlling interest**

	$000
Opening balance NCI	6,100
On acquisition (10% x $3,400,000)	340
Profit for the year	190
	6,630
Dividend paid (balancing figure)	(130)
Closing balance NCI	6,500

7   XYZ

Key answer tips

The key to the interpretation questions is to focus on the information given to you in the scenario rather than making generic comments. The background here is the comparison between two companies, A and B, with regards a potential takeover. We are specifically told that the companies are of a similar size and trade in similar economic environments and so neither of these will explain a difference in apparent performance. We are also told that the tax regimes for the two entities differ – hence it is not a great surprise that there are marks awarded for specifically commenting on the % tax paid and what this might mean to XYZ.

The question specifically asks for the calculation of five key ratios – you must work these out. There will be marks awarded for up to eight ratios in the exam. Notice here marks would be awarded for making adjustments to the ratios to ensure that entities A and B are compared on a like for like basis. Again the scenario with the additional information notes 1 and 2 gives the clues that this is what the model answer will comment on.

(a)   **REPORT**

To: The board of XYZ

Subject: Potential acquisitions

The gross profit margin of B, 36% is significantly higher than that of A, 29%, indicating that B has greater control over its core cost of sales. However A has managed to achieve 14% profit before tax compared with B's 11%. This would normally indicate that A has better control of administrative and distribution costs than B, however there have been two notable transactions that have had a significant impact on A's profit before tax:

1   A gain of $350,000 on the disposal of a non-current asset was offset against administrative expenses. Adjusting for this one-off gain increases administrative expenses by $350,000 and results in admin expenses of 14% of sales, which is line with B.

2   On the face of it both entities pay approximately 5% for finance (based on interest/long term borrowings). However A holds held for trading investments and has recorded gains of $20,000 in the year to finance costs. When this is removed the finance costs are $45,000, which means that A is paying around 9% for its borrowings. This indicates that A is considered by the lender(s) to be a riskier investment.

The gearing ratio of A is 53% compared with B's gearing of 43%. B is likely to be viewed as a less risky investment by financiers if additional funding was required.

B's gross margin is considerably higher than A's and yet only achieves 11% profit before tax percentage. This might be something that could be improved on acquisition if the combined entity could take advantage of economies of scale.

Based on the reported figures A makes profit before tax of 14% but if the non-current asset gain is removed (assuming that this is a non-recurring item) then this profit falls to less than 5%, which is significantly less than B.

Furthermore, the efficiency level of B appears to be higher than A when we compare non-current asset turnover, A's being 2.24 and B's being 2.93. A, however, recently refocused business activities and invested in non-current assets. These assets may not yet be providing return which would deflate the NCA turnover ratio. Entity B may have older assets and be in need of investment. This may suit us as we can align any investment with our own business strategy.

The tax regimes may play a significant role in the decision on acquisition. A pays approximately 28% tax based on tax/profit before tax. B pays approximately 35% tax. This is something that should be investigated further before proceeding with either acquisition.

Conclusion

On the basis of this initial review, I would recommend that entity B be considered further for acquisition, based on the profitability, efficiency and low risk indicated by the gearing and interest costs.

(b)   Although A and B operate in similar sectors, it is unlikely that any two entities will have the same operating environments and as a result will produce different results. Different activities and strategies will affect the comparability, e.g. A's decision to invest in held for trading investments will produce gains/losses.

The financial statements given are for one period only and are not necessarily covering the same 12 month period. The information provided may cover a period that is not typical of the trend of performance over a longer period of time and may be affected by non-recurring items, e.g. A's gain on the sale of non-current assets.

Despite the increasing levels of accounting guidance, entities still have considerable discretion in the way financial transactions are recorded. Adopting different accounting policies can affect comparability, e.g. equity of one entity could include revaluation of fixed assets and the other may hold non-current assets at depreciated historic cost. This would affect ratios such as return on capital employed and non-current asset turnover.

Before making an acquisition it is important to consider the non-financial factors. An entity's social and environmental policy may be in line with the acquirer's strategy and finding the best business fit may be as important as the financial information.

Appendix

	A	B
Gross profit margin GP/ sales	1,100/3,800 = 29%	1,580/4,400 = 36%
Profit margin PBT/sales	532/3,800 = 14%	484/4,400 = 11%
Profit margin after adjustments	(532 – 350 - 20)/3,800 = 4%	
Gearing Debt/equity	500/950 = 53%	650/ 1,500 = 43%
Non-current asset turnover	3,800/1,700 = 2.24	4,400/1,500 = 2.93
ROCE	(532 + 25)/1,450 = 38%	(484 + 32)/2,150 = 24%
ROCE after adjustment	(532 + 25 – 350)/1,450 = 14%	
Finance costs Interest/debt	25/500 = 5%	32/650 = 5%
Adjusted for HFT gain	(25 + 20)/500 = 9%	
Distribution costs/sales	375/3,800 =10%	420/4,400 =10%
Admin exps/sales	168/3,800 = 4%	644/4,400 = 15%
Adjusted for NCA gain	(168 + 350)/3,800 =14%	
Tax rate Tax/PBT	148/532 =28%	170/484 =35%

CIMA

Financial Pillar

F2 – Financial Management

24 November 2011 – Thursday Afternoon Session

Instructions to candidates

You are allowed three hours to answer this question paper.
You are allowed 20 minutes reading time **before the examination begins** during which you should read the question paper and, if you wish, highlight and/or make notes on the question paper. However, you will **not** be allowed, **under any circumstances**, to open the answer book and start writing or use your calculator during this reading time.
You are strongly advised to carefully read ALL the question requirements before attempting the question concerned (that is all parts and/or sub-questions).
ALL answers must be written in the answer book. Answers written on the question paper will **not** be submitted for marking.
You should show all workings as marks are available for the method you use.
ALL QUESTIONS ARE COMPULSORY.
Section A comprises 5 questions and is on pages 2 to 6.
Section B comprises 2 questions and is on pages 8 to 11.
Maths tables and formulae are provided on pages 13 to 15.
The list of verbs as published in the syllabus is given for reference on page 19.
Write your candidate number, the paper number and examination subject title in the spaces provided on the front of the answer book. Also write your contact ID and name in the space provided in the right hand margin and seal to close.
Tick the appropriate boxes on the front of the answer book to indicate the questions you have answered.

F2 – Financial Management

SECTION A – 50 MARKS

[You are advised to spend no longer than 18 minutes on each question in this section.]

ANSWER *ALL* FIVE QUESTIONS IN THIS SECTION

Question One

BG acquired 25% of the equity share capital of JV several years ago when the retained earnings of JV were $40,000. JV operates as a separate entity under a contractual agreement between BG and 3 other parties, each party holding an equal proportion of the equity share capital. The investment in JV is held at cost in BG's individual financial statements, and has been correctly classified as a joint venture.

Statement of financial position as at 31 March 2011	BG $000	JV $000
ASSETS		
Non-current assets		
Property, plant and equipment	322	280
Investment in JV	70	-
	392	280
Current assets		
Inventories	111	120
Receivables	115	132
Held for trading investment	35	-
Cash and cash equivalents	21	40
	282	292
Total assets	674	572
EQUITY AND LIABILITIES		
Equity attributable to owners of the parent		
Share capital ($1 shares)	120	200
Revaluation reserve	18	-
Retained earnings	213	120
Total equity	351	320
Non-current liabilities		
Long term borrowings	90	-
Current liabilities		
Payables	185	160
Income tax payable	48	92
	233	252
Total liabilities	323	252
Total equity and liabilities	674	572

Additional information:

1. During the year JV sold goods to BG for $200,000. Half of these goods remain in BG's inventories at 31 March 2011. JV makes a 20% margin on all sales. The most recent invoice for $24,000 sent from JV to BG in respect of these sales remains outstanding at the year end.

2. BG holds another investment, which it has correctly classified as held for trading. The fair value of this investment at 31 March 2011 was $42,000, although this has not yet been reflected in the financial statements.

Question Two

DRT has entered into the following agreements in the year to 31 May 2011:

Sale of land

On 31 May 2011 DRT sold land to NKL, an entity that provides DRT with long-term finance. The sale price was $1,600,000 and the carrying value of the land on the date of the sale was $1,310,000 (the original cost of the asset). Under the terms of the sale agreement DRT has the option to repurchase the land within the next four years for between $1,660,000 and $1,800,000 depending on the date of repurchase. NKL cannot use the land for any purpose without the prior consent of DRT. The land must be repurchased for $1,800,000 at the end of the four year period if the option is not exercised before that time.

DRT has derecognised the land and recorded the subsequent gain within profit for the year ended 31 May 2011.

TURN OVER

Set-up of payroll services entity, GHJ

Until 1 January 2011, DRT operated a payroll services division providing payroll services for itself and also for a number of external customers. On 1 January 2011 the business of the division and assets with a value of $300,000 were transferred into a separate entity called GHJ, which was set up by DRT. The sales director of GHJ owns 100% of its equity share capital. A contractual agreement signed by both the sales director of GHJ and a director of DRT, states that the operating and financial policies of GHJ will be made by the board of DRT. GHJ has acquired a long-term loan of $1 million with DRT acting as guarantor. Profits and losses of GHJ, after deduction of the sales director's salary, flow to DRT. The directors of DRT wish to avoid consolidating GHJ as the additional borrowings of GHJ would negatively impact DRT's gearing ratio.

Required:

(b) **Discuss** how the relationship with GHJ should be reflected in the financial statements of the DRT group. Your answer should make reference to any relevant international accounting standards.

(5 marks)

(Total for Question Two = 10 marks)

Question Three

On 1 July 2010 BNM, a listed entity, had 5,000,000 $1 ordinary shares in issue. On 1 September 2010, BNM made a 1 for 2 bonus issue from retained earnings. On 1 February 2011 BNM issued 3,000,000 $1 ordinary shares for $4.10 each, which was their full market price.

BNM generated profit after tax of $3.8m for the year ended 30 June 2011.

The basic earnings per share for the year ended 30 June 2010 was 48.2 cents.

At 1 July 2010 the ordinary shareholders of BNM held options to purchase 1,000,000 $1 ordinary shares at $3.10 per share. The options are exercisable between 1 July 2012 and 30 June 2014. No further options were issued in the year. The average market value of one $1 ordinary share of BNM during the year ended 30 June 2011 was $4.00.

Required:

(a) **Calculate** the basic earnings per share to be reported in the financial statements of BNM for the year ended 30 June 2011, including the comparative figure, in accordance with the requirements of IAS 33 *Earnings Per Share.*

(5 marks)

(b) **Calculate** the diluted earnings per share for the year ended 30 June 2011, in accordance with the requirements of IAS 33 *Earnings Per Share.* (A comparative figure is NOT required).

(3 marks)

(c) **Explain** why it is important for users to have diluted earnings per share presented in the financial statements.

(2 marks)

(Total for Question Three = 10 marks)

Question Four

Financial Instrument

QWS issued a redeemable debt instrument on 1 July 2009 at its par value of $6 million. The instrument carries a fixed coupon interest rate of 6%, which is payable annually in arrears. The debt instrument will be redeemed for $6.02 million on 30 June 2013. Transaction costs associated with the issue were $200,000 and were paid at the time of issue. The effective interest rate applicable to this liability is approximately 7.06%.

Required:

(i) **Explain** how this instrument will be initially and subsequently measured.

(ii) **Calculate** the carrying value of the liability to be included in QWS's statement of financial position as at 30 June 2011. (Round all workings to the nearest $000)

(5 marks)

Pension plan

QWS operates a defined benefit pension plan for its employees. At 1 July 2010 the fair value of the pension plan assets was $1,200,000 and the present value of the plan liabilities was $1,400,000. The interest cost on the plan liabilities was estimated at 7% and the expected return on plan assets at 4%.

The actuary estimates that the current service cost for the year ended 30 June 2011 is $300,000. QWS made contributions into the pension plan of $400,000 in the year.

The pension plan paid $220,000 to retired members in the year to 30 June 2011.

At 30 June 2011 the fair value of the pension plan assets was $1,400,000 and the present value of the plan liabilities was $1,600,000.

In accordance with the amendment to IAS 19 *Employee Benefits*, QWS recognises actuarial gains and losses in other comprehensive income in the period in which they occur.

Required:

Calculate the net expense that will be included in QWS's profit or loss AND the amounts that would be included in other comprehensive income in respect of actuarial gains or losses for the year ended 30 June 2011. (Round all workings to the nearest $000)

(5 marks)

(Total for Question Four = 10 marks)

TURN OVER

Question Five

The Financial Accounting Standards Board, the main standard-setting body in the USA, and the International Accounting Standards Board agreed, at their Norwalk meeting in 2002, to work towards making their existing and future financial reporting standards fully compatible.

Required:

(a) **Discuss** the progress made towards convergence, including how this has been achieved.

(6 marks)

(b) **Discuss** the benefits of convergence to BOTH investors and accounting students.

(4 marks)

(Total for Question Five = 10 marks)

(Total for Section A = 50 marks)

End of Section A

Section B starts on page 8

This page is blank

SECTION B – 50 MARKS

[You are advised to spend no longer than 45 minutes on each question in this section.]

ANSWER BOTH QUESTIONS IN THIS SECTION – 25 MARKS EACH

Question Six

The statements of comprehensive income for three entities for the year ended 31 March 2011 are presented below:

	BH	NJ	MK
	$000	$000	$000
Revenue	3,360	3,240	2,390
Cost of sales	(1,800)	(1,860)	(1,380)
Gross profit	1,560	1,380	1,010
Administrative expenses	(380)	(340)	(250)
Distribution costs	(400)	(300)	(150)
Investment income	80	-	-
Finance costs	(180)	(140)	(110)
Profit before tax	680	600	500
Income tax expense	(200)	(160)	(150)
Profit for the year	480	440	350
Other comprehensive income			
Revaluation of property, plant and equipment	70	40	30
Gains on investments in NJ and MK	96	-	-
Tax effect of OCI	(50)	(16)	(10)
Other comprehensive income for the year, net of tax	116	24	20
Total comprehensive income for the year	596	464	370

Additional information:

1. BH acquired a 25% investment in NJ on 1 September 2002 for $300,000. The investment was classified as available for sale and the gains earned on it have been recorded within other comprehensive income in BH's individual financial statements. The fair value of the 25% investment at 31 March 2010 was $400,000 and at 1 January 2011 was $425,000. BH was not able to exercise significant influence over the financial and operating policies of NJ.

   On 1 January 2011, BH acquired an additional 40% of the 1 million $1 equity shares of NJ for $680,000. The retained reserves of NJ at that date were $526,000. The group policy is to value the non-controlling interest at its fair value at the date of acquisition. The non-controlling interest had a fair value of $581,000 at 1 January 2011. NJ lost a key customer in February and BH's directors have decided that goodwill on acquisition is impaired by 10% at 31 March 2011. Impairment losses are charged to group administrative expenses.

   The investment in NJ continues to be held as an available for sale asset in BH's individual financial statements and recorded at its fair value of $1,170,000 at 31 March 2011. The total gains recorded to date in respect of NJ are $190,000, of which $90,000 occurred in the year and are included in the other comprehensive income of BH.

2. BH acquired 40% of the equity share capital of MK for $334,000 on 1 October 2010. The investment was classified as available for sale and the gains earned on it since its acquisition have been recorded within other comprehensive income in the year in BH's individual financial statements. The fair value of this available for sale asset at 31 March 2011 was $340,000. BH exercises significant influence over the financial and operating policies of MK.

   A new competitor has recently entered the market in which MK operates and it is likely that this will have an immediate impact on MK's profits in the coming period. As a result, the directors of BH have decided that the investment in MK should be subject to 10% impairment at 31 March 2011.

3. NJ sold goods to BH in January 2011 for $200,000. Half of these items remain in BH's inventories at the year end. NJ earns a 20% gross margin on all sales.

4. The profits of all three entities can be assumed to accrue evenly throughout the year. Assume there is no further impact to income tax figures.

5. MK paid a dividend of $80,000 to its equity shareholders on 31 March 2011. BH included its share of the dividend in investment income.

Required:

Prepare the consolidated statement of comprehensive income for the BH Group for the year ended 31 March 2011. (Round all figures to the nearest $000.)

(18 marks)

The directors of BH, with the backing of the non-controlling shareholders of NJ, are considering moving NJ to a new facility overseas. NJ would then source all raw materials locally, recruit a local workforce and would be subject to local taxes and corporate regulations. The facility identified is in a country that uses the KRON as its currency, whilst BH and the rest of the group use the $. Since acquisition, NJ has operated relatively autonomously within the group and this is expected to continue if the move takes place.

The directors are unsure about the currency that would be used to prepare the financial statements of NJ if the relocation was to go ahead and what implication this might have for the group financial statements.

Required:

Apply the principles of IAS 21 *The Effects of Changes in Foreign Exchange Rates*, to establish which currency should be used to prepare the financial statements of NJ, assuming that NJ moves to the overseas facility identified above.

(7 marks)

(Total for Question Six = 25 marks)

Section B continues on the next page

Question Seven

Mr X owned a highly successful technology business which he sold five years ago for $20 million. He then set up an investment entity that invests, primarily in smaller private businesses in need of short to medium term funding. Mr X sits on the board as a non-executive director of a number of the entities that his business has invested in and is often able to offer valuable business advice to these entities, especially in the area of research and development activities.

Mr X has been approached by the managing director of ABC, a small private entity looking for investment. ABC has been trading for more than 10 years manufacturing and selling its own branded perfumes, lotions and candles to the public in its 15 retail stores and to other larger retailing entities. Revenues and profits have been steady over the last 10 years. However 18 months ago, the newly appointed sales director saw an opportunity to sell the products on-line. Using long term funding, he therefore set up an online shop. The online shop has been operating successfully for the last 14 months. The sales director also used his prior contacts to secure a lucrative deal with a boutique hotel chain for ABC to manufacture products for the hotel, carrying the hotel chain name and logo.

The managing director of ABC now believes that the business has further opportunities and does not wish to lose the momentum created by the sales director. The bank that currently provides both a long-term loan and an overdraft facility has rejected ABC's request for additional funds on the basis that there are insufficient assets to offer for security (the existing funding is secured on ABC's property, plant and equipment).

Extracts from the financial statements for ABC are provided below:

Statement of comprehensive income for the year ended 30 June	2011	2010
	$'000	$'000
Revenue	6,000	3,700
Cost of sales	(4,083)	(2,590)
Gross profit	1,917	1,110
Administrative expenses	(870)	(413)
Distribution costs	(464)	(356)
Finance costs	(43)	(34)
Profit before tax	540	307
Income tax expense	(135)	(80)
Profit for the year	405	227

The revenues and profits of the three business segments for the year ended 30 June 2011 were:

	Retail operations	Online store	Hotel contract
	$'000	$'000	$'000
Revenues	4,004	1,096	900
Gross profit	1,200	330	387
Profit before tax	320	138	82

The online store earned a negligible amount of revenue and profit in the year ended 30 June 2010.

Statement of financial position as at 30 June	2011 $'000	2010 $'000
ASSETS		
Non-current assets		
Property, plant and equipment	380	400
Intangible assets – development costs	20	10
	400	410
Current assets		
Inventories	1,260	1,180
Receivables	455	310
Cash and cash equivalents	-	42
	1,715	1,532
Total assets	2,115	1,942
EQUITY AND LIABILITIES		
Equity		
Share capital ($1 equity shares)	550	550
Retained earnings	722	610
Total equity	1,272	1,160
Non-current liabilities		
Long-term borrowings	412	404
Current liabilities		
Payables	363	378
Short-term borrowings (overdraft)	68	-
	431	378
Total liabilities	843	782
Total equity and liabilities	2,115	1,942

As a member of Mr X's investment management team, you have been asked to analyse the financial performance and position of ABC and make a recommendation as to whether this request for investment should be considered further by Mr X.

Required:

(a) **Prepare** a report that analyses the financial performance of ABC for the year ended 30 June 2011 and its financial position at that date, and makes a recommendation as to whether the investment should be considered further. (8 marks are available for the calculation of relevant ratios)

(20 marks)

(b) **Discuss** the benefits and limitations to Mr X of relying on traditional ratio analysis when deciding whether or not to invest in ABC.

(5 marks)

(Total for Question Seven = 25 marks)

(Total for Section B = 50 marks)

End of Question Paper

Maths Tables and Formulae are on pages 13 to 15

TURN OVER

This page is blank

MATHS TABLES AND FORMULAE

Present value table

Present value of $1, that is $(1 + r)^{-n}$ where r = interest rate; n = number of periods until payment or receipt.

Periods	Interest rates (r)									
(n)	1%	2%	3%	4%	5%	6%	7%	8%	9%	10%
1	0.990	0.980	0.971	0.962	0.952	0.943	0.935	0.926	0.917	0.909
2	0.980	0.961	0.943	0.925	0.907	0.890	0.873	0.857	0.842	0.826
3	0.971	0.942	0.915	0.889	0.864	0.840	0.816	0.794	0.772	0.751
4	0.961	0.924	0.888	0.855	0.823	0.792	0.763	0.735	0.708	0.683
5	0.951	0.906	0.863	0.822	0.784	0.747	0.713	0.681	0.650	0.621
6	0.942	0.888	0.837	0.790	0.746	0.705	0.666	0.630	0.596	0.564
7	0.933	0.871	0.813	0.760	0.711	0.665	0.623	0.583	0.547	0.513
8	0.923	0.853	0.789	0.731	0.677	0.627	0.582	0.540	0.502	0.467
9	0.914	0.837	0.766	0.703	0.645	0.592	0.544	0.500	0.460	0.424
10	0.905	0.820	0.744	0.676	0.614	0.558	0.508	0.463	0.422	0.386
11	0.896	0.804	0.722	0.650	0.585	0.527	0.475	0.429	0.388	0.350
12	0.887	0.788	0.701	0.625	0.557	0.497	0.444	0.397	0.356	0.319
13	0.879	0.773	0.681	0.601	0.530	0.469	0.415	0.368	0.326	0.290
14	0.870	0.758	0.661	0.577	0.505	0.442	0.388	0.340	0.299	0.263
15	0.861	0.743	0.642	0.555	0.481	0.417	0.362	0.315	0.275	0.239
16	0.853	0.728	0.623	0.534	0.458	0.394	0.339	0.292	0.252	0.218
17	0.844	0.714	0.605	0.513	0.436	0.371	0.317	0.270	0.231	0.198
18	0.836	0.700	0.587	0.494	0.416	0.350	0.296	0.250	0.212	0.180
19	0.828	0.686	0.570	0.475	0.396	0.331	0.277	0.232	0.194	0.164
20	0.820	0.673	0.554	0.456	0.377	0.312	0.258	0.215	0.178	0.149

Periods	Interest rates (r)									
(n)	11%	12%	13%	14%	15%	16%	17%	18%	19%	20%
1	0.901	0.893	0.885	0.877	0.870	0.862	0.855	0.847	0.840	0.833
2	0.812	0.797	0.783	0.769	0.756	0.743	0.731	0.718	0.706	0.694
3	0.731	0.712	0.693	0.675	0.658	0.641	0.624	0.609	0.593	0.579
4	0.659	0.636	0.613	0.592	0.572	0.552	0.534	0.516	0.499	0.482
5	0.593	0.567	0.543	0.519	0.497	0.476	0.456	0.437	0.419	0.402
6	0.535	0.507	0.480	0.456	0.432	0.410	0.390	0.370	0.352	0.335
7	0.482	0.452	0.425	0.400	0.376	0.354	0.333	0.314	0.296	0.279
8	0.434	0.404	0.376	0.351	0.327	0.305	0.285	0.266	0.249	0.233
9	0.391	0.361	0.333	0.308	0.284	0.263	0.243	0.225	0.209	0.194
10	0.352	0.322	0.295	0.270	0.247	0.227	0.208	0.191	0.176	0.162
11	0.317	0.287	0.261	0.237	0.215	0.195	0.178	0.162	0.148	0.135
12	0.286	0.257	0.231	0.208	0.187	0.168	0.152	0.137	0.124	0.112
13	0.258	0.229	0.204	0.182	0.163	0.145	0.130	0.116	0.104	0.093
14	0.232	0.205	0.181	0.160	0.141	0.125	0.111	0.099	0.088	0.078
15	0.209	0.183	0.160	0.140	0.123	0.108	0.095	0.084	0.079	0.065
16	0.188	0.163	0.141	0.123	0.107	0.093	0.081	0.071	0.062	0.054
17	0.170	0.146	0.125	0.108	0.093	0.080	0.069	0.060	0.052	0.045
18	0.153	0.130	0.111	0.095	0.081	0.069	0.059	0.051	0.044	0.038
19	0.138	0.116	0.098	0.083	0.070	0.060	0.051	0.043	0.037	0.031
20	0.124	0.104	0.087	0.073	0.061	0.051	0.043	0.037	0.031	0.026

Cumulative present value of $1 per annum,

Receivable or Payable at the end of each year for n years $\dfrac{1-(1+r)^{-n}}{r}$

Periods (n)	Interest rates (r)									
	1%	2%	3%	4%	5%	6%	7%	8%	9%	10%
1	0.990	0.980	0.971	0.962	0.952	0.943	0.935	0.926	0.917	0.909
2	1.970	1.942	1.913	1.886	1.859	1.833	1.808	1.783	1.759	1.736
3	2.941	2.884	2.829	2.775	2.723	2.673	2.624	2.577	2.531	2.487
4	3.902	3.808	3.717	3.630	3.546	3.465	3.387	3.312	3.240	3.170
5	4.853	4.713	4.580	4.452	4.329	4.212	4.100	3.993	3.890	3.791
6	5.795	5.601	5.417	5.242	5.076	4.917	4.767	4.623	4.486	4.355
7	6.728	6.472	6.230	6.002	5.786	5.582	5.389	5.206	5.033	4.868
8	7.652	7.325	7.020	6.733	6.463	6.210	5.971	5.747	5.535	5.335
9	8.566	8.162	7.786	7.435	7.108	6.802	6.515	6.247	5.995	5.759
10	9.471	8.983	8.530	8.111	7.722	7.360	7.024	6.710	6.418	6.145
11	10.368	9.787	9.253	8.760	8.306	7.887	7.499	7.139	6.805	6.495
12	11.255	10.575	9.954	9.385	8.863	8.384	7.943	7.536	7.161	6.814
13	12.134	11.348	10.635	9.986	9.394	8.853	8.358	7.904	7.487	7.103
14	13.004	12.106	11.296	10.563	9.899	9.295	8.745	8.244	7.786	7.367
15	13.865	12.849	11.938	11.118	10.380	9.712	9.108	8.559	8.061	7.606
16	14.718	13.578	12.561	11.652	10.838	10.106	9.447	8.851	8.313	7.824
17	15.562	14.292	13.166	12.166	11.274	10.477	9.763	9.122	8.544	8.022
18	16.398	14.992	13.754	12.659	11.690	10.828	10.059	9.372	8.756	8.201
19	17.226	15.679	14.324	13.134	12.085	11.158	10.336	9.604	8.950	8.365
20	18.046	16.351	14.878	13.590	12.462	11.470	10.594	9.818	9.129	8.514

Periods (n)	Interest rates (r)									
	11%	12%	13%	14%	15%	16%	17%	18%	19%	20%
1	0.901	0.893	0.885	0.877	0.870	0.862	0.855	0.847	0.840	0.833
2	1.713	1.690	1.668	1.647	1.626	1.605	1.585	1.566	1.547	1.528
3	2.444	2.402	2.361	2.322	2.283	2.246	2.210	2.174	2.140	2.106
4	3.102	3.037	2.974	2.914	2.855	2.798	2.743	2.690	2.639	2.589
5	3.696	3.605	3.517	3.433	3.352	3.274	3.199	3.127	3.058	2.991
6	4.231	4.111	3.998	3.889	3.784	3.685	3.589	3.498	3.410	3.326
7	4.712	4.564	4.423	4.288	4.160	4.039	3.922	3.812	3.706	3.605
8	5.146	4.968	4.799	4.639	4.487	4.344	4.207	4.078	3.954	3.837
9	5.537	5.328	5.132	4.946	4.772	4.607	4.451	4.303	4.163	4.031
10	5.889	5.650	5.426	5.216	5.019	4.833	4.659	4.494	4.339	4.192
11	6.207	5.938	5.687	5.453	5.234	5.029	4.836	4.656	4.486	4.327
12	6.492	6.194	5.918	5.660	5.421	5.197	4.988	7.793	4.611	4.439
13	6.750	6.424	6.122	5.842	5.583	5.342	5.118	4.910	4.715	4.533
14	6.982	6.628	6.302	6.002	5.724	5.468	5.229	5.008	4.802	4.611
15	7.191	6.811	6.462	6.142	5.847	5.575	5.324	5.092	4.876	4.675
16	7.379	6.974	6.604	6.265	5.954	5.668	5.405	5.162	4.938	4.730
17	7.549	7.120	6.729	6.373	6.047	5.749	5.475	5.222	4.990	4.775
18	7.702	7.250	6.840	6.467	6.128	5.818	5.534	5.273	5.033	4.812
19	7.839	7.366	6.938	6.550	6.198	5.877	5.584	5.316	5.070	4.843
20	7.963	7.469	7.025	6.623	6.259	5.929	5.628	5.353	5.101	4.870

FORMULAE

Annuity

Present value of an annuity of $1 per annum receivable or payable for *n* years, commencing in one year, discounted at *r*% per annum:

$$PV = \frac{1}{r}\left[1 - \frac{1}{[1+r]^n}\right]$$

Perpetuity

Present value of $1 per annum receivable or payable in perpetuity, commencing in one year, discounted at *r*% per annum:

$$PV = \frac{1}{r}$$

Growing Perpetuity

Present value of $1 per annum, receivable or payable, commencing in one year, growing in perpetuity at a constant rate of *g*% per annum, discounted at *r*% per annum:

$$PV = \frac{1}{r-g}$$

This page is blank

This page is blank

This page is blank

LIST OF VERBS USED IN THE QUESTION REQUIREMENTS

A list of the learning objectives and verbs that appear in the syllabus and in the question requirements for each question in this paper.

It is important that you answer the question according to the definition of the verb.

LEARNING OBJECTIVE	VERBS USED	DEFINITION
Level 1 - KNOWLEDGE What you are expected to know.	List State Define	Make a list of Express, fully or clearly, the details/facts of Give the exact meaning of
Level 2 - COMPREHENSION What you are expected to understand.	Describe Distinguish Explain Identify Illustrate	Communicate the key features Highlight the differences between Make clear or intelligible/State the meaning or purpose of Recognise, establish or select after consideration Use an example to describe or explain something
Level 3 - APPLICATION How you are expected to apply your knowledge.	Apply Calculate Demonstrate Prepare Reconcile Solve Tabulate	Put to practical use Ascertain or reckon mathematically Prove with certainty or to exhibit by practical means Make or get ready for use Make or prove consistent/compatible Find an answer to Arrange in a table
Level 4 - ANALYSIS How are you expected to analyse the detail of what you have learned.	Analyse Categorise Compare and contrast Construct Discuss Interpret Prioritise Produce	Examine in detail the structure of Place into a defined class or division Show the similarities and/or differences between Build up or compile Examine in detail by argument Translate into intelligible or familiar terms Place in order of priority or sequence for action Create or bring into existence
Level 5 - EVALUATION How are you expected to use your learning to evaluate, make decisions or recommendations.	Advise Evaluate Recommend	Counsel, inform or notify Appraise or assess the value of Advise on a course of action

Financial Pillar

Management Level Paper

F2 – Financial Management

November 2011

Thursday Afternoon Session

CIMA

The Examiner's Answers –

F2 - Financial Management

Some of the answers that follow are fuller and more comprehensive than would be expected from a well-prepared candidate. They have been written in this way to aid teaching, study and revision for tutors and candidates alike.

SECTION A

Answer to Question One

(a) **Consolidated statement of financial position of BG group as at 31 March 2011**

All workings in $000	**BG**
Non-current assets	**$000**
Property, plant and equipment (322 + (25% x 280))	392
Goodwill **(W1)**	10
	402
Current assets	
Inventories (111 + (25% x 120) – 5 **(W2)**)	136
Receivables(115 + (25% x 132) – 6 **(W3)**)	142
Held for trading (35+7**(W4)**)	42
Cash and cash equivalents (21 + (25% x 40))	31
	351
Total assets	753
EQUITY AND LIABILITIES	
Equity attributable to owners of the parent	
Share capital ($1 shares)	120
Revaluation reserve	18
Retained earnings **(W5)**	235
Total equity	373
Non-current liabilities	
Long term borrowings	90
Current liabilities	
Payables (185 + (25% x 160) - 6 **(W3)**)	219
Income tax payable (48 + (25% x 92))	71
	290
Total liabilities	380
Total equity and liabilities	753

Workings

W1 Goodwill	**$000**	**$000**
Consideration transferred		70
Net assets acquired:		
25% of share capital of JV (25% x 200)	50	
Retained earnings at acquisition (25% x 40)	10	(60)
Goodwill		10

W2 Unrealised profit on intra-group trading   **$000**
Sales   200
Held by BG at year end – 50%   100
20% profit margin   20
25% group share   5
Dr   RE   5
        Cr   Inventories   5

W3 Intra-group balance   **$000**
Outstanding balance   24
Group share 25%   6
Dr   Payables   6
        Cr   Receivables   6

W4 Held for trading   **$000**
FV at 31 March 2011   42
Carrying value brought forward   35
Gain on HFT transferred to profit or loss (thru RE in SOFP)   7
Dr   HFT asset   7
        Cr   RE   7

W5 Retained earnings   **$000**
RE of BG   213
25% group share of post-acquisition RE of JV (25% x (120 – 40))   20
Less group share of unrealised profit on inventories (W2)   (5)
Increase in fair value of HFT asset (W4)   7
Consolidated retained earnings   235

(b)   IAS 31 permits equity accounting to be used as an alternative to proportionate
        consolidation when consolidating investments in joint venture entities. Equity
        accounting initially measures the interest at cost and then subsequently at cost plus the
        group share of post-acquisition profits and gains. Adopting equity accounting would
        have a significant effect on the consolidated financial statements of the BG group as
        the investment would be included as a one-line entry, Investment in Joint Venture,
        rather than the group share of all assets and liabilities being included on a line by line
        basis. Each element within the group statement of financial position would therefore be
        reduced and instead there would be an "Investment in Joint Venture" within non-current
        assets which would be measured at cost plus BG's share of post-acquisition reserves.

Answer to Question Two

(a) Sale of land

This is a form of sale and repurchase agreement and therefore under IAS 18 and the Framework we need to consider the substance of the transaction and ultimately who holds the majority of the risks and rewards of the ownership of the land.

The substance of this transaction would appear to be a financing arrangement, especially as NKL is already a provider of long term finance to DRT, with the land acting as security. The risks and rewards associated with the land have not actually been transferred to NKL. DRT continues to be subject to the principal risk of the asset, which is a fall in its value, as it would be forced to repurchase the land in 4 years' time at $1.8 million. DRT could, however, gain from the agreement if the value of the land increased beyond the agreed repurchase terms. In addition, DRT continues to determine how the land can be used.

The asset should not be derecognised by DRT and the gain on sale should be eliminated. The proceeds received represent finance and therefore a corresponding liability should be recognised in DRT's financial statements at 31 May 2011. In subsequent years the liability will be adjusted to include interest (which arises because the repurchase price is higher than the original "sale" price). However, no interest on this financing is recognised in the year to 31 May 2011 as the transaction occurred at the year-end date.

The correcting entry being:

Dr Property, plant and equipment		$1,310,000
Dr Gain on sale	$290,000	
Cr Liability		$1,600,000

(b) Set-up of payroll services entity, GHJ

The key question here is whether DRT has control of GHJ and hence it should be consolidated as part of the DRT group. In accordance with IAS 27 *Consolidated and Separate Financial Statements* and IFRS 3 *Business Combinations,* ownership of the majority of the equity share capital of an entity is normally sufficient to presume control, unless there is evidence to the contrary. The sales director holds all of the equity shares of GHJ which would normally infer control. However, he has no voting power, instead DRT effectively exercises control by way of the signed agreement. Other factors which would indicate that DRT effectively controls GHJ are as follows:

- The control over the financial and operating policies of GHJ enables DRT to ensure that the economic benefits flow from GHJ to DRT.
- GHJ is undertaking activities that DRT would be conducting itself if GHJ did not exist.
- DRT is acting as guarantor for the loan.

Taking all of this into account we can conclude that DRT controls GHJ, which is actually a special purpose entity and should be consolidated by DRT. The assets transferred are group assets and would be included in the consolidated statement of financial position. In addition the loan of $1 million should also be consolidated.

Answer to Question Three

(a) Basic eps:

Profit attributable to ordinary shareholders	$3,800,000
Weighted average number of issued ordinary shares during the year ended 30 June 2011:	
(5,000,000 x 7/12) + (8,000,000 x 5/12) + 2,500,000 (bonus)	8,750,000
Basic eps	**43.4 cents**
Basic eps for y/e 30 June 2010 (restated) 48.2 cents x 2/3	**32.1 cents**

(b) Diluted eps:

Profit attributable to ordinary shareholders		$3,800,000
Weighted average number of issued ordinary shares during the year ended 30 June 2011 from part a:		8,750,000
Shares held under option	1,000,000	
Shares that would have been issued at average market price (1,000,000 x 3.10/4.00)	(775,000)	
Shares effectively issued for no consideration and therefore dilutive		225,000
Weighted average number of issued ordinary shares and potential ordinary shares during the year ended 30 June 2011		8,975,000
		42.3 cents

(c) The diluted earnings per share measure includes the dilutive impact of any potential ordinary shares that a company has. Potential ordinary shares (such as the options in this scenario), when they are eventually issued, will increase the weighted average number of shares, the denominator of the basic eps calculation. This will have a negative impact on the reported eps. The diluted eps is presented alongside the basic calculation with equal prominence and shows investors the effect on eps if these dilutive shares were issued.

Answer to Question Four

(a) Financial instrument

(i)   This debt instrument will be initially measured at fair value less transaction costs, being the net proceeds of issue. It is subsequently measured at amortised cost using the effective interest rate.

(ii)

Year end 30 June	Opening balance $000	Effective interest 7.06% $000	Interest received $000	Closing balance $000
2010	5,800	409	(360)	5,849
2011	5,849	413	(360)	5,902

The carrying value of the liability as at 30 June 2011 is $5,902,000.

(b) Pension plan

Income statement expense	$000
Service cost	300
Interest cost (7% x $1,400,000)	98
Expected return (4% x $1,200,000)	(48)
Net expense	350

The net expense in profit or loss will be $350,000.

Actuarial gains and losses	FV of plan assets $000	PV of plan liabilities $000
Opening balance	1,200	1,400
Service cost		300
Interest cost (7% x $1,400,000)		98
Expected return (4% x $1,200,000)	48	
Benefits paid	(220)	(220)
Contributions	400	
	1,428	1,578
Actuarial loss on plan assets	(28)	
Actuarial loss on plan liabilities		22
Closing balance	1,400	1,600

Within other comprehensive income there will be an actuarial loss on plan assets of $28,000 and an actuarial loss on plan liabilities of $22,000.

Answer to Question Five

(a) **Progress towards convergence**

The FASB and the IASB at their Norwalk meeting agreed to work towards convergence using two main strategies:

- To eliminate minor differences between a list of target standards
- To develop new accounting standards jointly to ensure common approach and wording.

The work schedule towards convergence was entitled the Roadmap and included a list of the standards to be revised or amended to align their approaches and wording. This target was achieved and resulted in the revision of IAS 23 Borrowing costs and IAS 1 Presentation of Financial statements.

New standards, including IFRS 5, IFRS 8 and IFRS 9 have been developed jointly and incorporate new agreed definitions and wording. The FASB has agreed that its approach needs to switch from a rules-based system of reporting to a principles-based approach like that adopted by the IASB. This is the reason that the two bodies are jointly reviewing and revising the Framework for Preparation and Presentation of Financial Statements as the underlying basis for all future jointly developed accounting standards.

The progress of the convergence project has achieved objectives faster than expected and as a result the SEC in the US no longer requires entities to provide a reconciliation from IAS to US GAAP for entities adopting IAS and listed on the US stock exchange.

(b) **Possible benefits to investors and accounting students**

Financial statements prepared using accounting standards that follow the same principles can easily be compared. Prior to convergence, it would have been necessary to adjust certain figures in the accounts that would have been recognised or measured on different bases. Increased comparability and transparency should result in greater liquidity in investment markets and promote cross-border investment. This is all positive for investors, as it is easier to trade investments and realise capital gains.

Accounting students can also benefit from accounting across the world being based on similar and jointly developed accounting standards. This means there is one set of principles to be learned – increasing the chance of understanding and creating less confusion. One set of principles also increases the relevance of an accounting qualification – as an accounting qualification based on these principles is relevant across the world enabling an easy transfer of skills abroad.

Answer to Question Six

(a) Consolidated statement of comprehensive income for the BH Group for the year ended 31 March 2011.

All workings in $000	$000
Revenue (3,360 + (3/12 x 3,240) – 200**(W1)**)	3,970
Cost of sales (1,800 + (3/12 x 1,860) - 200 **(W1)** + 20 **(W1)**)	(2,085)
Gross profit	1,885
Administrative expenses (380 + (3/12 x 340) + 16**(W2)** + 41**(W3)**)	(522)
Distribution costs (400 + (3/12 x 300))	(475)
Gain on derecognition of AFS Investment **(W4)**	125
Investment income (80 – (40% x 80))	48
Finance costs (180 + (3/12 x 140))	(215)
Share of profit of associate (40% x 350 x 6/12)	70
Profit before tax	916
Income tax expense (200 + (3/12 x 160))	(240)
Profit for the year	676

Other comprehensive income:	
Revaluation of property, plant and equipment (70 + (3/12 x 40))	80
Gain on AFS investments – eliminated on consolidation **(W5)**	-
Tax effect of other comprehensive income (50 + (3/12 x 16))	(54)
Recycling of previously recognised gains on AFS investment **(W6)**	(100)
Share of other comprehensive income of associate, net of tax (40% x 20 x 6/12)	4
Other comprehensive income for the year, net of tax	(70)
Total comprehensive income for the year	606

Profit for the year attributable to:	
Equity holders of the parent (676 - 26)	650
Non-controlling interest **(W7)**	26
	676

Total comprehensive income attributable to:	
Equity holders of the parent (606 – 28)	578
Non-controlling interest **(W7)**	28
	606

Workings

W1 Elimination of intra-group trading	$000
Adjustment to revenue and cost of sales to eliminate intra-group trading	200
Total items remaining in inventories	100
Profit margin earned on these items 20% - adjustment to cost of sales	20

W2 Goodwill impairment - NJ

	$000	$000
Consideration transferred (for 40% purchased on 1 Jan 2011)		680
Previously held interest at fair value on 1 Jan 2011		425
Non-controlling interest at fair value at date control gained		581
Net assets at acquisition:		
Share capital	1,000	
Reserves at date control gained	526	
		(1,526)
Goodwill		160
10% impairment to be charged to administrative expenses		16

W3 Impairment of investment in associate

	$000
Investment at cost	334
Plus 40% share of post-acquisition TCI of associate (6/12 x 370) x 40%	74
	408
Impairment 10%	41

W4 Gain on derecognition of AFS investment in NJ

	$000
FV at date control is gained	425
Original cost of 25% investment	(300)
Gain on derecognition	125

W5 Gain on AFS investments

	$000
OCI gain in year reported in BH's accounts	96
Reverse post acquisition gain recognised on investment in MK(340,000-334,000)	(6)
Reverse post-acquisition gain recognised on investment in NJ $(90,000 – 25,000)	(65)
Recycling of pre-acquisition gain recognised in the year $(425,000 – 400,000)	(25)
	-

W6 Gains previously recognised in OCI (up to y/e 31/3/10)

	$000
FV of AFS Investment (25% holding in NJ) at 31 March 2010	400
Original cost of investment	(300)
Gains previously recognised in OCI to be recycled on de-recognition	100

W7 Non-controlling interest

	PFY $000	TCI $000
As per NJ accounts	440	464
Pro-rata for 3 months	110	116
Less adjustment for unrealised profit on inventories	(20)	(20)
Less goodwill	(16)	(16)
	74	80
NCI share 35%	**26**	**28**

(b) **Functional currency**

The functional currency of a foreign enterprise is the currency of the primary economic environment in which the entity operates. The key considerations would be:

- The currency which principally influences selling prices for goods and services;
- The country that most influences the selling prices of the entity's goods and services through its competitive forces and regulation;
- The currency that mainly influences labour, material and other costs.

If it is still unclear which currency should be the functional currency then consider the currency in which funding is primarily raised and in which operating receipts are retained. Where the subsidiary operates relatively autonomously, rather than as an extension of the parent, this provides evidence that the functional currency of this subsidiary should be the local currency in which it operates.

Based on the information provided it is likely that NJ would adopt the currency of the country in which it operates. If the move went ahead, NJ would be impacted by the local currency as it would be sourcing goods locally and recruiting local workforce. In addition, it would be subject to local corporate rules and regulations. Furthermore since NJ is expected to operate autonomously its local currency is most likely to be its functional currency. Therefore the KRON is likely to be the currency in which NJ will prepare its financial statements.

Answer to Question Seven

(a) **Report on ABC's financial performance and position**

To: Mr X
From: Member of Investment Team

ABC's revenue has grown by a considerable 62% from 2010 as a result of the new on-line store and the hotel contract. If these two new lines of business are stripped out revenues have actually increased in the core business by 8%, which is encouraging.

ABC is generating a healthy gross profit margin of 32%, up from 30% in 2010. The segments generating this overall profit, however, are generating different margins.
Both the retail operations and online store have generated the same gross margin, which you would expect as both are selling own-brand products. The online store however is benefiting from lower operating costs and generating a net profit margin (based on PBT) of 12.6% as opposed to the equivalent retail operations margin of 8%. Fewer sales staff and shop overheads are likely to be causing this difference. The hotel contract has achieved a 43% gross margin. The PBT margin is 9.1%, which is again more lucrative than the retail operations but lower than you would perhaps expect with such a high GP margin. It may be reasonable to assume that expenses related to setting up the hotel contract have been incurred and charged to profit (such as new labelling etc) and these expenses are unlikely to recur in future years, resulting in a higher profit before tax margin from this segment in the future. It would, however be necessary to investigate how expenses have been allocated to the segments to ensure the margin fairly reflects the economic reality. There is also an opportunity for ABC to capitalise on this development and approach other hotels about a similar deal.

Finance costs have increased as a result of ABC requiring short-term funding in the year, however the increased profitability has resulted in interest cover increasing in the year from 10 to 13.6 times. It appears that ABC's profits provide adequate cover for additional finance costs on debt, and so this is unlikely to be the cause of the bank's refusal to extend borrowing facilities. The lack of assets available for security appears to be the main issue.

The working capital is as you would expect for a principally retail based business with high levels of inventory and low receivables. Receivables of approximately 30 days seems high for a retail based business, however it must be noted that a significant part of the retail operations revenue comes from selling to other larger retailers, who will have negotiated favourable credit terms. There is no breakdown between the segments but clearly the terms of the hotel contract have no negative impact on the receivables of ABC as it hasn't changed. It is surprising to see that payables days have reduced from 53 days to 32 days from last year. This could result from a new supplier for the hotel own-label products negotiating faster payment or that a large payment to suppliers was made shortly before the year-end, causing payables to reduce and short-term borrowing to increase. It is difficult to determine accurately from just the year-end statement of financial position, however gaining the maximum credit possible from your suppliers could avoid the need for interest-bearing borrowings being required to fund working capital.

Inventories are the main asset of the business and investment in them dominates ABC's working capital. When inventories are removed in the calculation of the quick ratio, we see an increase from 0.9 to 1.1 in the period. The inventories days are high but have reduced from 166 days to 113 days. A reduction in the holding period of more than 50 days is a positive result for ABC and may be a result of the online business being set up. To conclude on working capital, it does appear that the working capital position is a result of changes in trading conditions rather than poor management controls which is a positive sign when considering investment.

ABC has improved efficiency in the year, increasing turnover with very little investment in non-current assets. Non-current asset turnover has increased from 9.0 to 15.0 in the year, which again reflects well on the management of the business.

The gearing has moved slightly as a result of the short-term borrowings, increasing from 34.8% to 37.7%. The gearing level itself is not a major issue but it is clear from the bank's refusal that lack of security is an issue and the bank was obviously not interested in utilising the inventories. ABC appears to be a well-managed, ambitious, profitable enterprise and additional investment is likely to provide the funds required to continue the expansion and bring additional returns.

There is sufficient interest cover for additional debt and coming from the technologies sector, Mr X has experience of entities that have a low non-current asset base and may be able to suggest alternative means of security. Alternatively, this analysis of ABC would suggest that an equity investment would also be viable, although perhaps less attractive to the existing owners. If an equity investment was sought then Mr X would need to agree terms of return with ABC.

One note of caution is that a dividend of $293,000 appears to have been paid which is 72% of the profit for the year. Given that ABC is looking for investment and is short of cash, such a large dividend pay-out appears on the face of it to be a poor management decision. However, I would recommend that the investment be considered further and in particular reasons for the large dividend be established.

(b)   Benefits and limitations of ratio analysis

The benefits to Mr X of using traditional ratio analysis for investment decisions include the ability to delegate the preliminary analysis to other members of his team. It can act as a first screening of investments by creating benchmarks and minimum targets that have to be achieved for investments to be considered further. It therefore can cut down time and costs associated with investment appraisal.

Traditional ratio analysis does not account for the different business sectors, and so using thresholds and target percentages may not work when comparing entities from different sectors or from different ends of the same sector. In the case of the investment in ABC, it does not take account of his personal interest in research and development activities and if ABC were to continue to expand it may invest more resources in developing new perfume recipes or formulae for cosmetic creams, etc. This may be an area of particular interest to Mr X and ratio analysis does not account for personal bias towards certain types of entity. Also coming from a technology background he may have an interest in web/online development. The ratios do not distinguish between different sources of revenue.